Brick & Mortar Shopping in the 21st Century

Advertising and Consumer Psychology
A Series sponsored by the Society for Consumer Psychology

Aaker/Biel: *Brand Equity & Advertising: Advertising's Role in Building Strong Brands* (1993)

Clark/Brock/Stewart: *Attention, Attitude, and Affect in Response Advertising* (1994)

Englis: *Global and Multi-National Advertising* (1994)

Goldberg/Fishbein/Middlestadt: *Social Marketing: Theoretical and Practical Perspectives* (1997)

Haugtvedt/Machleit/Yalch: *Online Consumer Psychology: Understanding and Influencing Consumer Behavior in the Virtual World* (2005)

Kahle/Chiagouris: *Values, Lifestyles and Psychographics* (1997)

Kahle/Kim: *Creating Images and the Psychology of Marketing Communication* (2006)

Kahle/Riley: *Sports Marketing and the Psychology of Marketing Communications* (2003)

Kardes/Herr/Nantel: *Applying Social Cognition to Consumer-Focused Strategy* (2005)

Lowrey: *Brick & Mortar Shopping in the 21ˢᵗ Century* (2008)

Mitchell: *Advertising Exposure, Memory, and Choice* (1993)

Schumann/Thorson: *Advertising and the World Wide Web* (1999)

Scott/Batra: *Persuasive Imagery: A Consumer Response Perspective* (2003)

Shrum: *The Psychology of Entertainment Media: Blurring the Lines Between Entertainment and Persuasion* (2004)

Thorson/Moore: *Integrated Communication: Synergy of Persuasive Voices* (1996)

Wells: *Measuring Advertising Effectiveness* (1997)

Williams/Lee/Haugtvedt: *Diversity in Advertising: Broadening the Scope of Research Directions* (2004)

Brick & Mortar Shopping in the 21st Century

Tina M. Lowrey
University of Texas at San Antonio

Lawrence Erlbaum Associates
Taylor & Francis Group

New York   London

Lawrence Erlbaum Associates
Taylor & Francis Group
270 Madison Avenue
New York, NY 10016

Lawrence Erlbaum Associates
Taylor & Francis Group
2 Park Square
Milton Park, Abingdon
Oxon OX14 4RN

© 2008 by Taylor & Francis Group, LLC
Lawrence Erlbaum Associates is an imprint of Taylor & Francis Group, an Informa business

Printed in the United States of America on acid-free paper
10 9 8 7 6 5 4 3 2 1

International Standard Book Number-13: 978-0-8058-6364-2 (Softcover) 978-0-8058-6394-9 (Hardcover)

Library of Congress Cataloging-in-Publication Data

Conference on Advertising and Consumer Psychology (25th : 2006 : Houston, Tex.)
    Brick & mortar shopping in the 21st century / editor, Tina M. Lowrey.
       p. cm. -- (Advertising and consumer psychology series ; 11)
    Includes bibliographical references and index.
    ISBN-13: 978-0-8058-6364-2 (alk. paper)
    ISBN-10: 0-8058-6364-8 (alk. paper)

    1. Consumer behavior--Congresses. 2. Shopping--Congresses. 3. Consumption (Economics)--Social aspects--Congresses. I. Lowrey, Tina M. II. Title. III. Title: Brick and mortar shopping in the 21st century.
HF5415.32.C653 2006   658.8'342--dc22   2007013601

Visit the Taylor & Francis Web site at
http://www.taylorandfrancis.com

Dedication

I would like to dedicate this book to my dear friend
and colleague Cele Otnes, with whom I've shared many
wonderful shopping-related research projects, and
to L. J., my favorite person to shop with and for.

CONTENTS

I

Mood and Cognition Effects on Shopping Behavior

II

New Findings in Retailing Strategy

III

The Influence of Social Identity Variables on Shopping Behavior

IV

Methodological Innovations for Studying Shopping Behavior

ABOUT THE EDITOR

Tina M. Lowrey (PhD, University of Illinois) is professor of Marketing at the University of Texas at San Antonio. Her main research interests include psycholinguistic analyses of advertising, and gift-giving and ritualistic consumption. Her work has appeared in numerous journals, including the *Journal of Consumer Research, Journal of Consumer Psychology,* and *Journal of Advertising.* She has chapters in *Contemporary Consumption Rituals: A Research Anthology* (which she co-edited with Cele C. Otnes); *Handbook of Qualitative Research Methods in Marketing; Marketing Communication: New Approaches, Technologies, and Styles; Gender Issues and Consumer Behavior; Gift Giving: A Research Anthology;* and *New Developments and Approaches in Consumer Behavior Research.* She serves on the editorial boards of *Journal of Advertising, Journal of Consumer Psychology, Media Psychology,* and *Psychology & Marketing.* She edited *Psycholinguistic Phenomena in Marketing Communications.*

LIST OF CONTRIBUTORS

David Allan
HAUB School of Business
Saint Joseph's University
Philadelphia, PA

Ray L. Benedicktus, III
Department of Marketing
College of Business
Florida State University
Tallahassee, FL

Michael K. Brady
Department of Marketing
College of Business
Florida State University
Tallahassee, FL

Oliver B. Büttner
Institute of Marketing and Retailing
Georg-August-Universität Göttingen
Göttingen, Germany

Sumire Crader
Waseda University
Tokyo, Japan

Peter R. Darke
Department of Marketing
College of Business
Florida State University
Tallahassee, FL

Velma A. R. Gooding
Department of Advertising
University of Texas at Austin
Austin, TX

Anne-Marie G. Hakstian
Berlon School of Business
Salem State College
Salem, MA

Margaret K. Hogg
Department of Marketing
Lancaster University
Management School
Lancaster, United Kingdom

Robert V. Kozinets
Schulich School of Business
York University
Toronto, Ontario, Canada

Tina M. Lowrey
Marketing Department
College of Business
University of Texas at San Antonio
San Antonio, TX

David Luna
Department of Marketing
Zicklin School of Business
Baruch College
New York, NY

May O. Lwin
School of Communication
and Information
Nanyang Technological University
Nanyang Link, Singapore

Rajesh V. Manchanda
I.H. Asper School of Business
University of Manitoba
Winnipeg, Manitoba, Canada

Cele C. Otnes
Department of Business Administration
University of Illinois at
Urbana-Champaign
Champaign, IL

Dale G. Paulson
Allegiance Research Group
Alexandria, VA

Elfriede Penz
Institute of International Marketing
and Management
Wirtschaftsuniversität Wien
(WU-Wien)
Vienna, Austria

Laura A. Peracchio
Sheldon B. Lubar School of Business
University of Wisconsin - Milwaukee
Milwaukee, WI

Julie A. Ruth
School of Business
Rutgers University
Camden, NJ

Najam U. Saqib
School of Business Management
Ryerson University
Toronto, Ontario, Canada

Günter Silberer
Institute of Marketing and Retailing
Georg-August-Universität Göttingen
Göttingen, Germany

Linda Tuncay
School of Business Administration
Loyola University Chicago
Chicago, IL

Clay M. Voorhees
Department of Marketing & Supply
Chain Management
Eli Broad College of Business
Michigan State University
East Lansing, MI

Kai-Yu Wang
Sheldon B. Lubar School of Business
University of Wisconsin - Milwaukee
Milwaukee, WI

Jerome D. Williams
Department of Advertising
University of Texas at Austin
Austin, TX

Judith Lynne Zaichkowsky
Faculty of Business Administration
Simon Fraser University
Vancouver, Canada

ABOUT THE CONTRIBUTORS

David Allan (PhD, Temple University) is assistant professor of Marketing in the Erivan K. Haub School of Business at Saint Joseph's University in Philadelphia, Pennsylvania. His primary research interests include advertising and popular culture, especially popular music. He has published numerous articles in the area of advertising cues and effects in journals such as the *Journal of Advertising Research, International Journal of Advertising, Journal of Advertising Society,* and *Popular Musicology.* In addition, he is frequently interviewed for his advertising and popular culture expertise by newspapers such as *The Philadelphia Inquirer, Sacramento Bee* and *The San Diego Union-Tribune.* Prior to his academic career, he spent over 20 years in the radio industry in various roles including general, programming, and marketing management.

Ray L. Benedicktus, III is a doctoral candidate at Florida State University. His research engages topics related to services strategy, multi-channel retailing, and consumer attitudes. He has published his research in the *Journal of Interactive Advertising* and presented papers at several conferences including AMS and Winter AMA. He is currently developing a dissertation exploring the mechanisms underlying the processing of physical store presence information in multi-channel retail environments.

Michael K. Brady (PhD, Florida State University) is associate professor of Marketing and doctoral program director at Florida State University. His research interests are in managing customer perceptions of service encounters and the strategic ramifications of branding for service firms. He has published over 20 articles in scholarly journals, including the *Journal of Marketing, Journal of Consumer Research, Journal of Service Research, Journal of Retailing, Journal of the Academy of Marketing Science,* and other outlets. He has won several research, teaching, and service awards, including the M. Wayne Delozier research award given by the Academy of Marketing Science, the Steven J. Shaw research award given by the Society for Marketing Advances, the Academy of Marketing Science outstanding teacher award, a University-wide teaching award, and an outstanding reviewer award given by the *Journal of Retailing.* Mike serves on the editorial review boards of the *Journal of Retailing, Journal of Service Research,* and *Journal of the Academy of Marketing Science.*

Oliver B. Büttner is a PhD candidate in marketing at the Georg-August-Universität Göttingen (Germany) and has graduated in psychology at the Friedrich-Alexander-Universität Erlangen-Nürnberg (Germany). His research interests revolve around shopping behavior in brick & mortar and electronic retail environments. His work has appeared in *Advances in Consumer Research*, *NeuroPsychoEconomics*, and as chapters in various German books.

Sumire Crader (BBA, Simon Fraser University) is currently researching Comparative Labor Economics at Waseda University in Tokyo, Japan in order to obtain her Master's degree. Her main research interests include visual aesthetics and consumer behavior, comparative human resources (U.S. and Japan) in a cultural context, and the convergence of international human resources practices.

Peter R. Darke (PhD, University of Toronto) is assistant professor of Marketing in the College of Business at Florida State University. He received his doctoral degree in Psychology from the University of Toronto. His current work focuses on consumer attitudes, judgment, and decision-making. He has published articles in the *Journal of Applied Psychology, Journal of Applied Social Psychology, Journal of Consumer Psychology, Journal of Consumer Research, Journal of Economic Psychology, Journal of Marketing Research, Journal of Personality and Social Psychology, Journal of Research in Personality, Journal of Retailing, Marketing Letters*, and *Personality and Social Psychology Bulletin*.

Velma A. R. Gooding is a doctoral student in advertising at the University of Texas, Austin. Her research has been about how stereotypical media affect shopping, perceptions, and opportunity. She also studies marketplace disparities experienced by African-American and Latino populations and dynamics between these groups as the U.S. population changes. She has vast experience in marketing communications and previously taught at Iowa State University, Drake University, Simpson College, and Washburn University. She previously owned and operated an ethnic marketing and research firm in the state of Kansas. She was instrumental in helping to rebrand the YWCA of the USA, and developed marketing materials for the national 50th anniversary of Brown v. Board of Education in Topeka. She holds a BA in print journalism from Hampton University and an MS in Journalism Mass Communications from Iowa State University.

Anne-Marie G. Hakstian (J.D., George Washington University Law School) is associate professor of Management at the Bertolon School of Business at Salem State College in Massachusetts. She is currently pursuing her doctorate in the Law, Policy, and Society program at Northeastern University. Her main research interests are sex and race discrimination. Her work has been published in several journals including the *University of Virginia Journal of Social Policy and the Law,* the *Journal of Public Policy and Marketing,* the *University of Michigan Journal of Race and Law,* the *Boston College Third World Law Journal* and the *American University Journal of Gender, Social Policy and the Law.* She serves on the editorial board of the *Business Law Review (North Atlantic edition).*

Margaret K. Hogg (PhD, University of Manchester, U.K.) is professor of Consumer Behaviour and Marketing at Lancaster University (U.K.). Her main research interests include identity, self, and consumption, particularly distastes, negative symbolic consumption and the undesired self; and evolving notions of the self amongst women as mothers (e.g., new mothers; empty nesters). Her work has appeared in *Consumption, Markets and Culture; European Journal of Marketing; and the Journal of Marketing Management.* She has chapters in *Handbook of Qualitative Research Methods in Marketing, Elusive Consumption,* and *Marketing and Feminism: Current Issues and Research.* She serves on the editorial boards of *Journal of Marketing Management* and *Marketing Theory.* She edited six volumes on *Consumer Behavior Research* for the Sage Library in Business and Management series; and is a co-author on the leading European text *Consumer Behaviour: A European Perspective* (3rd ed.).

Robert V. Kozinets (PhD, Queens University) is associate professor of Marketing at York University's Schulich School of Business in Toronto, Canada. An anthropologist by training, he has ethnographically studied themed retail environments like ESPN Zone and American Girl Place, as well as Star Trek, Star Wars, and X-Files fans, sports and automobile afficionadoes, coffee connoisseurs, online and offline videogamers, activists and culture jammers, technophiles, and other online or virtual community members. His articles have been published in the *Journal of Marketing,* the *Journal of Consumer Research,* the *Journal of Marketing Research,* the *Journal of Contemporary Ethnography, Consumption, Markets, & Culture* and the *Journal of Retailing.* He developed and continues to expand the technique of netnography or Internet ethnography, and has also been actively involved in developing videography as a marketing and consumer research method. He is currently editing a volume on Consumer Tribes along with Avi Shankar and Bernard Cova.

David Luna (PhD, University of Wisconsin-Milwaukee) is associate professor of Marketing at Baruch College (City University of New York). His main research interest is language and information processing in the context of marketing communications. Other interests include imagery processing, mental representation, and the role of automatic processes on judgment formation. His work has been published in academic journals like the *Journal of Consumer Research, Journal of Consumer Psychology, Journal of the Academy of Marketing Science*, and *Journal of Advertising*, among others. His research has also appeared in several edited books, including chapters in *Diversity in Advertising, Online Consumer Psychology: Understanding and Influencing Behavior in the Virtual World*, and *Persuasive Imagery: A Consumer Response Perspective*. His papers appear regularly in the proceedings of national and international conferences, like the *Society for Consumer Research* and the *Association for Consumer Research* proceedings.

May O. Lwin (PhD, National University of Singapore) is assistant professor and acting head at the Division of Public and Promotional Communication, Wee Kim Wee School of Communication and Information in Nanyang Technological University, Singapore. Her research interests are in the areas of sensory factors in advertising, and social and regulatory issues in marketing communications. She has published in leading international journals such as the *Journal of Public Policy & Marketing, Journal of the Academy of Marketing Science, Journal of Business Law, Marketing Letters, Journal of Current Issues and Research in Advertising* and *Journal of Consumer Affairs*. She has also authored a number of marketing books, including the best-selling Clueless Series (e.g., *Clueless in Advertising*). Her latest work (*Advertising: Principles and Effective IMC Perspective*) is the first major Western textbook adapted for the entire Asian and Asia-Pacific educational market.

Rajesh V. Manchanda (PhD, University of Illinois) is associate professor of Marketing at the University of Manitoba, Winnipeg, Canada. Dr. Manchanda has two broad areas of research, the first of which revolves around understanding the role of negative affect in marketing. His study of negative affect has included emotions such as embarrassment, guilt, and feeling offended (or shocked). His second area of research deals with pricing and consumer promotion issues. Dr. Manchanda's research has appeared in journals such as the *Journal of Consumer Research, Journal of Consumer*

Psychology, Journal of Advertising Research, Journal of Product and Brand Management, and *Marketing Letters.*

Cele C. Otnes (PhD, University of Tennessee) is professor in the department of Business Administration, the University of Illinois at Urbana-Champaign (UIUC). She is co-author with Elizabeth H. Pleck of *Cinderella Dreams: The Allure of the Lavish Wedding,* published by the University of California Press in 2003, and has co-edited two other books on rituals and consumption. She has published numerous articles on ritualistic consumption in general, and gift giving in particular, in the *Journal of Consumer Research, Journal of Business Research, Journal of the Academy of Marketing Science, Journal of Retailing, Journal of Advertising, Journal of Contemporary Ethnography* and *Psychology & Marketing,* among others. She has taught Principles of Retailing, Consumer Behavior, and Promotions Management in the College of Business at UIUC.

Dale G. Paulson (PhD, The American University, Washington, DC) is president of Allegiance Research Group in Alexandria, Virginia. He specializes in innovative research related to market segmentation and consumer motivations and has received several trademarks for his methodologies. His book on segmentation is entitled "Allegiance®: Fulfilling the Promise of One-to-One Marketing for Associations." His work on developing tag lines and quantifying the meaning of words has been published by *Association Management* magazine, "Tag Lines Create Powerful Images." He has written numerous research articles for the national trade publication *Association Trends* and has taught research seminars or given speeches at several meetings of national organizations such as the American Marketing Association and the Direct Marketing Association. He has done research for over one hundred organizations.

Elfriede Penz is associate professor at WU-Wien. She received a PhD in Psychology (University of Vienna) and a European PhD on Social Representations and Communications. She also holds an MAS as cultural manager from the University of Music and Performing Arts, Vienna. She received a best paper award (AIB-UK, 2006) and the Outstanding Paper in Marketing awarded by Emerald LiteratiNetwork in 2005. Elfriede Penz' research interests include consumer behaviour as well as methodological issues in international marketing and management. She has published in refereed international journals such as *Journal of Economic Psychology, International Marketing Review,* and *Psychology & Marketing.*

Laura A. Peracchio (PhD, Northwestern University) is professor of Marketing at the University of Wisconsin-Milwaukee. Her areas of research interest are automatic processing, visual persuasion, language and culture, and food and nutrition issues. Her work has appeared in the *Journal of Consumer Research*, *Journal of Consumer Psychology*, and *Journal of Advertising*. Laura is an Associate Editor of the *Journal of Consumer Research* and president of the Society for Consumer Psychology, an international organization composed of marketing and psychology scholars and a division of the American Psychological Association.

Julie A. Ruth (PhD, University of Michigan) is associate professor of Marketing at Rutgers University at Camden. Her main research interests include emotion-laden aspects of consumer behavior and marketing strategy including gift exchange, family relationships, and brand partnerships such as co-branding and joint sponsorship. Her work has appeared in numerous journals, including the *Journal of Marketing Research*, *Journal of Consumer Research*, *Journal of Consumer Psychology*, *Journal of Advertising*, and *Journal of the Academy of Marketing Science*. She has chapters in *Contemporary Consumption Rituals: A Research Anthology*; *Gift Giving: A Research Anthology*; and *Handbook of Qualitative Research Methods in Marketing*. She also serves on the editorial board of the *Journal of Advertising*. She is engaged in a long-term research program regarding the consumption landscape in South Africa and other markets in transition.

Najam U. Saqib (PhD, University of Manitoba) is assistant professor of Marketing at Ryerson University, Toronto, Canada. His research interests include consumer decision making, branding, and international marketing. His work has been accepted for publication in the *Journal of Public Policy and Marketing*.

Günter Silberer (Dr rer pol, University of Mannheim, Germany) is professor of Marketing and director of the Institute of Marketing and Retailing at the Georg-August-Universität Göttingen. His main research interests include consumer behavior, tracking research, point of sale marketing, online marketing, and retail management. His work has appeared in journals such as *Journal of Consumer Policy*, *Journal of Business Research* and *Marketing–Zeitschrift für Forschung und Praxis*. He has chapters in various German marketing readers and edited different publications concerning interactive marketing. He wrote books (in German) on mood as marketing factor, on multimedia in sales conversation, on value-oriented business management, and on the diffusion and use of comparative product test results.

Linda Tuncay (PhD, University of Illinois) is assistant professor of Marketing at Loyola University Chicago. Her main research interests include how gender influences identity construction, persuasion, and shopping behavior. Her work will be appearing in the *Journal of Consumer Research*. She has also presented at various conferences such as the Association for Consumer Research, Society for Consumer Psychology, and American Marketing Association.

Clay M. Voorhees (PhD, Florida State University) is assistant professor of Marketing at Michigan State University. His research interests include assessing the outcomes of service marketing strategies, managing the service decision making process, consumer complaining behavior, service failure and recovery, segmentation of service consumers, role of other customers in service experiences, and branding for service firms. His research has been published in the *Strategic Management Journal, Journal of the Academy of Marketing Science, Journal of Service Research*, and *Journal of Services Marketing.*

Kai-Yu Wang is a PhD candidate in Marketing at the University of Wisconsin-Milwaukee. He received his MBA degree from National Dong Hwa University and undergraduate degree in Psychology from Chung-Yuan Christian University in Taiwan. His research interests include information processing, consumer persuasion processes, and advertising effects.

Jerome D. Williams (PhD, University of Colorado) is the F. J. Heyne Centennial Professor in the Department of Advertising at the University of Texas at Austin. His current research interests focus on multicultural marketing and advertising strategies, marketplace discrimination, Internet privacy, and public health communication. Among the many journals in which his work has been published are the *Journal of Public Policy and Marketing, Journal of Marketing, Journal of Marketing Research, Journal of Retailing, International Journal of Research in Marketing, Journal of the Academy of Marketing Science, Marketing Letters*, and *Journal of Consumer Affairs*. He is co-editor of *Diversity in Advertising: Broadening the Scope of Research Directions*, and co-author of a forth-coming book on consumer racial profiling. He currently serves on the Editorial Board of the *Journal of Public Policy & Marketing* and *Journal of Macromarketing.*

Judith Lynne Zaichkowsky (PhD, University of California, Los Angeles) is professor of Marketing at Simon Fraser University, Canada. Her work in consumer research on involvement is recognized as one of the top articles in consumer behavior and one of the most influential articles in the field of advertising. More recently she is working on trademark issues as they relate to design, identification, and evaluation. She is author of *Defending Your Brand Against Imitation: Consumer Behavior, Marketing Strategies and Legal Issues (Quorum Books, 1995)* and *The Psychology Behind Trademark Infringement and Counterfeiting (Erlbaum 2006)*. She received a Centenary Alumni award from the University of Guelph in 2003 for outstanding contributions to research. She is a member of the editorial review boards for *Journal of Advertising, Journal of the Academy of Marketing Science, Psychology and Marketing, Journal of Promotion Management*, and *Asia Pacific Review of Marketing.*

PREFACE

BRICK & MORTAR SHOPPING IN THE 21ST CENTURY: AN OVERVIEW

Tina M. Lowrey

*I*N RECENT YEARS, research attention has turned away from traditional retailing toward an understanding of how consumer psychology can inform the e-tailing environment. Although this focus is understandable, traditional retailers obviously face an increasing amount of competition for customers, even if, at times, the competition is self-inflicted. That is, many traditional retailers offer electronic shopping options that compete with their own brick and mortar operations. In light of this situation, it is time to renew attention to how traditional retailing operates in the new competitive environment. It is important to understand which psychological theories can provide insights into why so many consumers still flock to traditional shopping environments, as well as situational factors that promote or inhibit brick and mortar shopping. It is also essential to understand which individual differences lead some customers to prefer shopping in traditional retailing venues. Finally, it is important to learn about new methodologies that best capture moderators and mediators of various shopping behaviors.

I had the honor of chairing the 25th Advertising & Consumer Psychology conference, which was designed to address these issues. This volume showcases the best papers from that conference, which was an intimate gathering of scholars interested in exploring the continued popularity of brick and mortar shopping. The conference was held in Houston, TX, at the Galleria Mall (selected for its topical inspiration). The keynote speaker, Robert Kozinets of York University, opened the conference with a comprehensive conceptualization of experiential retail, and also led an ethnographic tour of the Galleria. The conference drew scholars from Asia, Europe, Latin America, and North America, and included a presentation of data collected in South Africa—a truly global group of individuals with diverse perspectives and experiences. This volume should give readers a feel for the array of topics, methodological approaches, and theoretical underpinnings that were shared that weekend in Houston.

The volume is divided into four parts: Part I is devoted to affective and cognitive effects on shopping behavior. The first chapter (Kozinets) proposes a systematic framework for categorizing the different types of spaces that exist in the marketplace. Using data from more than a decade of field-work conducted at a variety of different retail locations, his chapter lays the groundwork for a deeper understanding of the strong relationships that can exist between consumers, brands, and the retail spaces that bring the two together. Chapter 2 (Wang, Peracchio, & Luna) investigates the theoretical and practical contributions that thin slice judgments can provide to those studying retailing and consumer behavior. Thin slice judgments (brief exposures to stimuli, p. 18) are explored in the context of information processing research. More specifically, the authors discuss potential foundations for thin slice judgment formation, the impact of such judgments on consumer behavior, and the potential usefulness of the concept for studying shopping behavior.

Allan's chapter (Chapter 3) provides a comprehensive overview of the effects that music can have on shopping outcomes, based on a review of the extant literature on this topic. Included in this overview is an analysis of the different settings used for data collection, the varying samples of respondents utilized, the different variables manipulated, and the various results obtained. The chapter ends with an identification of issues left unanswered for future research to address. In Chapter 4, Hogg and Penz investigate approach-avoidance conflicts in the context of brick and mortar versus online shopping scenarios. Their conceptualization includes key features of products and retail situations that lead to discomfort, which in turn lead to approach-avoidance conflict. The authors also outline the ways in which such conflicts impact actual purchasing strategies by individuals in various retail settings.

Part II moves on to recent findings that impact retailing strategy. Crader and Zaichkowsky (Chapter 5) discuss an approach to marketing at the retail level that incorporates various principles of art that appeal to all of the senses. They argue that an appropriate use of aesthetic considerations can activate consumers' emotions, thus creating pleasure and positively motivating purchasing behavior. Indeed, these pleasurable aesthetic experiences may be a major contributor to the continued popularity of brick and mortar shopping in an online world. Chapter 6 (Benedicktus, Brady, Darke, & Voorhees) investigates the impact of physical channel presence, brand factors, and consensus information on consumers' trusting beliefs and online purchase intentions for multi-channel firms. They suggest that brand strength is the primary trust cue, but the existence of consensus information can help newer companies that do not yet have established brands. Physical channel presence is also an important contributing factor to trust and purchase intent for online transactions. Saqib and Manchanda (Chapter 7) examine the effects of licensing brand alliances on consumers' attitudes and intentions to buy. They provide the psychological underpinnings to explain how such licensing effects may occur. The results of two experiments are briefly reviewed to support the theory they propose, and they provide future research directions for those interested in this topic.

Part III looks at the influence of social identity variables on shopping behavior, such as gender, race, and ethnicity. Chapter 8 (Tuncay & Otnes) examines the interplay between gender identity and consumption with regard to male consumers. Specifically, they discuss how conceptualizations of masculinity have evolved over time and how masculinity is a key influencer of men's consumption patterns. Williams, Lwin, Hakstian and Gooding's chapter (Chapter 9) proposes a power-responsibility equilibrium model for the assessment of retail discrimination. The model incorporates a variety of factors that contribute to discrimination, and takes into consideration business policy, government regulation, and consumer responses. Ruth's chapter (Chapter 10) reports the results of in-depth interviews with South African consumers, with particular attention paid to the effects of third parties on shopping experiences. Her research includes insights from experiences in both apartheid and post-apartheid South Africa, which allows for a comprehensive investigation of how the shopping environment may have changed as a result of sweeping social changes in that culture.

Part IV concludes the book with three methodological chapters. Two of these chapters present innovative new methods for studying shopping behavior, whereas the final chapter is an overview of classic and newer methods for studying behavior at the point-of-sale. Chapter 11 (Büttner & Silberer) provides a thorough explanation of using video-cued thought protocols to study shoppers' cognitions *in situ*—their field study provides evidence for the validity of such an approach, and they provide sufficient detail for those scholars who may be interested in utilizing the method in their own research. Paulson (Chapter 12) presents a novel methodology called Cartoon Sequence Research (CSR). The chapter outlines the theoretical underpinnings of CSR, explains exactly how to administer a CSR study, and describes various insightful sets of findings for clients across a variety of industries. Finally, Chapter 13 (Silberer) is a comprehensive review of classic methods for studying behavior *in situ* at the point-of-sale, as well as an introduction to some newer methods that may not be familiar to the audience. Silberer provides an in-depth discussion of the strengths and weaknesses of each method, and offers suggestions for how best to combine methods for more robust research designs.

This is the first book to present the latest research from a diverse group of scholars who continue to study brick and mortar shopping, despite the current popularity of research on e-tailing and online shopping. Although online shopping is thriving, people continue to flock to traditional shopping venues as well. I hope that the book will provide not only a broad overview of what is currently being studied, but also spark additional interest in the study of brick and mortar shopping in the 21st century. Despite the inherent difficulties of studying shopping behavior, it is a fun, fruitful, and fascinating topic of study.

ACKNOWLEDGEMENTS

I would like to acknowledge all of those who helped put this volume together, including of course the authors (who served as internal reviewers on one another's chapters). I would also like to thank Anne Duffy, Rebecca Larsen, and Tanya Policht, of Lawrence Erlbaum Associates, who provided guidance throughout the process. Thanks, also, to Dana Chen and Qifu Xiao, who assisted with the Author and Subject indices. Finally, many thanks to Steve Chisholm of MidAtlantic Books and Journals, Inc., and Glen Butler and Jonathan Pennell of Taylor and Francis who helped finalize the book's publication.

I

MOOD AND COGNITION EFFECTS ON SHOPPING BEHAVIOR

1

BRANDS IN SPACE: NEW THINKING ABOUT EXPERIENTIAL RETAIL

Robert V. Kozinets

Schulich School of Business, York University

ON SATURDAY MORNING, during my stay at the Westin Oaks hotel, located within the somewhat-familiar-yet-still-somewhat-surreal Galleria Mall in Houston, I received a copy of *USA Today*. Like the other contributors to this volume, I was in Houston for the 25th annual Advertising & Consumer Psychology Conference, a conference whose theme was Brick & Mortar Shopping in the 21st Century. The *USA Today* lead story was titled "Starbucks Nation" and in it the author was talking about the way that retail had become intertwined with entertainment and popular culture. The author, Bruce Horovitz, interviewed sociologist George Ritzer—the man who coined the catchy and culturally critical terms McDonaldization and Disneyfication. Ritzer talked about how Starbucks has created the impression that they can be arbiters of popular taste, selling music, and sponsoring and selling movies like the recent *Akeelah and the Bee*. Ritzer's term for this? He calls it—wait for it—"the Starbuckization of society" (Horovitz, 2006, p. 1A).

The news that retail is combining in many ways with popular culture and entertainment isn't really news. In the heyday of the Internet age, when Amazon.com looked to become the new Wal-Mart of the online set, e-tailing was a new and threatening phenomenon. A 1999 *BusinessWeek* cover trumpeted the term "Xtreme Retail" and compared retail to the Roman sophisticates being stormed by the e-tail hordes; how would existing brick and mortar stores fight "the Online Onslaught"?

In that *BusinessWeek* article, we are told that "In the new world of Xtreme Retailing, stores are combining the speed, convenience, and immediacy of e-commerce technology with the thrills of an amusement park. How? Essentially, by taking their core product or image and turning it into an experience. Thus, Vans becomes a skate park and not just a place to buy sneakers, while Bass Pro Shops becomes a fishing pond and archery range and not just a sporting-goods store" (Ginsburg & Morris, 1999).

Even in 1999, that was fairly old news. In the 1970s, with the publication of Kotler's (1974) investigation of store atmospherics, marketers had already tentatively begun to clue into the entire multisensory experience of retail, postulating that the entire physical experience does indeed affect consumers' shopping behaviors.

From there, it was a long trek (or should I say Odyssey?) by consumer researchers through various outdoor (Sherry, 1990) and indoor (Gottdeiner, 1986; Miller, 1998) markets, across the "highways and buyways" of America (Belk, 1991), and through the "malling of America" (Kowinski, 1985). Firat and Venkatesh (1995) speculated on the postmodern role of shopping, and linked it firmly to Debord's ([1967] 1995) Situationist concept of the spectacle. We discovered that markets had festal, sacral elements that combined in some mysterious ways with entertainment and leisure culture. Shopping itself was a leisure activity, often feminized in the literature and often anthropologized by comparisons of some innate hunter-gatherer instinct.

With the publication of Gottdeiner's (1997) sociological treatise on the "Theming of America" and Sherry's (1998) volume on retail "Service-Scape"—containing Sherry's (1998) brilliant hermeneusis of the spectacular Nike Town Chicago location—the intellectual ground had shifted incontrovertibly. Marketing and academia were ready to acknowledge the importance of the experiential domain in contemporary retailing.

Taken together, the notion that retail was transforming into an experiential and transformational setting was becoming easier to grasp. This way of thinking culminated in the publication of Pine and Gilmore's (1999) powerful work on the "Experience Economy" (also found in Wolf, 1999). What had been called "atmospherics" was now firmly established as the "experiential" domain of retail. The retail experience, still an ephemeral concept at best, affected not only point of sale shopping behavior but, in a service economy, was often the key aspect of what was purchased: the experience was the product, and it often changed emotions and even perspectives. By the 2000s, a number of critical books had followed, decrying the pervasive power and prevalence of the shopping mall. Malls had "seduced American shopping" creating "one nation under goods" (Farrell, 2003). We are told that shopping malls are "sacred places" (Pahl, 2003).

From my earliest work in 1995, which looked at the launch of Las Vegas' *Star Trek Experience*, a theme parkish infiltration of an entertainment franchise into physical space, I have been fascinated with the ways in which entertainment, leisure, brands, play and "themes," have merged with consumer culture, commercial society, public places, meeting spaces, and retail. Retail was changing—it had already changed—into something different; new forms of retail were emerging.

Although the X-plosion of X-treme X-periential retail has been proposed as an X-punging of the X-otic enticements of e-commerce, systematic frameworks were still scarce for understanding the dynamic contemporary relationship between brands, consumers, and the retail places that physically host their courtship. In this chapter, I play with the thinking of Yi-Fu Tuan and explore and expand its implications to help us conceptualize the contemporary retail scene. In this stage of thinking, I am attempting to provide a synthetic overview of my own thinking as it has been represented in various co-authored works in the *Journal of Retailing* (Arnold, Kozinets, & Handelman, 2001; Kozinets et al., 2002), the *Journal of Contemporary Ethnography* (Sherry et al., 2001), the *Journal of Consumer Psychology* (Sherry et al., 2004), and the *Journal of Consumer Research* (Kozinets et al., 2004), as well as several book chapters on this topic (e.g., Sherry, Kozinets, & Borghini, 2007). In the chapter, I explore four basic formats for experiential retail and then briefly consider some of their implications for our theoretical understanding and managerial practice.

Theoretical Overview

If we initially consider the etymology and meaning of the term "retailing," we might find some insights into the evolution of retail that I am charting in this chapter. The Oxford English Dictionary tells us that the term is about 650 years old, and dates from the Old French term "retaillier," which means to "cut off, pare, clip, divide." The word actually has the same origins as the word "tailor," the person who takes standard clothes and cuts them or trims them. In its more commonplace meaning of "selling in small quantities," the term is about 580 years old, still quite ancient, and retains the meaning of cutting a piece off, shredding, or scraping (think of a modern cheese store or butcher, cutting a big wheel or loin into family-sized portions). The basic idea is that items were large (not merely mass produced, but produced en masse) and that the retailer needed but to apportion them more appropriately to sell them directly to the consumer. It was a question of quantities; mainly, the retailer bought larger lots of product than needed by consumers. These were the days before strong brands; the retailer was the local brand. The retail experience essentially inhered in the merchant individualizing the product for the consumer—usually simply by breaking it down into a smaller quantity.

Many early trading cultures were nomadic, traveling with their wares. The trader was not a permanent part of communities although hypercommunities gathered around them. As a merchant class began to develop and own land, to become fixed in place, they became a part of the community. As sociologists like Mark Granovetter (1985) and Ray Oldenburg (1989) have informed us, the commercial spaces provided by these retailers also had an important social function: the retailer was a member of the community and also, in some sense, a provider of a place where community could form, both geographically (on a certain piece of land) as well as culturally (through the goods and meanings provided). The retail space as a gathering place and a place for social and intellectual stimulation is actually an ancient imperative. The ground that the original malls and stores were built upon was mystery: markets were bounded, distant places, set up on the frontier, where tricksters, magic, and gambling presided.

This sense of sacred magic bounded in place has a long trajectory in human history, stretching from the most ancient cave painting in Chauvet, to still-powerful relics like the Pyramids and Stonehenge, to disputed contemporary mysteries like the Glastonbury crop circles. According to architectural and cultural critic Ada Huxtable (1997), the contemporary conjunction of magic, history, and retail "theming" began in the 1920s and 1930s when Colonial Williamsburg in Virginia was "restored" to its 1770 splendor. This restoration was made all the more remarkable by the fact that 412 buildings that no longer existed were somehow "restored."

This may have been an initial spark, but in my estimation the big bang that truly created the themed retail explosion as we know it occurred in 1953, when Walt Disney proposed Disneyland as a utopian playplace. In his initial proposal, he wrote: "The idea of Disneyland is a simple one. It will be a place for parents and children to share pleasant times in one another's company: a place for teachers and pupils to discover greater ways of understanding and education. Here the older generation can recapture the nostalgia of days gone by and the younger generation can savor the challenge of the future." Disney's massive success was built upon what I believe was a utopian sincerity, an ability to transcend and blend space and time into a sort of retail timelessness, as well as a deft ability to execute on themed vision. It was a product of Disney's time and place, and it created one hell of an infectious meme.

As we all know, Disneyland was a massive, high profile, highly lauded success. Soon after its success was apparent, Disney became even more ambitious and began developing Walt Disney World, whose original centerpiece was to be an actual experimental prototype community of tomorrow, a group of scientific-consumer time travelers who would use cutting edge technology to develop and experiment with lifestyles a decade or more ahead of their time (imagine using TiVo, plasma TVs, and iPods in the 1980s!). It was a bold vision of a technoconsumption empire, a Promised Land that Walt—like Moses—never lived to see. His vision for EPCOT died with him in 1966, but Walt Disney World, the largest and most successful themed environment on the planet, opened to even more resounding success in 1971.

Consider Pine and Gilmore's (1999) assertion that retailers and companies were driven to move up a progression of economic value from commodities to goods to services to experiences. This evolution seemed to imply a return to a more mysterious frontier, where not only what was experiential was encountered, but what was unexpected and even personally transformational. This was the Wheel of Retailing rolling from basic transactions to high-end services and customization to spin into something that resembled a "variation on a theme park" (Sorkin, 1992), offering high levels of interactivity, communal content, and play. In the following section, I develop this idea and stretch these conceptions by building on the conception of space and place.

Space, Place, and Brands

The boundary-spanning geographer Yi-Fu Tuan was interested in topophilia, the emotional connection that inheres between human beings and physical environments. In *Place and Space*, Tuan (1977) emphasizes experience and the experiential conception of physical location. He proposes that "Place is security, space is freedom: we are attached to the one and long for the other" (Tuan, 1977, p. 3). Like nonhuman animals, we appreciate boundaries of space that are "marked off and defended against intruders" and we also have places that "are centers of felt value where biological needs, such as those for food, water, rest, and procreation are satisfied."

The descriptions dovetail well with the two most fundamental dimensions of human values and motivation: a need for an alternation of security/familiarity/comfort and excitement/stimulation. Building upon this initial idea and crossing it with the brand consciousness that drives retail, I conceive of a way to understand retail themes that splits our understanding into the retailer's goal and the consumers' particular frame of retail or shopping experience.

Walt Disney made a huge intuitive leap when he crossed the idea of an amusement park or carnival with his powerhouse entertainment house of brands. He realized that he could leverage his entertainment brands outside of the movie theater or the home living room television context to create physical experiences that the consumer would pay for. Moreover, these 3-D expressions of entertainment would be experiences that had far more potential to be memorable, and were higher value added (and priced at a higher margin).

Brand spaces. The theming formula became lodged in the business mind. In 1971, at the same time Roy Disney was putting the finishing touches on his late brother's Florida vision, two Americans opened the first Hard Rock Café in London. Using a theme based upon the unmitigated glory of rock and roll, the restaurant chain expanded a decade later into Houston, Chicago, Los Angeles, and San Francisco. It currently has 143 locations in 38 countries, spawned a rush of t-shirt collecting, and now has successful hotels and casinos. In an inevitable return, Hard Rock Café is now building a theme park at Myrtle Beach, South Carolina.

Also in the early 1970s, the Medieval Times chain of chow-and-joust themed entertainment and dining complexes opened in Spain. By 2006, they had built seven more locations across North America and served over 35 million guests. A rush of theming hit in the 1990s, much of it either unsuccessful or only a marginal, quick-lived hit: the Rainforest Café in 1994, Planet Hollywood in 1995, the Fashion Café in 1996, and Stephen Spielberg's Dive in 1999.

The aspects of the theming formula emphasized by these retailers were spatial. The consumer wanted an enlarged vista, somewhere that offered a little more adventure, a little something different. The consumer would pay for ambience. For example, these restaurants were not renowned for their food, but for their atmosphere. The consumer knows that they are purchasing entertainment along with their Planet of the Apes Banana Daiquiri or Fashion Tarte, they are getting a taste of Hollywood or history, glamour, or glory. However, there is a type of disconnect here. The consumer buys stuff and entertainment, but the producer is selling stuff differentiated by entertainment, at a higher margin. The issue is that these are commodities tenuously differentiated; once the entertainment content is gone, the concept implodes.

Brand stores. Marketers of all stripes were realizing that retail could offer something more than just the "stuff" that was being purchased, that theming could add value to what was more or less a commodity: theming was branding. Across many retail categories we saw retailers who were still trying to sell products or services, but who had vamped the level of the service up to include notions of theming that could be wide-ranging enough to encompass branding and brand performances. Krispy Kreme enacted donut theater and presented a red light to get consumers slavering for fresh hot donuts whose immediate eating was an act of immaculate consumption. Ed Debevic's restaurants in Los Angeles and Chicago offered wait staff that tormented their customers (see Brown, 2001) with saucy, sassy service, and took the time out of their busy days to dance on the counters.

Hooters offered just enough sexual innuendo to attract male consumers' interest. Even mundane McDonald's themes itself, catering to local landmarks as with the baseball-fitted McDonald's directly across from Chicago's Wrigley Field on Clark Street. Target's branding of community, graphics, and colored space raises retail to high art, where store is brand and brand is store. As I've written about elsewhere, even Wal-Mart is ideologically and geographically branded with notions of nostalgia and small-town Americana (see Arnold, Kozinets, & Handelman, 2000). In each of these examples, consumers pay for shopping, but not entertainment. There is a solid convergence of interests here. The retailer's goal is to make transactions, and so is the consumer's. The consumer goes to buy stuff, and the retailer intends to sell stuff. However, the retail experience itself becomes meaningful, or is recognized as meaningful, and is itself branded.

Brand Places. Things start to get more complicated as the intentionality behind branding efforts such as Target's and Krispy Kreme's begin to enter strongly into the retail equation. In this case, we have familiar places which sell product, but whose main intention is to be a type of 3-D promotion, a tool for branding. This is destination shopping, flagship store building; it is a place where trusted brands are recharged with excitement.

A classic example of a Brand Place would be the Toys R Us flagship store in Times Square, New York. Toys R Us opened the store in November, 2001, signing an unbelievable 20-year lease for the massive 110,000 square foot site. Filling in some of the vacuum left by the untimely death of FAO Schwartz, inside they placed a "life size" animatronic dinosaur straight out of a Universal or Disney theme park ride. They installed a multithemed, operational 60-foot Ferris wheel, a huge Candyland board, a massive King Kong Lego sculpture, and much more. Awesome in scale and scope, managerial intention was not merely to sell a lot of toys, but to blow the wad and build the value of the Toys R Us brand in the face of fierce price challenges from discounters Wal-Mart and Target.

Nike Town, especially in its original incarnation as a type of mythic sports space (see Sherry, 1998) was another such location that sought through inspirational experiential design to build brand value. Likewise, the original Apple stores were not only the company's first attempt to sell directly to consumers, but a chance to wrest away control of the Apple brand image from the likes of Sears and CompUSA and set it straight. Mission accomplished.

M&M World in Las Vegas is four floors and 26,000 square feet of prime real estate, containing a 3-D movie theater, an M&M racing team area, and a merchandise store. Even charging admission to the theater, selling plush M&M figures, and offering a full 21 colors and flavors of M&Ms cannot possibly hope to capture the costs of running such an enterprise; the store's main purpose is to build the brand.

Another powerful example of the Brand Place is American Girl Place, a museum-like store that offers a high production-value play, themed dining experiences, and detailed museum-like displays of the historical and modern American Girl dolls, clothing lines, and accessories. In these spaces, buying and branding are intertwined. The producer has built a meticulous place devoted to building the already familiar brand and charges or recharges it with cultural and emotional energy. The consumer comes to the place in order to shop, to transact and buy, but also gains emotional brand experience.

Brand Scape.   We are seeing an intensification of this brand building to the point where the realm of branding itself has crossed over to the world of entertainment. Being immersed in the lived world of the brand is in itself a form of entertainment and being surrounded by entertainment is indisputably an act of immersive branding. Coming full-circle, consumers will now pay for the privilege of walking around inside living 3-D ads that interact with them.

Predating Disney World, Legoland opened in Billund, Denmark, in 1968 and featured miniature towns built entirely of Lego. The Legoscape attracted 625,000 visitors in its first year and grew over 20 years to eight times its original size, and has grown to encompass multiple locations. Hershey's Chocolate World opened in 1973, originally as a replacement of the Hershey chocolate plant tour that was becoming unwieldy due to high customer demand. It now includes a free tour of Chocolate Town, a ticketed 3-D show, ticketed Trolley Works ride, a Factory Works Experience for the kids, shops, and restaurants.

Legoscape. Chocolatescape. But wait, there's more. Downtown Atlanta hosts the World of Coca Cola, a museum, originally opened in 1990, dedicated to Coca Cola, its invention, its association with Americana, its global reach. ESPN Zone is another powerful example. With a restaurant, sports bar, virtual reality style video arcade, 21 commissioned Chicago sports-themed art works and 140 high definition television monitors spread over 35,000 square feet, ESPN Zone Chicago is a sports lover's paradise and the three-dimensional incarnation of the television network (see Kozinets et al., 2002; Kozinets et al., 2004).

The store is no longer a store and the mall no longer a mall. They are both "entertainment complexes" that include as necessary ingredients such things as museum cases, guided tours, themed plays, large screen presentations, animatronics, figures, costumes and garb, themed dining, and of course the mandatory memorabilia gift store. Consumers seek experience and retailers sell them the experience, which include the bundle of goods and services (or not). The retail Ur-space is Disneyland. Branding is so complete and complex in these places that they have become landscapes all their own, Brand Scapes: lifestyle/brands that people will pay to delve deeper into.

Cursory Considerations

I offer no conclusions in this chapter, but only a small set of initial and tentative considerations. I present these four "brands in space" in the framework in Figure 1.1, whose vertical dimensions are a continuum intended to capture retailer objectives (either seeking to build the iconic status of the brand, or building transactions) and horizontal reach seeking to convey the continuum of consumers' retail framing, either as a place for shopping or a space in which to purchase entertaining new experiences.

In this chapter, I have developed and crossed the idea of theming and brands with those of space and place, blending these elements with contemporary retail configurations. This yields four contemporary themed retail

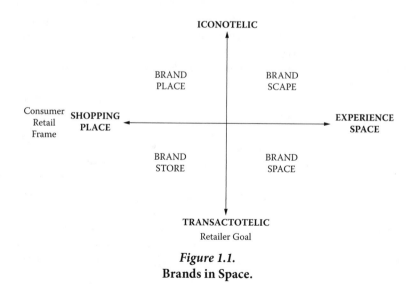

Figure 1.1.
Brands in Space.

archetypes: Brand Store, Brand Place, Brand Space, and Brand Scape. Brand Stores add just a dash of drama and theme to familiar products and places. Brand Spaces, at the risk of seeming cheesy, up the ante by purveying themed experiences wrapped around commodities to excitement-seeking consumers. Brand Places are spectacular shopping places, large-scale three-dimensional promotional projects where brand building occurs. Brand Scapes are retail environments that sell brands-as-entertainment and entertainment-as-brands, locations in which consumers seek enchanted experiences and retailers fulfill this need with iconic brands-writ-large.

My intent for this chapter and its ideas is to enlarge our sense of retail and to open up the discussion on the complex variety of forms of themed retail. Retail can and should now be conceptualized as an opportunity for revenue generation or promotion/advertising (or any combination of the two); the implications of this for marketers and consumer researchers have barely begun to be explored. There are many implications for consumer researchers, psychologists, sociologists, and anthropologists alike. What, for example, does it mean to think of place as promotion? What are the budgetary impacts of this? What are the metrics for understanding it?

A more general question is, How can our measures be adjusted for these transformations of retail? As we have developed a range of scales designed to measure constructs like "Attitude towards the Ad" (Edell & Burke, 1983), should we develop scales to measure "Attitude towards the Theme"? Should we relate Attitude Toward the Ad to retail spaces that are intended as promotions, and try to understand their effects? Does the realm of "shoppertainment" [(Wolf, 1999) or "retailtainment," you can pick your catch phrase] have an impact on memorability? Does shoppertainment affect Schemer's Schema (Friestad & Wright, 1994)? We could use better measures and better process model understandings of how themes work to build brand loyalty and the passionate intention to purchase. What are the anthropological sensibilities behind commercial pilgrimages to places such as the World of Coca Cola or American Girl Place? We need ethnographies of such important consumption journeys.

Brand Stores are quickly becoming the norm. Wandering through the Galleria Mall, stores like M.A.C. offered a highly theatrical approach to makeup sales, where salespeople were paid as makeup design consultants and taught to treat their customers accordingly. An attractive artist created an artwork live in the Oh My Godard Gallery, and many stores—from Dylan's Candy Bar and Aveda to the Movado store through to The Cheesecake Factory—had distinctive design and accents that employed museum casing, costuming, and a sense of all-encompassing branding. The retail store itself as brand is ascendant.

Another important trend that we see is Brand Stores raising the retail stakes and morphing into Brand Places (for example, Toys R Us's huge Times Square gamble or the multi-million dollar, super high-tech Prada store). Brand Places seem on the surface to be the up-and-comers of the themed retail world. Creating a concept like an Apple Store, or a M.A.C. showcase store, or any of the hundreds of the brand-building retail incarnations of established brands like Armani, Gucci, or Sony, seems relatively easy to operationalize. Success, however, is still elusive. The road is littered with the desiccated husks of ambitious retail marketers like Viacom, Warner Brothers, and General Mills.

On the pragmatic side, it seems at first glance that the space opened up by Brand Spaces like Planet Hollywood, Rainforest Café, and the Fashion Café is drying up and dying, but this may be an illusion. Major franchises like the Hard Rock Café and Medieval Times are thriving and growing. This may be simply a themed survival of the hippest. I was unfortunate enough to attend a dinner at my local, extremely well situated Rainforest Café last weekend (in Toronto's booming Yorkdale Mall), and it was packed full of people, mostly families with screaming children, and it was every bit as awful as I remember it. But its profitability is not in question.

Brand Scapes are still experimental and difficult gambles, not for the financially faint of heart. However, their promise seems virtually untapped. Experiential retail is an extremely exciting and active area in retail and while marketers are using these entertainment-oriented tools to revive their brands and re-awaken the consumers' attention, we as scholars would benefit from a deeper study of their forms, functions, and implications.

References

Arnold, S. J., Kozinets, R. V., & Handelman, J. M. (2001). Hometown ideology and retailer legitimation: The institutional semiotics of Wal-Mart flyers. *Journal of Retailing, 77*(2), 243–271.

Belk, R. (Ed.) (1991). *Highways and buyways: Naturalistic research from the consumer behavior odyssey.* Provo, UT: Association for Consumer Research.

Brown, S. (2001). Torment your customers (they'll love it). *Harvard Business Review, 79*(9), 82–88.

Debord, G. ([1967] 1995). *The society of the spectacle.* Donald Nicholson-Smith (trans.). New York: Zone Books.

Edell, J. A., & Burke, M. C. (1983). The moderating effect of attitude toward an ad on ad effectiveness under different processing conditions. In T. C. Kinnear (Ed.), *Advances in Consumer Research, 11,* 644–649.

Farrell, J. J. (2003). *One nation under goods: Malls and the seduction of American shopping.* Washington, DC: Smithsonian Institution Press.

Firat, A. F., & Venkatesh, A. (1995). Liberatory postmodernism and the reenchantment of consumption. *Journal of Consumer Research, 22* (December), 239–267.

Friestad, M., & Wright, P. (1994). The persuasion knowledge model: How people cope with persuasion attempts. *Journal of Consumer Research, 21* (June), 1–31.

Ginsburg, J., & Morris, K. (1999). Xteme retailing: stores fight the online onsaught. *BusinessWeek*, December 20.

Gottdiener, M. (1986). Recapturing the center: a semiotic analysis of shopping malls. In M. Gottdiender and A. P. Lagopoulos (Eds.), *The city and the sign: An introduction to urban semiotics* (pp. 289–302). New York: Columbia University Press.

Gottdeiner, M. (1997). *The theming of America.* Boulder, CO: Westview Press.

Granovetter, M. (1985). Economic action and social structure: The problem of embeddedness. *American Journal of Sociology, 91* (November), 481–510.

Horovitz, B. (2006). Starbucks nation. *USA Today*, May 19–21, p. 1A–2A.

Huxtable, A. L. (1997). *The unreal America: architecture and illusion.* New York: New Press.

Kotler, P. (1974). Atmospherics as a marketing tool. *Journal of Retailing, 49* (Winter), 48–61.

Kowinski, W. S. (1985). *The malling of America: An inside look at the great consumer paradise.* New York: William Morrow.

Kozinets, R. V., Sherry, J. F., Jr., Storm, D., Duhachek, A., Nuttavuthisit, K., & DeBerry-Spence, B. (2004). Ludic agency and retail spectacle. *Journal of Consumer Research, 31* (December), 658–672.

Kozinets, R. V., Sherry, J. F., Jr., Storm, D., Duhachek, A., Nuttavuthisit, K., & DeBerry-Spence, B. (2002). Themed flagship brand stores in the new millennium: Theory, practice, prospects. *Journal of Retailing, 78* (Spring), 17–29.

Miller, D. (Ed.) (1998*). Shopping, place, and identity.* New York: Routledge.

Oldenburg, R. (1989). *The great good place.* New York: Paragon House.

Pahl, J. (2003). *Shopping malls and other sacred places: Putting God in place.* Grand Rapids, MI: Brazos.

Pine, B. J., II, & Gilmore, J. H. (1999). *The experience economy: Work is theatre and every business a stage.* Boston: Harvard.

Sherry, J. F., Jr. (1998). The soul of the company store: Nike Town Chicago and the emplaced brandscape. In J. F. Sherry, Jr. (Ed.), *Servicescapes: The concept of place in contemporary markets* (pp. 109–146). Lincolnwood, IL: NTC Business Books.

Sherry, J. F., Jr. (1990). A sociocultural analysis of a Midwestern flea market. *Journal of Consumer Research, 17*(1), 13–30.

Sherry, J. F., Jr., Kozinets, R. V., & Borghini, S. (2007). Agents in paradise: experiential co-creation through emplacement, ritualization, and community. In A. Carù and B. Cova (Eds.), *Consuming experiences* (pp. 17–33). London: Routledge.

Sherry, J. F., Jr., Kozinets, R. V., Duhachek, A., DeBerry-Spence, B., Nuttavuthisit, K., & Storm, D. (2004). Gendered behavior in a male preserve: Role playing at ESPN Zone Chicago. *Journal of Consumer Psychology, 14*, 151–158.

Sherry, J. F., Jr., Kozinets, R. V., Storm, D., Duhachek, A., Nuttavuthisit, K., & DeBerry-Spence, B. (2001). Being in the zone: Staging retail theater at ESPN Zone Chicago. *Journal of Contemporary Ethnography, 30*(August), 465–510.

Sorkin, M. (Ed.) (1992). *Variations on a theme park: The new American city and the end of public space.* New York: Hill and Wang.

Tuan, Y. (1977). *Space and place: The perspective of experience.* Minneapolis: University of Minnesota Press.

Wolf, M. (1999). *The entertainment economy: How mega-media forces are transforming our lives.* New York: Random House.

2

THE ROLE OF THIN SLICE JUDGMENTS IN RETAIL ENVIRONMENTS

Kai-Yu Wang
Laura A. Peracchio
University of Wisconsin-Milwaukee

David Luna
Baruch College

YOU ENTER THE COAT DEPARTMENT of a retail store thinking about whether you will need a new winter coat this season. You are greeted warmly by a salesperson. Immediately, you sense that this salesperson is helpful and informative—you like her. You talk with her for a few minutes about your potential coat purchase. The salesperson shows you a coat and it immediately appeals to you. Although you try on a few more coats, you buy the initial coat along with a hat, gloves, and new pair of boots the salesperson has recommended. You leave the store feeling as though your shopping experience was successful and productive, intending to go back to that salesperson in the future.

Judgments and decisions based upon first impressions of people and products impact consumer shopping behavior in retail environments. According to Ambady, Krabbenhoft, and Hogan (2006), in the initial seconds of an encounter, salespeople convey much about themselves and their intentions, often before verbal contact is initiated. Shoppers make immediate judgments about people and products based on these first impressions. And, it would seem that salespeople too may make such immediate judgments about customers upon first meeting. First impression judgments based on brief exposure to a stimulus have been called thin slice judgments (Ambady et al., 2006). A significant body of research suggests that thin slice judgments can be highly accurate and have a significant influence on consumers' decisions and behaviors (Ambady, Bernieri, & Richeson, 2000; Ambady et al., 2006).

In this chapter, we highlight a number of potential theoretical and practical advances that an understanding of thin slice judgments may bring to the study of retailing and consumer shopping behavior. As Ambady et al. (2006) advise, "First impressions are . . . essential in the realm of consumer decision-making." We would add that they are also essential to the study of consumer shopping behavior. We begin by defining thin slice judgments and focusing on thin slice judgments in the context of information processing theory and the study of non-conscious processes. Then, we identify some of the factors that impact the formation of thin slice judgments including nonverbal communication and affect. Finally, we describe several potential applications of thin slice judgments to consumer shopping behavior and retailing. The goal of this approach is to illustrate how the study of thin slice judgments offers the potential for theoretical and substantive progress in our understanding of consumer shopping behavior.

Thin Slice Judgments

Thin slices are first impressions based on brief exposure to expressive behavior containing dynamic information (Ambady et al., 2006). Typically, these thin slices are formed following a very short exposure, often only a few seconds; although they can be as long as 5 minutes. In our daily life, we form first impressions of people from their speech, posture, or even eye contact. Most of these judgments are formed during very brief social interactions. That is, we form thin slice judgments of people from their verbal or non-verbal behavior in a very short time period. In a retail setting, consumers may form thin slice judgments of salespeople and products, and salespeople may form thin slice judgments of customers. Several studies have found that thin slice judgments formed based on these very brief exposures are highly accurate (Ambady & Rosenthal, 1992).

Through an individual's nonverbal behavior, such as facial expressions, voice, or body movements, we make judgments about emotions, personality, and other individual characteristics (Ambady et al., 2000). We are able to form thin slice judgments of people from brief exposures during social interactions. Similarly, nonverbal cues (eye gaze, speech hesitations, gestures, clothing, and posture) also impact certain dimensions of buyers' impressions of a salesperson (Leigh & Summers, 2002). When we extend the domain of thin slice judgments to retailing, it is important to consider customers' perceptions of salespeople's and salespeople's perceptions of customers' nonverbal behavior within the retail environment.

Ambady, Hallahan, and Rosenthal (1995) identified several individual difference traits, such as personality, nonverbal skills, and gender that moderate the accuracy of thin slice judgments. From a legibility perspective, individuals who are more expressive, more sociable, higher in self-esteem, and less shy were found to be judged more accurately by others. That is, more extraverted people reveal much about themselves through their nonverbal behavior. However, these more extraverted people are less accurate at judging others. Instead, those who are less sociable and lower in self-esteem can more accurately decode people's nonverbal behavior, even without interpersonal interactions. This research also found that females, in general, make more accurate thin slice judgments than males.

How accurate are thin slice judgments? Through a meta-analysis, Ambady and Rosenthal (1992) found that short observations of expressive behavior from 30 seconds to 5 minutes in duration yield predictive accuracy of an average effect size of $r = .39$. Thin slice judgments have been shown to have remarkable predictive accuracy in a variety of educational, organizational, and health care settings, within interpersonal relationships, and in determining sales performance (Ambady et al., 2000; Ambady et al., 2006; Curhan, Pentland, Caneel, Eagle, & Martin, 2005). In a negotiation setting, Curhan et al. (2005) obtained impressive effect sizes over .50 for the accuracy of thin slice judgments. In the selling domain, Ambady et al. (2006) found that thin slice judgments of sales managers' performance based on twenty-second audio clips accurately predicted sales performance. In this study, effect sizes were over .50, far beyond chance. Although thin slice judgments may not be accurate in every aspect of our daily life, the information gleaned from brief slices of verbal and nonverbal behavior sometimes allows us to form accurate judgments.

A series of studies have been conducted to examine the effects of mood on the accuracy of thin slice judgments (Ambady & Gray, 2002). This research found that judgments of participants in a sad mood were less accurate than those of participants in a neutral or a happy mood. In addition, they found that depressed people were less accurate in decoding nonverbal behavior, providing additional support for accuracy deterioration caused by sadness. However, if sad participants were assigned a cognitive load task, which distracted their attention away from their current mood, they performed as well as those in a neutral mood in making thin slice assessments. These findings suggest that sadness impairs the accuracy of thin slice judgments, and that allocation of cognitive resources to other tasks can alleviate the deteriorative effects of sadness on thin slice judgment accuracy.

Information Processing and Thin Slice Judgments

The cognitive information-processing paradigm has dominated consumer behavior research for the past two decades (Johar, Maheswaran, & Peracchio, 2006). As Jacoby, Johar, and Morrin (1998) have described, this approach generally characterizes information processing as conscious and deliberative. More recently, consumer psychologists have questioned this conscious processing paradigm and have called for more research into the role of non-conscious processes (Johar et al., 2006; Zaltman, 2000). Findings from consumer behavior research suggest that shopping decisions can occur in an automatic manner that would seem consistent with the notion of thin slice judgments (Bargh, 2002).

Automatic processes have typically been characterized as possessing four distinguishing features: a lack of intention, of conscious awareness, and of control, as well as a great deal of efficiency in that these judgments occur without deliberative effort on the part of an individual and are immune to conditions that tax an individual's cognitive resources (Bargh, 1996). As Ambady and colleagues suggest (Ambady et al., 2000; Ambady et al., 2006), thin slice judgments seem to fit the requirements for an automatic process. By contrast, conscious processing consumes cognitive resources and is intentional, controllable, and within the awareness of an individual.

Recent consumer research supports the contention that many consumer psychological processes may have both automatic and conscious components. Hence, consumer researchers have begun to provide a variety of empirical demonstrations of the impact of automatic and non-conscious processes on judgments (Raghubir & Krishna, 1996; Raghubir & Srivastava, 2002; Yorkston & Menon, 2004). For example, Raghubir and Krishna (1996) introduced to the consumer domain research on the impact of spatial perception biases on distance judgments. Their findings indicate that, immediately after initial exposure, when consumers estimate the direct distance between two points in a path, they use the perceptual salience of direct distance measurement in an automatic manner. Only later, in a second stage characterized by deliberative, systematic processing, are those distance estimates updated. This two-stage model of cognition suggests that consumer judgments are formed and framed in an initial automatic stage and then followed by conscious, deliberate processing.

The automatic nature and speed of thin slice judgments presupposes that they occur during the earliest stage of consumer judgment formation. Future research examining consumer shopping behavior should explore how such automatically formed thin slice judgments frame and impact subsequent deliberative processing. For instance, thin slice judgments may prime certain concepts, activating them in memory, and inhibit other concepts, causing subsequent judgments to be either more or less accurate. Under these conditions, it may require a great deal of cognitive resources to move beyond an initial thin slice judgment, making deliberative processing only feasible in certain situations, such as when consumers are highly involved.

The Formation and Application of Thin Slice Judgments

Perhaps the most relevant and intriguing aspect of thin slice judgments for consumer shopping behavior is how these short observations seem to allow for accurate prediction of outcome variables such as judgments about particular features and overall judgments of effectiveness. As Ambady and Rosenthal (1992) point out, this finding offers several implications, all of which are of theoretical and substantive interest to researchers studying consumer shopping behavior. First, this research implies that many of our day-to-day consumer judgments, at an aggregate level, may be more accurate than we previously expected. These findings also suggest that the judgments and perhaps the behavior of buyers, sellers, and customer service personnel may be predictable in some contexts. Thin slice judgments may assist us in accurately assessing and predicting outcomes in consumer buying situations. Finally, thin slice judgment research implies that people non-consciously communicate much information that may be, as DePaulo (1992) proposes, more accessible to the observer than to the sender and quite difficult for the sender to suppress.

In the next section, we review evidence regarding why thin slices may allow accurate judgment formation in a retailing environment.

Formation of Thin Slice Judgments

Ambady and Rosenthal (1992) have offered several explanations for the type of processing that may underlie thin slice judgments. First, adopting an ecological approach to thin slice judgments, they have suggested that successfully decoding nonverbal information is essential to accurate thin slice assessments. For example, Laplante and Ambady (2002) found that nonverbal cues such as tone of voice and facial expression provide much information about personality and internal state. Ambady and Rosenthal contend that certain features or attributes are quickly and accurately recognizable and decodable because immediate recognition of these features is necessary for successful navigation of the environment. For example, immediate identification of anger or fear may be important to survival.

Another explanation offered by Ambady and Rosenthal (1992) for the type of processing underlying thin slice judgments is an automatic comparison process. This comparison process employs categories in memory that are activated immediately upon a respondent's exposure to a stimulus. For example, they suggest that thin slices may activate stereotypes that are accurate or relevant to a particular context. Ambady et al. (2000) contend that thin slice judgments may arise from implicit knowledge of category exemplars. To achieve efficiency and conserve cognitive resources, individuals rely on quick and immediate categorization of stimuli in making a thin slice judgment. This type of categorization process has been examined in consumer research (Meyers-Levy & Tybout, 1989; Peracchio & Tybout, 1996). Future research should examine the use of these categorization judgments in retail environments and explore the type of processing that underlies such thin slice judgment formation.

Finally, Ambady and Rosenthal (1992) suggest that aspects of the judgment context may increase the accuracy of thin slice judgments. For example, judgments based on videotaped stimuli have been found to be more accurate than face-to-face judgments. This effect may emerge because actual face-to-face interactions place additional cognitive demands on participants including impression management and self-presentation (Ambady & Rosenthal, 1992). Thus, reducing the amount of distraction in the judgment context, focusing the attention of the decision-maker on relevant stimuli, and/or decreasing the number of task demands may increase the accuracy of thin slice judgments.

Relying on the affect as information paradigm, Pham, Cohen, Pracejus, and Hughes (2001) offer another, complementary explanation for the type of processing that may underlie thin slice judgments. They write, "The remarkable ability of feelings to predict spontaneous thoughts helps explain why immediate judgments based on very brief exposure to other individuals' nonverbal cues can be highly predictive of judgments based on much more extensive information about these individuals" (p. 185). Pham et al. suggest that nonverbal information produces an initial affective response that frames subsequent thoughts and thin slice judgments. This explanation is related to Ambady and Rosenthal's ecological approach regarding the usefulness of nonverbal information and introduces affect as a causal agent in the formation of a thin slice judgment. Future research employing indirect approaches rather than direct measurement should explore the role of affect in thin slice consumer shopping judgments.

Application of Thin Slice Judgments to Consumer Shopping Behavior

Exploring the accuracy of evaluative judgments based on thin slices in retail environments has the potential to yield interesting and valuable findings. As Ambady et al. (2006) point out, the more observable a trait, the more accurate thin slice judgments about that trait tend to be. In many shopping-related situations, important traits are easily observable or made salient by retailers, stimulating accurate thin slice judgments. The quest for most retailers is to break through the clutter by making a store's or a product's diagnostic traits (e.g., price discount) stand out. For example, in-store promotions make pricing information both salient and easily available to consumers. Thus, it would seem that thin slice judgments are bound to be relatively accurate in consumer shopping situations—as long as retailers do not provide misleading cues about their store's or a product's traits. For example, retailers may feature promotions (e.g., in-store product displays), but they do not offer price discounts. Unaware consumers may mistakenly infer that such promotion activities also reflect price discounts.

In the next section, we explore the potential application and extension of thin slice judgments to consumer shopping behavior. Our purpose is not to be inclusive of every application of thin slice judgments to consumer shopping behavior but rather to illustrate how research based on thin slice judgments can offer theoretical and substantive progress to that discipline. To this end, we consider the application of thin slice judgments to relationship marketing, language use, internet marketing, and customer service.

Relationship Marketing: Is There a Longer-Term Impact of Thin Slices?   Much attention in the retailing literature has focused on the cognitive antecedents of trust (Nicholson, Compeau, & Sethi, 2001), but little research has focused on trust as an automatic, thin slice process. It would seem viable that stage one of the trust process may be a thin slice assessment of the relationship partner. Nicholson et al. (2001) identified the importance of liking in building trust in long-term channel relationships. Their research suggests that when the relationship between buyer and sales representative is beginning, liking plays an important role in trust formation. It mediates how the similarity of the buyer and seller's business values and the frequency of buyer-seller interaction impact the development of the buyer's trust in the seller. As the buyer-sales representative relationship develops, liking becomes quite important in the channel relationship and influences the buyer's trust in the sales representative, and similarity of business values and personal interaction between buyer and seller become less important. This research raises interesting questions regarding the impact of thin slice judgments over time in a consumer shopping relationship. How do initial thin slice assessments anchor longer term relationships? Do thin slice assessments have a long-term impact throughout the relationship?

As Crosby, Evans, and Cowles (1990) point out, salespeople often perform the role of relationship manager when buyers and sellers interact. Jap, Manolis, and Weitz (1999) found evidence that higher quality relationships exhibit higher degrees of trust and fewer incidences of opportunitistic behavior. New products are accepted more readily in these high quality relationships. Can positive thin slice judgments have a beneficial impact on measures of longer term relationship quality such as new product acceptance? The impact of initial thin slice judgments in longer-term relationships between buyers and sellers is worthy of investigation. Future research should investigate whether initial thin slice judgments of salespeople's trustworthiness is positively related to new product acceptance.

Thin Slice Judgments and Language. Do consumers form judgments based on thin slices of language used in a shopping transaction? Can they form thin slice judgments based on sound, such as a speaker's tone of voice? For instance, does it matter whether a salesperson speaks with a bilingual customer in a first or second language? Anecdotal evidence, and increasing empirical research, suggests it would—consumers make judgments about people and brands based on various aspects of the language used during a shopping interaction.

Research on language and its influence on consumer behavior have identified automatic processes that influence judgments based on verbal stimuli (Luna, Ringberg, & Peracchio, 2005). Different languages, accents, language varieties (e.g., vernacular vs. "academese"), or intonations seem to activate different schemas, mental frames, or cultural models. These knowledge structures, which can contain unique associations, are cued by a particular language or language feature. For example, retailers targeting bilingual consumers may switch from one language (A) to another (B), in the process activating the knowledge structures associated with language B. Those associations then become readily accessible and can influence subsequent judgments (Luna & Peracchio, 2005). Indeed, the language used in a shopping transaction could influence how consumers feel about the retailer. Interpretations of the world around us in general, and interpretations of consumer shopping behavior in particular, depend on the cultural models activated by the language processed at any given time (Holland, Quinn, & Quinn, 1993; Hong, Morris, Chiu, & Benet-Martínez, 2000). Language may serve to elicit an associated mental frame or cultural model, resulting in the activation of certain values contained in that frame (e.g., independence vs. interdependence). Those values, then, influence an individual's interpretation of reality in an automatic fashion (Quinn & Holland, 1993). As Ambady and colleagues suggest, these interpretations and judgments can be made very quickly and accurately, based on thin slice judgments of verbal or auditory stimuli.

The application of the thin slice process to the language employed in a retailing environment can yield significant insights, extending current research on psycholinguistics in the area of marketing. For instance, one might predict that if auditory thin slices are used to form judgments, those judgments would be more accurate in alphabetic languages (e.g., English) than in logographic languages (e.g., Chinese). Conversely, judgments based on visual thin slices might be more accurate when consumers are operating in a logographic language (see Tavassoli & Lee, 2003). A moderator of these effects may be type of processing—data-driven or conceptually driven (Luna, Lerman, & Peracchio, 2005). That is, unless consumers are engaging in data-driven processing and attending to the language of an exchange, language may not be salient enough to trigger these effects.

Different types of judgments may be influenced by verbal thin slices. Trustworthiness ratings for salespeople or customer service representatives may be influenced by small samples of speech (Tsalikis, DeShields, & LaTour, 1991; Tsalikis, Ortiz-Buonafina, & LaTour, 1992). Also, the accents of salespeople or customer service personnel could lead to different perceptions and purchase intentions early on in the relationship (DeShields, Kara, & Kaynak, 1996), perhaps leading consumers to disregard the content of subsequent verbal communications. Altogether, the study of the impact of thin slices of speech and language on consumer shopping-relevant judgments could be studied systematically by examining the different aspects of language and their interactions—from phonetics, the study of sounds in speech, to morphology and syntax; from semantic to pragmatic and symbolic perspectives. For example, a salesperson's use of certain sounds or morphemes may make them appear more/less masculine or influence a product's perceived size and fit with one's needs (Shrum & Lowrey, 2007; Yorkston & de Mello, 2005; Yorkston & Menon, 2004). Similarly, a salesperson's use of certain syntactic structures in a verbal thin slice could influence consumers' judgments. According to the above discussions, we expect that thin slice judgments of the language used in a shopping transaction in terms of phonetics, morphemes, and syntax may impact consumers' perceptions and purchase intentions.

Language also impacts consumers' judgments of authenticity. Coupland (2003, p. 417) writes, ". . . language is every bit as much a means of achieving authenticity as it is a means to discrediting it. Specific ways of speaking and patterns of discursive representation can achieve the quality of experience that we define as authentic." It would seem that how salespeople speak with customers during a shopping transaction influences consumers' perceptions of authenticity. Further, research has found that salespeople who speak in the native language of customers become more accepted by them (Jaworski, Ylänne-McEwen, Thurlow, & Lawson, 2003). Language affects whether people perceive individuals as in-group or out-group members impacting judgments of authenticity.

Thin Slice Judgments on the Web. The World Wide Web represents an important tool, allowing retailers to interact with customers by providing information, presenting products, and facilitating purchases. Research on consumer shopping behavior on the web suggests that 80 percent of web surfers spend only a few seconds looking at a Web site before clicking through to the next site (Tweedy, 2002), and the average web surfer is unlikely to look past the first two pages of a Web site (Powell, 2003; Thompson, 2004). Thus, online consumers seem to be forming evaluative judgments of web sites in a manner consistent with thin slice judgments. As Ambady et al. (2006) suggest, perceptual judgments are accurate, "even in the absence of any personal interaction" (p. 4). On the web, the dynamic interaction between the user and the Web site may allow the formation of a thin slice judgment even without interpersonal interaction. Perhaps, just as thin slice judgments of people are accurate, thin slice judgments of a Web site's usefulness, effectiveness, and trustworthiness are also quite accurate.

Chiravuri and Peracchio (2003) have proposed that consumers can accurately judge the security and ease of use of a Web site from a brief thin slice encounter with that Web site. Based on research suggesting that trusting beliefs online form very quickly (McKnight, Choudhury, & Kacmar, 2002), Haried (2005) contends that consumers form accurate thin slice judgments of the trustworthiness of a Web site during brief exposure to that site. Haried relies on a cognitive view of trust that suggests that trust on the web is based on perceived competence, benevolence, integrity, openness, attraction, and predictability of a Web site. Other researchers have found that some person perception processes do operate on the Internet—for example, the Bystander Effect (Markey, Wells, & Markey, 2001) and the Deindividuation Effect (Postmes, Spears, Sakhel, & de Groot, 2001). Hence, researchers interested in consumer shopping behavior should investigate the potential application of thin slice judgments in an e-tailing environment.

Thin slice judgments and customer service. Much research in marketing has acknowledged the importance of customer service and service quality to the consumer's experience of and associations to a retail environment (Iacobucci, 2001). Customers' evaluative judgments of service quality affect many consumer behaviors that are important to retailers, such as customer loyalty and price sensitivity (Doucet, 2004). Researchers studying service quality have emphasized the importance of the service provider in delivering excellent customer service and presenting a face for an organization—in essence, personifying the brand (Barker & Hartel, 2004). Other research on the service-profit chain has identified relationships between the attitude of service providers, customer satisfaction, and achieving the organization's goals (Heskett, Sasser, & Schlesinger, 1997).

Research on customer service would benefit from examining, applying, and extending the concept of thin slice judgments. How do customers' thin slice judgments impact perceptions of service providers? And, how do thin slice judgments of service providers impact customers? Hecht and LaFrance (1995) found that the tone of voice of directory assistance operators determines customer perceptions of enthusiasm, sympathy, confidence, professionalism, and friendliness. Similarly, Levi and Pisoni (2007) indicate that voice characteristics (e.g., accent, speech rate) have an impact on listeners' attitudes toward a message.

If service providers are considered representatives of the retailer, how do these thin slice judgments impact retailer assessments? Are these thin slice effects short term or do they have longer term implications for how people think and feel about a retailer? Pugh (2001) has identified emotional contagion effects in customer service situations such that customers "catch" the affect of service providers. This research finds that the positive affect of service providers is related to customers' positive perceptions of service quality. Do thin slice judgments underlie this emotional contagion effect? Or, as Pham et al.'s (2001) research suggests, does the emotional contagion effect underlie thin slice judgments? These and other questions relating to service quality and thin slice judgments await investigation. We propose that thin slice judgments of customer service representatives are related to consumers' perceptions of the service quality of retailers.

Conclusion

Our examination of thin slice judgments reveals opportunities for researchers studying retailing to make theoretical and substantive contributions to our understanding of consumer shopping behavior. Examining thin slice judgments offers the possibility of augmenting and extending information processing theory. Gaining an understanding of how thin slice judgments are formed presents the potential for enhancing our understanding of consumer shopping behavior. Understanding the applications of thin slice judgments to consumer shopping behavior offers many opportunities for both theoretical as well as managerial and public policy advances within retailing. Calder and Tybout (1987) have suggested that consumer behavior research should advance theoretical knowledge about the consumer. Research focusing on thin slice judgments presents an opportunity to accomplish this research objective as well as to make substantive contributions to the discipline of retailing.

In their review of the past fifteen years of consumer behavior research, Johar et al. (2006) contend that most consumer behavior research has focused on one-shot events. However, the study of retailing is a dynamic discipline concerned with continuous exchange over time with consumers forming and reforming judgments in response to many different types of information. These researchers have called for an examination of how a sequence of events, for example, initial thin slice judgment formation and subsequent deliberative processing, affects consumer information processing. The study of thin slice judgments in a retailing environment offers the opportunity to examine how initial judgments are formed and then updated after exposure to subsequent information that may or may not be consistent with the initial thin slice judgment.

Many consumer researchers have called for a comprehensive model of information processing incorporating our understanding of both deliberative and implicit processes (Bettman, 1979; Johar et al., 2006). Research on thin slice judgments and the processing that underlies them should be included in such a model. Incorporating judgment accuracy into a model of information processing may open new avenues of research for consumer research and the study of retailing. Studying thin slice judgments and the accuracy of these evaluative judgments offers opportunities to contribute to knowledge in consumer research and information processing.

References

Ambady, N., Bernieri, F. J., & Richeson, J. A. (2000). Towards a histology of social behavior: Judgmental accuracy from thin slices of behavior. In M. P. Zanna (Ed.), *Advances in experimental social psychology* (pp. 201–272). San Diego, CA: Academic Press.

Ambady, N., & Gray, H. M. (2002). On being sad and mistaken: Mood effects on the accuracy of thin slice judgments. *Journal of Personality and Social Psychology, 83*, 947–961.

Ambady, N., Hallahan, M., & Rosenthal, R. (1995). On judging and being judged accurately in zero-acquaintance situations. *Journal of Personality and Social Psychology, 69*, 518–529.

Ambady, N., Krabbenhoft, M. A., & Hogan, D. (2006). The 30-second sale: Using thin slice judgments to evaluate sales effectiveness. *Journal of Consumer Psychology, 16*, 4–13.

Ambady, N., & Rosenthal, R. (1992). Thin slices of expressive behavior as predictors of interpersonal consequences: A meta-analysis. *Psychological Bulletin, 111*, 256–274.

Bargh, J. A. (1996). Automaticity in social psychology. In E. T. Higgins & A. W. Kruglanski (Eds.), *Social psychology: Handbook of basic principles* (pp. 169–183). New York: Guilford Press.

Bargh, J. A. (2002). Losing consciousness: Automatic influences on consumer judgment, behavior, and motivation. *Journal of Consumer Research, 29*, 280–285.

Barker, S., & Hartel, C. (2004). Intercultural service encounters: An exploratory study of customer experiences. *Cross Cultural Management, 11*, 3–14.

Bettman, J. R. (1979). Memory factors in consumer choice: A review. *Journal of Marketing, 43*, 37–53.

Calder, B. J., & Tybout, A. M. (1987). What consumer research is. . . . *Journal of Consumer Research, 14*, 136–140.

Chiravuri, A., & Peracchio, L. A. (2003, August). *Investigating online consumer behavior using thin slices of usability of Web sites.* Paper presented at the Americas Conference on Information Systems, Tampa, Florida.

Coupland, N. (2003). Sociolinguistic authenticities. *Journal of Sociolinguistics, 7*, 417–431.

Crosby, L. A., Evans, K. R., & Cowles, D. (1990). Relationship quality in services selling: An interpersonal influence perspective. *Journal of Marketing, 54*, 68–81.

Curhan, J. R., Pentland, A., Caneel, R., Eagle, N., & Martin, M. C. (2005, August). *Thin slices of negotiation: Predicting outcomes from conversational dynamics within the first five minutes.* Paper presented at the Annual Meeting of the Academy of Management, Honolulu, Hawaii.

DePaulo, B. M. (1992). Nonverbal behavior and self-presentation. *Psychological Bulletin, 111*, 203–243.

DeShields, O. W., Jr., Kara, A., & Kaynak, E. (1996). Source effects in purchase decisions: The impact of physical attractiveness and accent of salesperson. *International Journal of Research in Marketing, 13*, 89–102.

Doucet, L. (2004). Service provider hostility and service quality. *Academy of Management Journal, 47*, 761–771.

Haried, P. (2005). Understanding online consumer trust using thin slices of web sites (Working Paper). Milwaukee: University of Wisconsin-Milwaukee.

Hecht, M. A., & LaFrance, M. (1995). How (fast) can I help you? Tone of voice and telephone operator efficiency in interactions. *Journal of Applied Social Psychology, 25*, 2086–2098.

Heskett, J. L., Sasser, W. E., & Schlesinger, L. A. (1997). *The service profit chain.* New York: Free Press.

Holland, D., & Quinn, N. (Ed.) (1993). *Cultural models in language and thought.* New York: Cambridge University Press.

Hong, Y., Morris, M. W., Chiu, C., & Benet-Martínez, V. (2000). Multicultural minds: A dynamic constructivist approach to culture and cognition. *American Psychologist, 55*, 709–720.

Iacobucci, D. (2001). Services marketing and customer service. In D. Iacobucci (Ed.), *Kellogg on marketing* (pp. 320–329). New York: Wiley.

Jacoby, J., Johar, G. V., & Morrin, M. (1998). Consumer behavior: A quadrennium. *Annual Review of Psychology, 49*, 319–344.

Jap, S. D., Manolis, C., & Weitz, B. A. (1999). Relationship quality and buyer-seller interactions in channels of distribution. *Journal of Business Research, 46*, 303–313.

Jaworski, A., Ylänne-McEwen, V., Thurlow, C., & Lawson, S. (2003). Social roles and negotiation of status in host-tourist interaction: A view from British television holiday programmes. *Journal of Sociolinguistics, 7*, 135–163.

Johar, G. V., Maheswaran, D., & Peracchio, L. A. (2006). *MAP*ping the frontiers: Theoretical advances in consumer research on *M*emory, *A*ffect, and *P*ersuasion. *Journal of Consumer Research, 33*, 139–149.

Laplante, D., & Ambady, N. (2002). Saying it like it isn't: Mixed messages from men and women in the workplace. *Journal of Applied Social Psychology, 32*, 2435–2457.

Leigh, T. W., & Summers, J. O. (2002). An initial evaluation of industrial buyers' impressions of salespersons' nonverbal cues. *Journal of Personal Selling & Sales Management, 22*, 41–53.

Levi, S. V., & Pisoni, D. B. (2007). Indexical and linguistic channels in speech perception: Some effects of voiceovers on advertising outcomes. In T. M. Lowrey (Ed.), *Psycholinguistic phenomena in marketing communications.* Mahwah, NJ: Lawrence Erlbaum Associates.

Luna, D., Lerman, D., & Peracchio, L. A. (2005). Structural constraints in code-switched advertising. *Journal of Consumer Research, 32*, 416–423.

Luna, D., & Peracchio, L. A. (2005). Advertising to bilingual consumers: The impact of code-switching on persuasion. *Journal of Consumer Research, 31*, 760–765.

Luna, D., Ringberg, T., & Peracchio, L. A. (2007). Mental frames and language use: Frame-switching among biculturals. Manuscript in preparation.

Markey, P. M., Wells, S. M., & Markey, C. N. (2001). Personality and social psychology in the culture of cyberspace. In S. P. Shohov (Ed.), *Advances in psychology research* (pp. 103–124). Hauppauge, NY: Nova Science Publishers, Inc.

McKnight, D. H., Choudhury, V., & Kacmar, C. (2002). The impact of initial consumer trust on intentions to transact with a web site: A trust building model. *Journal of Strategic Information Systems, 11,* 297–323.

Meyers-Levy, J., & Tybout, A. M. (1997). Context effects at encoding and judgment in consumption settings: The role of cognitive resources. *Journal of Consumer Research, 24,* 1–14.

Nicholson, C. Y., Compeau, L. D., & Sethi, R. (2001). The role of interpersonal liking in building trust in long-term channel relationships. *Journal of the Academy of Marketing Science 29,* 3–15.

Peracchio, L. A., & Tybout, A. M. (1996). The moderating role of prior knowledge in schema-based product evaluation. *Journal of Consumer Research, 23,* 177–192.

Pham, M. T., Cohen, J. B., Pracejus, J. W., & Hughes, G. D. (2001). Affect monitoring and the primacy of feelings in judgment. *Journal of Consumer Research, 28,* 167–188.

Postmes, T., Spears, R., Sakhel, K., & de Groot, D. (2001). Social influence in computer-mediated communication: The effects of anonymity on group behavior. *Personality and Social Psychology Bulletin, 27,* 1243–1254.

Powell, W. (2003). The Web. *T + D, 57, 8;* 22–24.

Pugh, S. D. (2001). Service with a smile: Emotional contagion in the service encounter. *Academy of Management Journal, 44,* 1018–1027.

Quinn, N., & Holland, D. (1993). Culture and cognition. In D. Holland & N. Quinn (Eds.), *Cultural models in language and thought* (pp. 1–40). New York: Cambridge University Press.

Raghubir, P., & Krishna, A. (1996). As the crow flies: Bias in consumers' map-based distance judgments. *Journal of Consumer Research, 23,* 26–39.

Raghubir, P., & Srivastava, J. (2002). Effect of face value on product valuation in foreign currencies. *Journal of Consumer Research, 29,* 335–347.

Shrum, L. J., & Lowrey, T. M. (2007). Sounds convey meaning: The implications of phonetic symbolism for brand name construction. In T. M. Lowrey (Ed.), Psycholinguistic phenomena in marketing communications. Hillsdale, NJ: Lawrence Erlbaum Associates.

Tavassoli, N. T., & Lee, Y. H. (2003). The differential interaction of auditory and visual advertising elements with Chinese and English. *Journal of Marketing Research, 40,* 468–481.

Thompson, C. (2004). Search engines invite new problems. *Marketing Management, 13*, 52–53.

Tsalikis, J., DeShields, O. W., Jr., & LaTour, M. S. (1991). The role of accent on the credibility and effectiveness of the salesperson. *The Journal of Personal Selling & Sales Management, 11*, 31–41.

Tsalikis, J., Ortiz-Buonafina, M., & LaTour, M. S. (1992). The role of accent on the credibility and effectiveness of the international business person: The case of Guatemala. *International Marketing Review, 9*, 57–72.

Tweedy, D. G. (2002). How do we get visitors to visit our website? Or what's new in homepages? *DGT Internet Marketing.* Retrieved June 10, 2005, from http://www.dgtinternetmarketing.com/newsletter1.php

Yorkston, E., & Menon, G. (2004). A sound idea: Phonetic effects of brand names on consumer judgments. *Journal of Consumer Research, 31*, 43–51.

Yorkston, E., & de Mello, G. E. (2005). Linguistic gender marking and categorization. *Journal of Consumer Research, 32*, 224–234.

Zaltman, G. (2000). Consumer researchers: Take a hike! *Journal of Consumer Research, 26*, 423–48.

3

SOUND RETAILING: A REVIEW OF EXPERIMENTAL EVIDENCE ON THE EFFECTS OF MUSIC ON SHOPPING BEHAVIOR

David Allan

Saint Joseph's University

*O*VER 30 YEARS AFTER Kotler (1973) called it an atmospheric effect, music is still being played in retail establishments for the enjoyment and engagement of customers and employees. To many of us it is simply a form of entertainment. But to the retailer, music continues to be a key element in the retail environment. Bitner (1992) suggested that it was *the* key ambient condition of the servicescape. From a psychological perspective, it has been shown that music can affect everything from the moods of shoppers to their attitude toward the store and its employees. From a marketing perspective, it can position the retail establishment and help differentiate it from its competitors by stimulating the development of what Robert Kozinets called in Chapter 1 the "brand scape." Now with increasing competition that retailing is facing from e-tailing, music may be the at-*mus*-pheric effect that interacts with other atmospheric effects to distinguish bricks from clicks and result in *sound retailing*.

Music and marketing are popular literature topics. Music and advertising has attracted a considerable amount of academic attention, especially with regard to music variables and advertising effects. Some of the most notable effects include loudness (Kellaris & Rice, 1993); mood (Alpert & Alpert, 1990; Bruner, 1990); music preference (Gorn, 1982); tempo (Brooker & Wheatley, 1994; Kellaris & Kent, 1991, 1994); time (Kellaris & Mantel, 1996); and variation (Kellaris & Cox, 1989; Kellaris, Cox, & Cox, 1993; Park & Young, 1986) just to name a few (see also Bruner, 1990, pp. 96–97).

Music and shopping behavior has also received a great deal of scholarly focus. Not surprisingly, music is in fact believed to be the most commonly studied retail environmental cue (Turley & Milliman, 2000). What is surprising is that past reviews of experimental evidence in this area have included music and retail only as part of a larger review of atmospheric effects (Lam, 2001; Turley & Milliman, 2000), or consumer behavior (North & Hargreaves, 1997). Yet, most retailers would agree that music is one of their most important considerations. However, it is expensive, contrary to what many believe (Yalch & Spangenberg, 1993, p. 632). Worldwide, retailers spend billions of dollars on music (North & Hargreaves, 1998). This includes music systems, music providers like Muzak (e.g., Eroglu, Machleit, & Chebat, 2005; Yalch & Spangenberg, 1988), and royalty fees. In the case of Muzak all types of music are available for one general fee (usually between $80 and $120 per month). As for royalties, a license fee is paid to the American Society of Composers, Authors, and Publishers (ASCAP) or Broadcast Music Inc. (BMI). These companies provide residuals collected from the source and the retail establishment to song writers and composers each time a song is played. They consider the playing of CDs or radio to be public performance with licensing fees from $200 to $2,000 per year depending on square footage. A new alternative is satellite radio (Sirius or XM) offering a variety of music services for around $300 with ASCAP and BMI fees included.

It is clear, therefore, based on the amount of importance and attention researchers and retailers have placed on music in the retail environment, that music has earned a solo. This review will shine the whole spotlight on music and its effect on shopping behavior.

Purpose

This chapter has three purposes. First, it is a review of the most relevant studies involving music effects on shopping behavior. Second, it is a synthesis and comparison of variables and findings. Third, based on what has been done and how it has been executed, it is roadmap of future travel down this very important research stream.

Literature Review

A summary table of 29 published empirical studies on the effects of music on shopping behavior is presented chronologically in Table 3.1. Each of these studies observed characteristics or elements of music observing some type of effect on consumer behavior in the retail environment. What follows is a summary of theoretical backgrounds, variables and findings.

Theories and Models. A brief look at the studies in this group shows that many referenced in some way environmental psychological theory. This involves a stimulus-organism response (S-O-R) model where the music is the stimulus that causes a shopper's evaluation and some type of behavioral response. The most utilized has been Mehrabian and Russell's (1974) Pleasure-Arousal-Dominance (PAD) model of environmental psychology (e.g., Baker, Levy, & Grewal, 1992; Milliman, 1982, 1986; Yalch & Spangenberg, 1990). This model suggests that the environment affects individuals' moods or emotions by altering their state of pleasure, arousal, and dominance. Individuals, therefore, respond emotionally to the environmental stimulus of music, which results in some type of approach-avoidance behavior. This approach-avoidance behavior has four aspects: a desire to stay (approach) or not stay (avoid); a desire to explore (approach) or not explore (avoid); a desire to communicate with others (approach) or not communicate with others (avoid); and a desire to enhance satisfaction with tasks performed (approach) or not enhance satisfaction (avoid) (see Chapter 4, this volume).

The Mehrabian-Russell (1974) model was first suggested as an explanation for the interaction of environmental effects on shopping behavior by Donovan and Rossiter (1982). They suggested that in-store variables, like music, are represented psychologically by consumers in terms of pleasure (pleasant-unpleasant) and arousal (arousing-sleepy). These two emotional states act then as mediators of shopping behaviors. This provides a mechanism for retailers to explain and predict changes to in-store variables like music. Many studies observed the interaction of music on pleasure and arousal (e.g., Baker et al., 1992; Yalch & Spangenberg, 1988).

Some additional theories included Berlyne's (1971) theory of aesthetic response that was referenced in two studies (North & Hargreaves, 1996a, 1996b). This states that preference for stimuli is related to their potential to arouse in an inverted-U relationship with an intermediate degree of arousal potential being liked most. The functional theory of attitudes was also mentioned (Schlosser, 1998). This states that influences are most persuasive when they address the motives underlying an attitude targeted for change.

Independent Variables. The impact of music has been observed on a variety of shopping behaviors when mediated either individually or through the interaction of a number of variables. Those related directly to music characteristics included tempo (Caldwell & Hibbert, 2002; Chebat, Gelinas-Chebat, & Filiatrault, 1993; Eroglu et al., 2005; Oakes 2003; Herrington & Capella, 1996; Milliman, 1982, 1986; Oakes, 2003); volume (Babin, Chebat, & Michon, 2004; Herrington & Capella, 1996; Smith & Curnow, 1966), background, not as a focal point or foreground, as a focal point (Areni & Kim, 1993; Herrington & Capella, 1996; Yalch & Spangenberg, 1988, 1990, 1993), and genre.

Table 3.1 Summary of Relevant Research Involving Retail and Music

Citation	Sample Setting	Independent Variables	Dependent Variables	Results
Donovan & Rossiter (1966)	30 graduate students	Music tempo	Pleasure Arousal	Up tempo music most effective when pleasure and arousal high; slow tempo or no music most effective when pleasure and arousal low.
Smith & Curnow (1966)	1100 shoppers in a supermarket	Music volume	Time spent Money spent	High volume music resulted in less time spent but no difference in sales or customer satisfaction.
Milliman (1982)	216 shoppers in a supermarket	Music tempo	Pace of in-store traffic flow Sales volume	Slow tempo music resulted in a slower pace of in-store traffic and a higher sales volume.
Milliman (1986)	1392 customers in a restaurant	Music tempo	Service time Customer time Customer leaving Food purchased Liquor purchased	Slow tempo music resulted in longer service time; longer customer time; fewer customers leaving before seated; more food and liquor purchased; more sales volume.
Yalch & Spangenberg (1988)	86 shoppers in a clothing store	Background/ foreground	Department shopped Time spent Money spent Pleasure Arousal Dominance	Background music resulted in younger shoppers perceiving more time shopping; foreground music resulted in older shopping; background music was less desirable and arousing.

Yalch & Spangenberg (1990)	86 shoppers in a clothing store	Background/foreground	Mood Unplanned purchases Perception of shopping time	Clothing store shoppers preferred foreground music but moods and unplanned purchases were not affected; perception of shopping time varied with music and age but not time of day.
Baker, Levy, & Grewal (1992)	147 undergraduate students watching a video of a card-and-gift store	Background/ foreground Music genre (Classical/Top 40)	Willingness to buy Arousal Pleasure	Music and retail salespeople interacted to affect arousal and willingness to buy.
Areni & Kim (1993)	64 observations (16 for each dependent variable) at wine store in a restaurant	Music genre (Classical/ Top 40)	Information search Purchase behavior Consumption behavior Shopping time	Classical music influenced customers to purchase more expensive wines but did not affect the search or the time spent shopping.
Chebat, Gelinas-Chebat, & Filiatrault (1993)	427 undergraduate students in a simulated bank environment	Music tempo	Attention level Mood Time spent	Music acts as mediator and affects attention level, mood and time estimation: Music detracts from the effects of visual stimuli in bank.
Yalch & Spangenberg (1993)	105 shoppers in a department within a store	Music genre Background/foreground	Mood Perceptions of the store Time spent Money spent Music preference	Music that fit a department resulted in more purchases and money spent; music interacted with age but not gender. Younger shoppers showed a preference for foreground music and older shoppers preferred background.

(continued)

Table 3.1 (Continued)

Citation	Sample Setting	Independent Variables	Dependent Variables	Results
Gulas & Schewe (1994)	76 supermarket shoppers	Music genre (Classic Rock/Big Band)	Time spent Store attributes Emotions Items purchased Money spent	Classic Rock music resulted in more purchases by baby boomers than Big Band music for older shoppers.
Dube, Chebat, & Morin (1995)	270 undergraduates in a simulated bank environment	Music pleasure/arousal	Desire to affiliate	Music-induced pleasure and arousal affected consumers' desire to affiliate with bank personnel.
Herington & Capella (1996)	140 supermarket shoppers	Music tempo Music volume Music preference	Musical preference Mood state Time pressure	Tempo and volume did not affect shopping time or expenditure. Preference did influence shopping time and expenditure.
North & Hargreaves (1996a)	236 students in a cafeteria	Music genre/ complexity (New Age/Organ)	Music preference/appeal	As dislike became more extreme, music became more salient as a feature of the environment that subjects might like to change.
North & Hargreaves (1996b)	285 subjects in a dining area seeking advice on welfare	Music genre (New Age/Organ)	Evaluation of environment	Response to the dining area. Responses to music associated with response to the dining area.

Hui, Dube, & Chebat (1997)	116 students in a simulated bank environment	Music valence	Perceived wait duration; Emotional evaluation of the service environment; Emotional response to the wait	Music positively affects consumers' approach behaviors towards the service organization; valenced music stimulates a more positive emotional response (and perceived wait duration) to waiting and a stronger approach behavior towards the service organization.
North & Hargreaves (1998)	300 students in a cafeteria	Music genre (Classical/Pop/Easy Listening)	Evaluation of environment; Purchase intention	Musical genre affected perception of environment; Classical music associated with paying more; Classical and Pop might have increased sales.
North, Hargreaves, & McKendrick (1999)	82 shoppers bought wine/44 completed postpurchase questionnaire in a supermarket	Music genre (French/German)	Selection	French music led to French wines outselling German wines; German music led to German wines outselling French wines.
Chebat, Valiant, & Gelinas-Chebat (2000)	593 business students watching a travel service exchange on video	Background/foreground	Salesperson perception; Intent to buy; Argument acceptance; Desire to affiliate	Background music did not moderate the effects of the salesperson on the intent to buy but did influence the effects of acceptance of the salesperson's arguments and the desire to affiliate.
North, Hargreaves, & McKendrick (2000)	331 people in a bank; 328 people in a bar	Music fit	Bank/bar perception	Positive correlation between perception of the music and the bank and the bar.

(*continued*)

Table 3.1 (Continued)

Citation	Sample Setting	Independent Variables	Dependent Variables	Results
Chebat, Gelinas-Chebat, & Valiant (2001)	593 business students watching a travel service exchange on video	Background/foreground Music fit	Store perception Salesperson perception	Background music that is cognitively processed and fits affects attitude toward the store, the salesperson, and the visit to the store.
Dube & Morin (2001)	110 mall shoppers	Background/foreground Pleasure/arousal	Attitude toward environment Attitude toward personnel Store evaluation	Background music exerted influence on store evaluation due to variations in the intensity of pleasure by a mediating effect of attitude towards the servicescape and sales personnel.
Mattila & Wirtz (2001)	270 department store shoppers	Music/scent arousal	Store evaluation	When music and scent arousal levels are congruent, shoppers rate the environment more positively.
Baker, Parasurraman, Grewal, & Voss (2002)	297/169 business students watching a video of a simulated card-and-gift store environment	Music genre	Customer service	Music perceptions of slow Classical and Top 40 music were independent of customer service.
Caldwell & Hibbert (2002)	62 restaurant customers	Music tempo/Music preference	Actual time spent Effect on perceived time Money spent Affected enjoyment Intentions to return Intentions to recommend	Music preference affected actual time not tempo; neither affected perceived time; time spent was the best predictor of money spent; music preference, but not tempo, affected enjoyment and intentions to return and recommend.

North, Shilcock, & Hargreaves (2003)	393 total restaurant customers/141 investigated	Music Genre (Classical/ Top 40)	Customer spending Time spent	Music style (Classical) affected customer spending.
Oakes (2003)	335 undergraduate students during course resignation	Music tempo	Perception of wait time Affective responses	Music tempo resulted in temporal perception (perceived–actual wait duration); slow-tempo digitally-produced original music enhanced affective response (satisfaction, expectations, and relaxation).
Babin, Chebat, & Michin (2004)	800 mall shoppers	Music genre Music volume	Perceptual appropriateness	Changes in music genre and volume caused diminishing perceptual appropriateness resulting in lower positive affect, product quality, shopping value, and fewer approach behaviors.
Eronglu, Machleit, & Chebat (2005)	347 mall shoppers	Music tempo	Shopping experience	Shopping experience most favorable under conditions of slow music/high density and fast music/low density. Significant main effects of music tempo for approach/ avoidance tendency.

Although genre has received a considerable amount of attention, only a few genres have been observed, including Classical or Top 40 (Areni & Kim, 1993; Babin et al., 2004; Baker et al., 1992, 2002; North, Shilcock, & Hargreaves, 2003; North, Hargreaves, & McKendrick, 2000); Classic Rock or Big Band (Gulas & Schalewe, 1994), New Age or Organ (North & Hargreaves, 1996a, 1996b); Classical, Top 40, and Easy Listening (North & Hargreaves, 1998); and French or German (North, Hargreaves, & McKendrick, 1999).

Those that related more to music perception, either generally or specifically by a demographic included: fit (e.g., a consumer's perception of the music's relevance to a product or store) in a bar and bank (North et al., 2000), and in a store (Chebat, Gelinas-Chebat, & Vaillant, 2001); pleasure or arousal (Chebat, Valliant, & Gelinas-Chebat, 2000, 2001; Dube & Morin, 2001; Dube, Chebat, & Morin, 1995); preference (Herrrington & Capella, 1996, Yalch & Spangenberg, 1993); and age of the shopper (Yalch & Spangenberg, 1990; Gulas & Schewe, 1994).

Dependent Variables. When mediated with the above variables, the effects of music on a variety of behaviors have been observed during the shopping experience. The initial and intermediary variables included: mood (Chebat et al., 1993; Herrington & Capella, 1996; Yalch & Spangenberg, 1990, 1993); pleasure/arousal (Baker et al., 1992; Donovan & Rossiter, 1982; Yalch & Spangenberg, 1988); salesperson perception/affiliation (Baker et al., 2002; Chebat et al., 2000; Dube et al., 1995); store perception (Dube & Morin, 2001; Gulas & Schewe, 1994; North & Hargreaves, 1996b, 1998); time waiting (Hui, Dube, & Chebat, 1997; Oakes, 2003); and time spent (Areni & Kim, 1993; Caldwell & Hibbert, 2002; Chebat et al., 1993; Gulas & Schewe, 1994; North et al., 2003; Smith & Curnow, 1966; Yalch & Spangenberg, 1988, 1990, 1993). The outcome variables included: willingness to buy (Baker et al., 1992) and money spent (Milliman, 1982, 1986; North et al., 2003; Smith & Curnow, 1966; Yalch & Spangenberg, 1988). A schematic along a DV continuum can be seen in Figure 3.1 and provides the structure for a review of what we know from the research that has been conducted.

Results

Much has been learned since Kotler (1973, p. 64) termed the phrase "atmospherics" to describe, among other things, music. He suggested the need for further research into the use of atmospherics as a communication tool, as a competitive edge, and as a customer behavior solution (see Chapter 5, this volume). Now, over thirty years later, here is what has been found.

mood	pleasure/ arousal	salesperson perception/affiliation	store perception	time waiting	time spent	willingness to buy	money spent
background/ foreground fit genre preference tempo volume	background/ foreground genre tempo	background/ foreground fit pleasure/ arousal volume	background/ foreground fit w/smell genre pleasure/ arousal tempo volume	tempo valence	background/ foreground preference tempo volume	background/ foreground genre	background/ foreground genre preference tempo volume

Figure 3.1.
DV/IV Continuum

Mood. The research on mood suggests that some music variables can have an effect on shopping behavior. It has been observed that background and foreground music does not affect mood (Yalch & Spangenberg, 1990), but when the genre of music fits the shopper it can enhance mood (Yalch & Spangenberg, 1993). Herrington and Capella (1996) observed that preference for either background or foreground music can affect mood thereby influencing behavior, but Yalch and Spangenberg (1993) argued that moods did not explain the music effects (but store perceptions did). The results on tempo are also varied, with Chebat et al. (1993) suggesting that tempo acts as a mediator and can affect mood but Herrington and Capella (1996) were not able to confirm this finding for either tempo or volume.

Pleasure and Arousal. Whether music can enhance pleasure and arousal has received some attention with varying results. Yalch and Spangenberg (1988) observed that background music was less desirable and resulted in shoppers reporting that they were less aroused. This was observed to be dependent on age and time of day. Baker et al. (1992) observed that ambient cues (Classical-background/Top 40-foreground music) interacted with social cues (salesperson interaction) to influence pleasure. Donovan and Rossiter (1982, 1994) suggested that fast and slow tempo can interact with high and low pleasure and arousal to increase shopping-related intentions.

Salesperson Perception and Affiliation. It was observed that background music influenced the acceptance of the salesperson's arguments and the desire to affiliate with travel (Chebat et al., 2000), and bank personnel (Dube et al., 1995). This was extended to the consumer's attitude toward the sales personnel (Dube & Morin, 2001). This suggests that low or moderately arousing music may help salespeople significantly in selling to and affiliating with the consumer.

Additionally, Baker et al. (2002) observed that when the music fits, it can positively affect perceptions of customer service and when it doesn't fit, or there are changes in the volume of music, the result is diminished perceptual environmental appropriateness resulting in fewer approach behaviors (Babin et al., 2004).

Store Perception. Not surprisingly, the effect of music on the perception of the store has received a considerable amount of attention. The results tell us that background music that is highly pleasurable can positively affect store evaluation (Dube & Morin, 2001). It appears that the fit of the music to the retail environment is an important consideration. It was observed that when the music fit, it affected the perceptions (positively) of a bar and bank (North et al., 2000), and a store (Chebat et al., 2001). Fit has also been shown to interact with scent to enhance store evaluation (Mattila & Wirtz, 2001). Finally, genre has been observed to interact with fit/age of the shopper to (positively) affect perception of the store (North & Hargreaves, 1998; Yalch & Spangenberg, 1993).

Tempo also appears to be an important music variable. It was observed that fast tempo negatively influenced attention level (Chebat et al., 1993), but had no effect on enjoyment (Caldwell & Hibbert, 2002). It was also observed that slow tempo enhanced satisfaction, expectations, and relaxation (Babin et al., 2004), and that slow tempo interacted with high retail density and fast tempo interacted with low retail density to enhance the overall shopping experience (Eroglu et al., 2005). Finally, changes in volume (and genre) of music were shown to diminish perceptual environmental appropriateness resulting in lower perceptions of personal shopping value (Babin et al., 2004).

Time Waiting. As for the real and perceived time that a consumer waits for service, Milliman (1986) observed that slow tempo resulted in longer customer actual time. It was also shown that slow tempo can increase perceived wait time by the consumer (Oakes, 2003). Another variable to consider is music valence (e.g., liked versus disliked) which was suggested as a possible stimulus of lower perceived wait duration (Hui et al., 1997).

Time Spent. As for time spent shopping, background (older consumers) and foreground music (younger consumers) affected perceived time shopping depending on age but not gender (Yalch & Spangenberg, 1988, 1990). It was also observed that background music did not affect the amount of time spent shopping in a wine store (Areni & Kim, 1993).

It was shown and confirmed that tempo had no effect on shopping time, either real or perceived (Caldwell & Hibbert, 2002; Herrington & Capella, 1996), but music preference did (Caldwell & Hibbert, 2002). Milliman (1982, 1986) observed that slow tempo resulted in a slower pace of in-store traffic, service time, and customer time. Similar results were observed by Kellaris and Altsech (1992) for fast and liked music when used to increase the turnover of tables in a busy restaurant.

The results on volume are contradictory with Smith and Curnow (1966) finding that variation (high) resulted in less time spent, but Herrington and Capella (1996) observing that volume did not affect time spent in a supermarket.

Willingness to Buy. Although purchase intention has always been difficult to research and predict, a few researchers have attempted to investigate it with regard to music variables. Chebat et al. (2000) concluded that background music did not appear to moderate the relationship between salesperson's perception and the intent to buy. Baker et al. (1992) observed that genre variation interacted with salesperson interaction to enhance willingness to buy. North and Hargreaves (1998) also suggested that genre (Classical and Top 40) was associated with subjects being prepared to pay the most for food in a cafeteria.

Money Spent. Of course a positive outcome is ultimately the purchase. It appears that background and foreground does not affect unplanned purchases (Yalch & Spangenberg, 1990).

Some music variables, however, have been shown to have some type of an influence here. It was observed that genre (Classical) influenced customers to purchase more expensive wines than Top 40 did (Areni & Kim, 1993), and has been shown to be associated with paying and spending more in a cafeteria (North & Hargreaves, 1998; North et al., 2000; North et al., 2003). Classic Rock background music resulted in more purchases by Baby Boomers in a supermarket but fewer purchases for older shoppers, suggesting some type of interaction between genre and age (Gulas & Schewe, 1994). French music was shown to increase French wine sales and German music to increase German wine sales suggesting some type of relationship between music fit and product (North et al., 1999). Music preference was shown to influence total spending and the amount spent on food and drink in a restaurant (Caldwell & Hibbert, 2002). Slow tempo was observed to have resulted in higher sales volume in a cafeteria (Milliman, 1982, 1986), but had no affect on sales volume in a restaurant (Caldwell & Hibbert, 2002), or a supermarket (Herrington & Capella, 1996). Similarly, music volume was not observed to affect money spent at a supermarket (Smith & Curnow, 1966).

Future Research

Often with discovery comes more questions. While there is obviously much we know based on the preceding review of results, there is also much we still do not. What follows are future research suggestions made but never pursued beginning with Smith and Curnow (1966) and ending the way this review started with Kotler (1974).

Settings. Since Smith and Curnow (1966, p. 265) suggested that some "unanswered questions" included the application of their findings on the effect of music volume on time/money spent to purchasing situations other than supermarkets, only Harrington and Capella (1996) further researched these variables (disputing the findings) and again it was at a supermarket. Location for most of the field experiments, on all aspects of music and retail, has been limited primarily to supermarkets (Gulas & Schewe, 1994; Herrington & Capella, 1996; Milliman, 1982; Smith & Capella, 1966); restaurants/cafeterias/bars (Caldwell & Hibbert, 2002; Milliman, 1986; North & Hargreaves, 1996a, 1996b, 1998; North et al., 2000; North, 2003); malls/department stores (Babin et al., 2004; Dube & Morin, 2001; Eroglu et al., 2005: Mattila & Wirtz, 2001; Yalch & Spangenberg, 1988, 1990, 1993); banks (Chebat et al., 1993; Dube et al., 1995; Hui, 1997; North et al., 2000) and wine shops (Arena & Kim, 1993; North et al., 1999). It is necessary to expand this to a wider variety of field locations. Some possibilities include sporting good stores (e.g., investigating the impact of the sports radio genre) and women's lingerie stores such as Victoria's Secret (e.g., investigating the impact of the genre of romantic music). Another interesting field environment would be Starbucks. With the introduction of music retail into their cafes, it would be interesting to investigate the music's (both CD and satellite) effect on time and money spent.

Samples.   Gulas and Schewe (1994) found that age-linked music can be differentially target marketed and called for future research into a possible nostalgia effect. Much of the research has been done using demographic segmentations involving limited ages (mostly student samples) with some gender manipulations. Future research could focus on more race/ethnicity-based preferences, along with other demographic variables that have yet to be investigated.

Variables.   While a wide variety of variables have been manipulated and observed, a larger scope within certain music variables provides future possibilities of interest and investigation.

Genre.   North and Hargreaves (1998) agreed there was a need for future research utilizing additional listening environments and "a broader range of musical styles" (p. 2268). Genre did garner a considerable amount of study but it was primarily limited to Classical versus Top 40. More attention needs to be given to other genres of music appealing to a wider range of demographics and subcultures. Additional research in this area could also introduce new forms of delivery other than broadcast radio and Muzak, such as satellite or cable radio. Fit has also received a considerable amount of attention in regard to music (North et al., 1999), the workplace (Grayston, 1974) and advertising (MacInnis & Park, 1991), but not enough attention with respect to the retail environment. Only a few studies have focused on fit (e.g., Areni

& Kim, 1993; Chebat et al., 2001; North et al., 2000), and those again were primarily concerned with Classical and Top 40. Future research should further investigate what constitutes fit effectiveness in the retail environment for a wider range of genres.

Music preference. Herrington and Capella (1996) observed that music preference could affect such things as time spent shopping and suggested that not enough is currently known about the effects of music preferences of consumers. Most of the research in this area has been experiments that provided the music. Future research could be conducted where the shopper actually chooses the music using some type of iPod or jukebox, providing the ability to customize the music for an individualistic approach. The possibilities of music variables here are many, including genre, tempo, and volume.

Ethical Implications. Kotler (1974) suggested the need for an investigation into the social and ethical implications of "man's growing power to create atmospheres to motivate purchase" (p. 64). This suggestion has been largely ignored. Future research could investigate the ethical and social implications of the persuasion powers and manipulation opportunities of music in the retail environment. In addition to the obvious ones, one other alternative could be the use of music as a discriminatory atmospheric effect (e.g., an extreme genre of music like heavy metal that appeals to one race but can be unappealing to another resulting in intimidation and/or avoidance).

Conclusion

It is clear that much has been accomplished with regard to the effects of music on shopping behavior. This review of the experimental evidence summarizes the most relevant research from 1966–2006. By shining the spotlight on music, it not only shows the potential of music in the retail environment but further solidifies the argument that it may be the most important atmospheric consideration.

It is also clear that much is left to do in this area from both a theoretical and practical perspective. There is a great deal to be learned by the future exploration of new settings, with varied samples, using yet untested variables. More importantly, now that so much has been learned, it is probably the perfect time to reflect on the social and ethical implications of our gained knowledge. Hopefully, this review provides the foundation and incentive for future research and leads to even more sound retailing.

REFERENCES

Alpert, J. I., & Alpert, M. I. (1990). Music influences on mood and purchase intentions. *Psychology & Marketing, 7*(2), 109–133.

Areni, C. S., & Kim, D. (1993). The influence of background music on shopping behavior: Classical versus top-forty music in a wine store. In L. McAlister & M. L. Rothschild (Eds.), *Advances in consumer research,* (Vol. 20, pp. 336–340). Provo, UT: Association for Consumer Research.

Babin, B. J., Chebat, J. C., & Michon, R. (2004). Perceived appropriateness and its effect on quality, affect, and behavior. *Journal of Retailing and Consumer Services, 11*(5), 287–299.

Baker, J., Levy, M., & Grewal, D. (1992). An experimental approach to making retail decisions. *Journal of Retailing, 68*(4), 445–460.

Baker, J., Parasuraman, A., Grewal, D., & Voss, G. B. (2002). The influence of multiple store environment cues on perceived merchandise value and patronage intentions. *Journal of Marketing, 68*, 120–141.

Berlyne, D. E. (1971). *Aesthetics and psychobiology.* New York: Appleton Century Crofts.

Bitner, M. J. (1992). Servicescapes: The impact of physical surroundings on customers and employees. *Journal of Marketing, 56*, 57–71.

Brooker, G., & Wheatley, J. J. (1994). Music and radio advertising: Effects of tempo and placement. In C. T. Allen & D. R. John (Eds.), *Advances in consumer research,* (Vol. 21, pp. 286–290). Provo, UT: Association for Consumer Research.

Bruner, G. C. (1990). Music, mood, and marketing. *Journal of Marketing, 54*, 94–104.

Caldwell, C., & Hibbert, S. A. (2002). The influence of music tempo and musical preference on restaurant patrons' behavior. *Psychology & Marketing, 19*(11), 895–917.

Chebat, J.-C., Gelinas-Chebat, C., & Filiatrault, P. (1993). Interactive effects of musical and visual cues on time perception: An application to waiting lines in banks. *Perceptual and Motor Skills, 77*(3), 995–1020.

Chebat, J.-C., Gelinas-Chebat, C., & Vaillant, D. (2001). Environmental background music and in-store selling. *Journal of Business Research, 54*, 115–123.

Chebat, J.-C., Vaillant, D., & Gelinas-Chebat, C. (2000). Does background music in a store enhance salespersons' persuasiveness. *Perceptual and Motor Skills, 91*(2), 405–424.

Donovan, R. J., & Rossiter, J. R. (1982). Store atmosphere: An environmental psychology approach. *Journal of Retailing, 58*(1), 34–57.

Donovan, R. J., Rossiter, J. R., Marcoolyn, G., & Nesdale, A. (1994). Store atmosphere and purchasing behaviour. *Journal of Retailing, 70*(1), 283–294.

Dube, L., Chebat, J.-C., & Morin, S. (1995). The effects of background music on consumers' desire to affiliate in buyer-seller interactions. *Psychology & Marketing, 12*(4), 305–319.

Dube, L., & Morin, S. (2001). Background music pleasure and store evaluation intensity effects and psychological mechanisms. *Journal of Business Research, 54,* 107–113.

Eroglu, S. A., Machleit, K. A., & Chebat, J.-C. (2005). The interaction of retail density and music tempo: Effects on shopper responses. *Psychology & Marketing, 22*(7), 577–589.

Gorn, G. J. (1982). The effects of music in advertising on choice behavior: A classical conditioning approach. *Journal of Marketing, 46,* 94–101.

Grayston, D. (1974). Music while you work. *Industrial Management, 4,* 38–39.

Gulas, C. S., & Schewe, C. D. (1994). Atmospheric segmentation: managing store image with background music. In R. Acrol & A. Mitchell (Eds.), *Enhancing knowledge development in marketing* (pp. 325–330). Chicago: American Marketing Association.

Herrington, J. D., & Capella, L. (1996). Effects of music in service environments: A field study. *The Journal of Services Marketing, 10*(2), 26–41.

Hui, M. K., Dube, L., & Chebat, J.-C. (1997). The impact of music on consumers' reactions to waiting for services. *Journal of Retailing, 73*(1), 87–104.

Kellaris, J. J., & Altsech, M. B. (1992). The experience of time as a function of musical loudness and gender of the listener. In J. Sherry & B. Sternthal (Eds.), *Advances in consumer research,* (Vol. 19, pp. 725–729). Provo, UT: Association for Consumer Research.

Kellaris, J. J., & Cox, A. D. (1989). The effects of background music in advertising: A reassessment. In T. K. Srull (Ed.), *Advances in consumer research,* (Vol. 16, pp. 113–118). Provo, UT: Association for Consumer Research.

Kellaris, J. J., Cox, A. D., & Cox, D. (1993). The effect of background music on ad processing: A contingency explanation. *Journal of Marketing, 57,* 114–125.

Kellaris, J. J., & Kent, R. J. (1991). Exploring tempo and modality effects on consumer responses to music. In R. H. Holman & M. R. Solomon (Eds.), *Advances in consumer research,* (Vol. 18, pp. 243–248). Provo, UT: Association for Consumer Research.

Kellaris, J. J., & Kent, R. J. (1994). An exploratory investigation of responses elicited by music varying in tempo, tonality, and texture. *Journal of Consumer Psychology, 2*(4), 381–401.

Kellaris, J. J., & Mantel, S. P. (1996). Shaping time perceptions with background music: The effect of congruity and arousal on estimates of ad durations. *Psychology & Marketing, 13*(5), 501–515.

Kellaris, J. J., & Rice, R. C. (1993). The influence of tempo, loudness, and gender of listener on responses to music. *Psychology & Marketing, 10*(1), 15–29.

Kotler, P. (1973). Atmospherics as a marketing tool. *Journal of Retailing, 49*(4), 48–64.

Lam, S. Y. (2001). The effects of store environment on shopping behavior: A critical review. In M. C. Gilly & J. Meyers-Levy (Eds.), *Advances in consumer research,* (Vol. 28, pp. 190–197). Provo, UT: Association for Consumer Research.

MacInnnis, D., & Park, C. W. (1991). The differential role of characteristics of music on high- and low-involvement consumers' processing ads. *Journal of Consumer Research, 18,* 161–173.

Mattila, A. S., & Wirtz, J. (2001). Congruency of scent and music as a driver of in-store evaluations and behavior. *Journal of Retailing, 77,* 273–289.

Mehrabian, A., & Russell, J. A. (1974). *An approach to environmental psychology.* Cambridge, MA: MIT Press.

Milliman, R. E. (1982). Using background music to affect the behavior of supermarket shoppers. *Journal of Marketing, 46*(2), 86–91.

Milliman, R. E. (1986). The influence of background music on the behavior of restaurant patrons. *Journal of Consumer Research, 13,* 286–289.

North, A. C., & Hargreaves, D. J. (1996a). The effects of music on responses to a dining area. *Journal of Environmental Psychology, 16,* 55–64.

North, A. C., & Hargreaves, D. J. (1996b). Responses to music in a dining area. *Journal of Applied Social Psychology, 26*(6), 491–501.

North, A. C., & Hargreaves, D. J. (1997). Music and consumer behaviour. In D. J. Hargreaves & A. C. North (Eds.), *The Social Psychology of Music* (pp. 268–289). Oxford: Oxford University Press.

North, A. C., & Hargreaves, D. J. (1998). The effect of music on atmosphere and purchase intention in a cafeteria. *Journal of Applied Social Psychology, 28*(24), 2254–2273.

North, A. C., Hargreaves, D. J., & McKendrick, J. (1999). The influence of in-store music on wine selections. *Journal of Applied Psychology, 84*(2), 271–276.

North, A. C., Hargreaves, D. J., & McKendrick, J. (2000). The effects of music on atmosphere in a bank and a bar. *Journal of Applied Social Psychology, 30*(7), 1504–1520.

North, A. C., Shilcock, A., & Hargreaves, D. J. (2003). The effect of musical style on restaurant customers' spending. *Environment and Behavior, 35*(5), 712–718.

Oakes, S. (2003). Musical tempo and waiting perceptions. *Psychology & Marketing, 20*(8), 685–705.

Park, C. W., & Young, S. M. (1986). Consumer response to television commercials: The impact of involvement and background music on brand attitude formation. *Journal of Marketing Research, 23*, 11–24.

Schlosser, A. (1998). Applying the functional theory of attitudes to understanding the influence of store atmosphere on store inferences. *Journal of Consumer Psychology, 7*(4), 345–369.

Smith, P. C., & Curnow, R. (1966). Arousal hypotheses and the effects of music on purchasing behavior. *Journal of Applied Psychology, 50*(3), 255–256.

Turley, L. W., & Milliman, R. E. (2000). Atmospheric effects on shopping behavior: A review of experimental evidence. *Journal of Business Research, 49*, 193–211.

Yalch, R. F., & Spangenberg, E. (1988). An environmental psychological study of foreground and background music as retail atmospheric factors. In A. W. Walle (Ed.), *AMA Educators' Conference Proceedings* (pp. 106–110). Chicago: IL: American Marketing Association.

Yalch, R., & Spangenberg, E. (1990). Effects of store music on shopping behavior. *The Journal of Services Marketing, 4*(1), 31–39.

Yalch, R., & Spangenberg, E. (1993). *Using store music for retail zoning.* Paper presented at the Association for Consumer Research, Provo, UT.

4

ONLINE AND OFFLINE PURCHASING STRATEGIES: A PRELIMINARY INVESTIGATION AND CONCEPTUALIZATION OF APPROACH-AVOIDANCE CONFLICTS IN SHOPPING BEHAVIOR

Margaret K. Hogg

Lancaster University, U.K.

Elfriede Penz

Wirtschaftsuniversität Wien (WU-Wien), Austria

*O*UR CHAPTER EXTENDS CURRENT WORK in psychological theory on approach-avoidance conflicts via an investigation of online and offline shopping behavior. Approach-avoidance conflicts have attracted significant attention in psychology. At the same time there have been some studies into consumers' approach-avoidance behaviors in retail environments (Donovan & Rossiter, 1982). However, very little research attention has been paid to the approach-avoidance conflicts that shoppers experience when faced with the *combination* of personal, environmental, and product features in offline and online settings. We seek to address that gap in research because these multi-dimensional approach-avoidance conflicts could have a significant impact on shoppers' willingness to purchase offline or online. Our aim was to identify, firstly, the influential characteristics of the retail situations; secondly, the key features of the products; and thirdly the personal characteristics and predispositions (e.g., moods, emotions, attitude to risk) that led consumers to identify their experiences as uncomfortable, and which thus stimulated behavior in approach-avoidance conflicts. Our starting point was a small-scale empirical study, using written stories to elicit shoppers' experiences of approach-avoidance conflicts. The 'fight or flight' conflicts which individuals typically confront in other areas of their lives were paralleled by the approach-avoidance conflicts experienced by individuals when they are shopping (whether online or offline), and the pattern of approach-avoidance behaviors could be broadly classified into 'engage or escape.' From our analysis we identified two main categories of approach-avoidance conflicts. The approach-avoidance conflicts were either *other-oriented* (type 1 and type 2) or *self-oriented* in terms of the needs to be met by purchasing the product or service itself. From our study we conceptualized the main components of approach-avoidance conflicts in consumption in order to clarify the main drivers and inhibitors of consumers' approach-avoidance shopping behaviors in offline and online retail settings respectively.

Context

Whilst shoppers' interest in the Internet has accelerated in growth as a retail channel over the past 10 years, several critical incidents (for instance cyber crime) have contributed to the attenuation of much of the early consumer excitement that surrounded shopping online (Lee, 2004). Current research into shopping behavior has largely failed to capture the complexity of the psychological conflicts that consumers face when choosing whether to shop online and/or offline. Most consumer studies of approach-avoidance behavior have concentrated on shoppers' experiences *within* the retail environments, rather than examining the complex *interaction* between the individual, the environment (offline or online), and the nature of the product or service to be purchased. It is crucially important to understand what motivates or stops consumers making purchases either online or offline. This will also potentially contribute to a greater understanding of consumer ambivalence (Otnes, Lowrey, & Shrum, 1997).

Literature Review

Consumers' decisions can involve both positive and negative aspects. This means that purchase decisions can often (but not always) be linked to a psychological conflict, because of the positive as well as negative consequences caused by a "competition between incompatible responses" within an individual (Miller, 1944, p. 431). Differences between approach and avoidance motivation have been linked to valence: "in approach motivation, behavior is instigated or directed by a positive/desirable event or possibility, whereas in avoidance motivation, behavior is instigated or directed by a negative/undesirable event or possibility" (Elliot & Thrash, 2002, p. 804). Approach-avoidance conflict theory potentially helps us understand how consumers think about and manage the potential negative aspects or consequences (avoidance factors) when making a purchase decision (approach factors).

In our initial conceptualization from the literature, we propose that behavior in approach-avoidance conflicts is derived from three sources (Figure 4.1). Whereas considerable research has been undertaken to understand behaviors in approach-avoidance conflicts in response to (i) situational cues, rather less attention has been paid to the role played by (ii) the nature of the product or service or (iii) of a consumer's predispositions in approach-avoidance conflicts; or of the potential impact which the interaction between the environmental cues, the nature of the product or service, and the consumer's personal characteristics might have on individuals' purchase decisions.

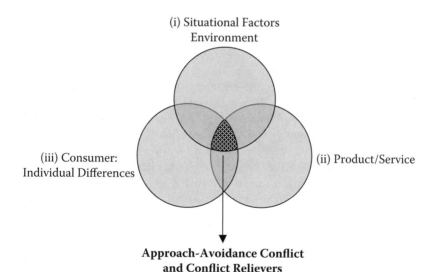

Figure 4.1.
Approach-avoidance conflicts: The intersection between
environment (channel), product, and consumer.

(i) Behavior in approach-avoidance conflicts in response to situational cues is captured in the Mehrabian and Russell (M-R) model (1974):

> Approach behaviors relate to willingness or desire to move towards, stay in, explore, interact supportively in, perform well in, and return to the environment. Avoidance behaviors relate to the opposites of the above: deteriorated performance and dissatisfaction; feelings of anxiety or boredom; unfriendliness to others; and a desire to leave the environment and not to return. [Donovan & Rossiter, 1982, p. 41]

Donovan and Rossiter (1982), drawing on Mehrabian and Russell (1974), argued that all responses to an environment can be considered as approach or avoidance (AP-AV) behaviors. Donovan and Rossiter (1994) distinguished four aspects of AP-AV in a retail environment. The AP aspects include the desire to stay in the store, to explore the store, to communicate with others, and the degree of enhancement of and satisfaction with the shopping performance. The AV aspects include the desire to get out of the store, to avoid the store and the communication in a store, and the hindrance of performance. Next to these behavioral responses, emotional states are induced by the physical store environment, i.e., pleasure-displeasure (PL), and arousal-non arousal (AR). PL describes feelings of joy and happiness while AR refers to excitement, alertness and stimulation (Van Kenhove & Desrumaux, 1997).

Baker (1986) focuses on how ambient, design, and social factors affect the ways consumers perceive their physical environment (see Chapter 5 in this volume). *Ambient factors* are not noticed unless they reach an unpleasant level, as for example in the case of too much lighting or a high temperature in a shop, and these factors can then encourage avoidance behavior. Music that is too loud, for instance, can distract consumers from their task (see Chapter 3 in this volume), but an acceptable temperature in a store, on the other hand, does not necessarily motivate purchase behavior. *Design factors* are actively evaluated by consumers and therefore have a greater potential to influence both approach and avoidance behavior. Aesthetic elements such as architecture, color, and style can increase a consumer's sense of pleasure when entering a store. Functional elements, such as layout or comfort, can also contribute to the sense of well-being and so increase the probability of approach. *Social factors* include the presence of an audience and/or service personnel. These can influence either approach or avoidance behavior. Some services, such as concerts, require a capacity audience for generating the atmosphere, whereas busy queues at checkouts and crowded sale floors generate atmospheres that can lead to dissatisfaction. The attractive appearance and the pleasant behavior of service personnel can both motivate approach behavior. The number of personnel and also the presence of other customers can also be reassuring components in a retail environment. Eventually, Baker et al. (1992) examined the M-R model in connection with the effects of ambient and social cues and supported Donovan and Rossiter's (1982) finding that the M-R model is applicable to a retail setting: "affective states produced by the store environment do influence consumers' willingness to buy" (Baker et al., 1992, p. 457).

Purchasing in an online shop is recognized as being rather different from traditional brick and mortar shopping (Dennis, Harris, & Sandhu, 2002). Effective Web site design represents a key factor for success whereas poor interface design has caused the failure of high profile sites (Palmer, 2002; Sinkovics & Penz, 2005). For consumers in an online shop, in order to experience approach rather than avoidance, it is important to develop relationships with companies; identify objective company data and information; feel secure; not be flooded with information; and not get lost when browsing through particular sites. Consumers want to be stimulated, and also to be able to personalize the online environment. Online retailers therefore need to offer a different set of appeals to consumers and emphasize simple and clear purchase-related aspects of the online experience, compared to offline channels (Sinkovics & Penz, 2005).

(ii) Some goods or services (Figure 4.1) have specific characteristics that make them more suitable for online shopping than others, such as standardized goods (books, CDs) that require only limited examination (Chiang & Dholakia, 2003; Kwak, Fox, & Zinkhan, 2002; Monsuwe, Dellaert, & Ruyter, 2004; Shim, Eastlick, Lotz, & Warrington, 2001) compared to experience goods which usually have to be experienced personally (Chiang & Dholakia, 2003) and thus are better suited for brick and mortar shops.

The concept of risk encompasses both potentially positive and negative outcomes, associated with the product or service (Mitchell, 1999), with a focus mainly on potentially negative outcomes. Risk thus can be seen as "subjective expectations of loss" (Stone & Gronhaug, 1993, p. 42) and occurs when preferring one product over another. It encompasses several dimensions such as product performance, financial, psychological, time, social, and also physical risk (Kaplan, Szybillo, & Jacoby, 1974).

Alongside the characteristics of the goods and services available online, and the atmosphere of online shops (e.g., design of the web-page) (McCarthy & Aronson, 2000; Wang & Tang, 2003), there is also evidence that (iii) individual psychological aspects and motives (Figure 4.1) all determine to some degree whether consumers experiment with shopping online or prefer to continue shopping in the offline environment (Forsythe & Shi, 2003; Joines, Scherer, & Scheufele, 2003; Korgaonkar & Wolin, 1999; Teo & Yeong, 2003; Wolfinbarger & Gilly, 2001). How consumers manage the contradictory pressures involved in the approach-avoidance conflicts which arise from any combination of these three aspects (Figure 4.1), in offline and online retail settings, is the focus of this research (cf., Sobh, Lee, & Vaughan, 2006).

Methodology

The objectives of the research were first, to explore the specific facets of the conflict in the purchase situation; secondly to identify products/services that potentially involve approach-avoidance conflicts; and thirdly to examine how shoppers manage the different approach and avoidance aspects of their purchasing decisions in offline and online settings.

In this international study (Austria and U.K.) we applied theoretical sampling (Miles & Huberman, 1994, p. 28) to achieve cross-national comparability and homogeneous samples to examine young adult consumer behavior. Most participants were students (aged 18+). They were approached either in person or via e-mail.

Following the recent debate in marketing scholarship (Vargo & Lusch, 2004) about the movement towards a new services dominant logic, and Deighton and Narayandas' subsequent call (2004, p. 19) to use stories in order to examine "value not frozen in objects but flowing in events"* we used stories as our data collection method. In order to get an overview of differences and similarities in offline and online purchase experiences, we employed the critical incident technique (Flanagan, 1954; Hopkinson & Hogarth-Scott, 2002). A series of questions was developed. These were designed to evoke associations with regard to past purchase situations. We 'controlled' for approach behaviors by asking about situations that were important for respondents and had potentially positive and often important consequences for them.

In a pilot study we asked respondents to think of two purchase instances where they had experienced potential approach-avoidance conflicts within the same store (offline purchase situation). However, this proved difficult for respondents. Many of them could not remember the second occasion when they had gone back to the store. Therefore we changed the scenario. In our main study we only asked respondents to provide one story which described either their offline or online experiences.

---

* "Stories can be read as illustrations of theory. . . . Stories can also be read as challenges to theory . . . telling stories is a tradition in anthropology, history, and some of the other interpretive social sciences, and if V & L [(Vargo & Lusch, 2004)] are correct that marketing scholarship must increasingly contend with value not frozen in objects but flowing in events, then, as anthropologists and historians do, marketing scholars may find that offering stories to one another to support or repudiate claims about the meaning of a sequence of events is a useful way to perform scholarship. . . ." (Day et al., 2004, p. 19).

We collected written stories (Hopkinson & Hogg, 2006) which included 41 offline stories (20 U.K. and 21 Austrian) and 37 online stories (17 U.K. and 20 Austrian). There was an approximate gender balance (44 percent men; 56 percent women). Most of the stories were written in English; a few stories were written in German. The stories took two forms. Most respondents (n = 64) wrote up to a page of straight descriptive prose which incorporated their answers to the question probes into their own accounts. A few of the respondents (n = 14) adopted the alternative style of writing a few sentences in direct response to the questions as set out, rather than producing a passage of prose. All these stories were content analyzed by both researchers in order to establish aspects of approach-avoidance conflicts and behaviors including: aspects of the purchase situation and the product; the sources of discomfort and conflict experienced by the consumers in relation to both the product and the situation; the social setting and circumstances surrounding the purchase situation; the emotions experienced by the consumers in relation to the conflicts linked to the purchase situation; and how consumers managed and/or resolved the levels of discomfort and conflicts which they experienced.

Findings

Our opening conceptualization (Figure 4.1) provides the framework for presenting our results. We begin firstly by outlining briefly the main approach-avoidance conflicts which we identified from our respondents' stories. Secondly, we discuss and illustrate the main findings, summarized from the content analysis into a flowchart (Figure 4.2), in order to draw some direct comparisons between the two channels. Thirdly, we move on to use examples from our participants' stories to show the *interactions* amongst the three components identified in Figure 4.1. In this way we use our original conceptualization (Figure 4.1) to demonstrate the importance of examining the *combination* of environmental with personal and product (or service) features when investigating AP-AV conflicts and behaviors; and we thus illustrate how the multi-dimensionality of the conflicts faced by consumers in online and offline shopping channels generate consumers' approach-avoidance behaviors.

Main Types of Approach-Avoidance Conflicts and Behaviors

Our participants described events which revolved around reconciling one or more personal needs and wants, and thereby achieving some personal goals, sometimes at the cost of relinquishing other personal goals. Approach-avoidance conflicts experienced by shoppers could be approximated to the 'fight or flight' conflicts found in other roles and/or settings (e.g. *inter alia* parent-child conflicts in a family setting; teacher-pupil disagreement in a school environment; lovers' quarrels in either public or private contexts). The approach-avoidance psychological conflicts experienced by shoppers often generated similar 'fight or flight' approach-avoidance behaviors. These might be described as a range of 'engage or escape' behaviors. Where shoppers chose to approach (i.e., 'engage') they would stay in the retail environment (whether offline or online) and complete the purchase, responding to a predominant (and positive) need to obtain the goods or services, despite the presence of negative aspects related to either the product and/or the environment and/or their own predisposition. When shoppers chose to avoid (i.e. 'escape') they left the retail environment and did not complete the purchase. In this case their response was dominated by their negative experience of the interactions within the purchase event (i.e., nature of product and/or environmental factors and/or personal dispositions), and the personal need to avoid these experiences overrode their need for the particular product or service.

Approach-avoidance conflicts in online and offline situations seemed to fall into two main categories in our dataset: they were either '*other-oriented*' or '*self-oriented*'. Two types of approach-avoidance conflict typified the '*other-oriented*' category, i.e., purchasing *for* someone else (e.g., a gift); or purchasing *on behalf of* someone else (non-gift situation). In the first '*other-oriented*' category (purchasing *for* another person, e.g., a gift), one overriding need represented in our respondents' stories was the desire to remain in the shopping channel and complete the purchase in order to please someone else [approach/engage] (e.g., by staying and purchasing a gift). However, this desire to please someone else was often offset by the desire to 'escape or flee' the shopping channel [avoidance/escape]. The second type of '*other-oriented*' approach-avoidance conflict (purchasing *on behalf of* another) was generated by our participants' desire to stay and complete a purchase on someone else's behalf [approach/engage] but this need was offset by the desire to escape or flee the shopping channel in order to avoid the embarrassment of making the purchase in a public setting. Both these '*other-oriented*' conflicts were characterized by role conflict, often linked to "peer and reference group interaction" (Otnes et al., 1997, p. 88). '*Self-oriented*' types of approach-avoidance conflicts tended to revolve around the desire to complete the purchase because of the personal need for the goods [approach/engage]. However, this drive to meet these particular needs and wants was often offset by other needs which generated avoidance (and the desire to flee).

Risk aversion and attitudes to perceived risk were central to many of the behaviors in approach-avoidance conflicts reported by our respondents (e.g., performance risk, social risk, financial risk, time risk, psychosocial risk). However, consumers' perceived risk relates to *cognitive* rather than *emotional* dissonance; and "induces a selective search for congruent information and an active avoiding of potentially dissonant information" (Mitchell & Boustani, 1994, p. 59). Donovan et al.'s (1982) research emphasized the importance of understanding the *emotional* drivers of behaviors in approach-avoidance conflicts. Risk aversion therefore only explains part of the story. If perceived risk (and its cognitive aspects) had predominated in all cases then our participants would have been largely describing events which ended in avoidance of purchase (negative end states), whereas many of our stories ended in making the purchase (positive end states), where emotional rather than cognitive reasons often prevailed in the purchase setting.

Comparison of Main Findings—Online versus Offline

The main findings from the content analysis are summarized in comparative, tabular form (Figure 4.2); and reflect the three components (Figure 4.1) which were identified as the main sources of approach-avoidance conflicts for consumers, i.e., the situational and environmental factors; the nature of the product and service; and individual consumer differences. In addition, we sketch in the different strategies and tactics which consumers used to relieve the conflicts they experienced in the different stages of the consumption process.

The Environment as a Source of Conflict. The environment is traditionally identified in the AP-AV model (Donovan & Rossiter, 1982) as the major source of conflict experienced by consumers, and this was confirmed by our research. However our findings indicated that there were different sources of environmental conflict across the two settings (Figure 4.2, first box). In the online setting the environmental factors which affected our respondents were mainly the website design and navigation, confirming previous findings. The respondents mentioned the importance of clear interfaces (representing the considerable amount of research already undertaken into human interactions with computer screens for shopping online) (e.g., Palmer, 2002; Sinkovics & Penz, 2005), and the ease of navigating the site to find the desired items. This was often contrasted with the time, effort, and frustration which could be experienced (e.g., Chen & Dubinsky, 2003; Dennis et al., 2002). Yvonne's account is typical of the online stories which we collected about the amount of time involved in purchasing tickets online. Yvonne outlined

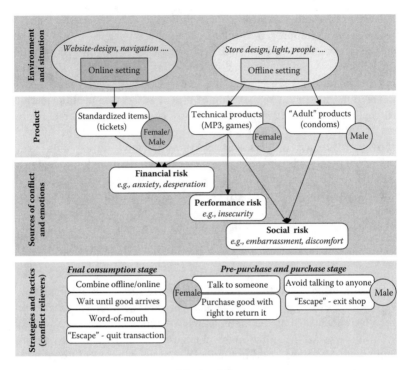

Figure 4.2.
Summary of main findings from the content analysis of the stories.

her frustration with all the stages when buying online (e.g., registering with the site; waiting for a confirmation email; remembering the login name and password for the site; finding they did not accept her credit card after she had started entering her details) and she ended by saying:

> I was desperate because there is no one to ask (Yvonne, Austrian female online customer).

Damien's online story also neatly illustrated the importance of being able to navigate around sites, and access information easily without having to keep *"awkwardly switching between screens"* in the search for information and prices for a field hockey kit which:

> is quite expensive, so I couldn't really afford to make a mistake. . . . I trawled through several websites. Some were very useful: they were clearly laid out,

with all of the information on the same screen and the labels and price tags next to a picture of the kit. Other websites simply had all the kits laid out in one picture at the top, and then the prices and information below, so you had to scroll between the picture and the information. This made comparison difficult . . . . (Damien, U.K. male online shopper).

The offline shopping environments which evoked uncertainty and approach-avoidance conflicts were characterized by the atmosphere, e.g. lights which went from 'horribly over-lit' and bright lights (*"would have preferred a darker room"*) to 'very little light', both of which were viewed negatively; indicating the continuing relevance of earlier studies in the area of store atmospherics (Donovan & Rossiter, 1982; Donovan et al., 1994). When describing the shopping environment, some participants were put off by the store itself; others by the staff or by their fellow customers. Carl's story about buying lingerie as a gift, for instance, captures many of these aspects well:

A few years ago at Christmas I went to a lingerie store to buy something for my girlfriend . . . The shop was very busy, fairly bright lights and bras and knickers everywhere; probably because of the time of year. In a way I would have preferred a darkened room! I did not want people to see me lurking around the lingerie . . . (Carl, U.K. male offline shopper).

Tara expresses similar feelings of embarrassment and frustration when faced with the difficulties of mastering a new system (in her newly refurbished local shop) for topping up her e-card:

A new machine was installed for self-service use and there were no "human" relations to be established with it, to ask questions or help in general . . . I felt confused over what to do actually with the machine, what to press, where to put my card . . . I was embarrassed to show that I was unable to do it myself. . . . I think I was red with embarrassment, The shop was . . . much bigger than before, all lit up, shiny and clean and really technologically advanced somehow . . . Very embarrassing, I laugh about it now but then I wanted to cry . . . (Tara, U.K. female offline shopper).

The environment seemed to generate equal amounts of discomfort for both men and women across both offline and online channels. The social context (Otnes et al., 1997) was important for both men and women. Embarrassment often flowed from social risk linked to others' evaluation of their competence. For women they were anxious about showing their lack of experience or expertise to other expert users (e.g., shop assistants) in their use of technical equipment, or in their choice amongst technically complex products. The predominant feelings of discomfort and embarrassment for men seemed to flow from fear of showing lack of expertise or inadequacy in front of others (whether their friends, their fellow shoppers, or the sales assistants) when purchasing products like lingerie or condoms.

The Nature of the Product or Service as a Source of Conflict. The second main source of conflict (Figure 4.1) was the nature of the product or service (Figure 4.2, box 2). The conflicts generated by the nature of the purchase did not vary by gender in the online channel. The main products described in online purchases were usually (but not always) standardized items, such as subscriptions, tickets for travel or concerts, accommodation, and travel packages. Other online purchases included technical products (e.g., MP3 player, TV, digital music player, Apple I-Pod) and specialty products (e.g., hockey kit, Arsenal football shirt, DJ desk). These are all fairly standardized items, when compared with fashion items such as clothing, lingerie, shoes and handbags which embody quality aspects that often require 'touch-and-feel' tests. The sources of conflict around the products typically purchased online tended to be linked to the cost (financial risk) and uncertainty about delivery (performance risk associated with the channel) rather than with the constitution of the product itself (e.g. material); although Damien's description of his concern about purchasing a field hockey kit online related not just to the financial but also to the performance risk linked to the product:

> However, having never bought any upper body protection before, I didn't know quite what I was looking for, and wasn't able to try anything on for size in the shop. Hockey kit is especially difficult because the kit reaches its 'peak' of comfort and protection after you have broken it in. The kit is quite expensive, so I couldn't really afford to make a mistake. (Damien, U.K. male online shopper).

The nature of the product or service as a source of conflict in the offline channels varied more by gender, with women mentioning technical products in particular, compared with men's description of 'adult' products (e.g., condoms, cigarettes, lingerie, and car services). However there was not a neat and definitive split between men and women in their discussion of products as the source of conflict (and thus approach-avoidance behaviors). This can be seen when Helga's story about purchasing a sex manual (Kamasutra book) for her brother's friend is compared with Rich's story about purchasing condoms for his friend [see next section for Rich's story]:

> I felt a slight discomfort searching for a book like this . . . there is a big choice. The range scopes aesthetic expensive books as well as slightly

disgusting books with cheap pictures and absolutely no sophisticated text (Helga, Austrian female offline customer).

Within the umbrella category of 'adult' products, some product categories linked to sexual activity clearly created approach-avoidance conflicts for both men and women. This suggests the importance of acknowledging that men's and women's consumption behaviors do not always necessarily line up neatly with gendered notions of consumption (Fischer, 2002; Fischer & Arnold, 1994; Hughes & Hogg, 2006), providing additional support for problematizing (Freed, 1996) the tendency to polarize gender into "mutually exclusive scripts for being male and female" (Bem, 1993, 81).

Individual Differences as a Source of Conflict. Thirdly, individual differences (Figure 4.1) represented another important influence on the conflicts experienced by consumers and their subsequent approach-avoidance behaviors in both online and offline channels, linked particularly to emotions and attitudes to perceived risk (Figure 4.2, box 3). In terms of the emotions that they experienced, some offline customers reported positive feelings such as trust. However offline customers overwhelmingly described negative feelings including embarrassment, worry, disappointment, confusion, anger, ridicule, nervousness, stress, annoyance, and feeling uncomfortable or silly. Rich's story captures many of these elements:

> The first time I ever actually had to buy condoms, . . . I got served by a nice girl and I didn't feel any embarrassment . . . [but then because of my friends messing around] . . . I felt absolutely mortified. The girl behind the counter seemed to find it quite funny as did a few people in the queue, but I felt incredibly embarrassed and dropped my change, which only worsened the situation (Rich, U.K. male offline customer).

Emotions amongst the online customers showed a mixture of positive and negative reactions to the purchase situation. In contrast to the offline stories, the online stories reported more excitement and arousal in general. Online male customers reported feeling concerned, anxious, worried, nervous, insecure and annoyed, but alongside excitement and satisfaction. This compared with the online female customers who also reported feeling anxious, but also suspicious, worried, angry, scared, desperate, insecure, disappointed, and frustrated along with the positive feelings of excitement and curiosity. Some interesting differences emerged here. Overall, the online stories described more positive feelings than the offline stories.

Perceived risk varied between offline and online situations, both in terms of different *types* of risk, and the *stages* within the purchase cycle at which perceived risk was experienced (confirming and extending Mitchell & Boustani, 1994, p. 57). Financial risk was a paramount concern for both online and offline shoppers, and generated feelings of anxiety and desperation in relation to both the product (would it be worth the cost, i.e., would it represent value for money?) and the channel (would the goods arrive?). Online and offline purchases were associated with different types of performance risk, for online purchasing the performance risk was associated with the channel itself (would it deliver the goods?); whilst performance risk offline tended to be more associated with the product or service, which often created feelings of consumer insecurity. Social risk was particularly important in offline settings when consumers often experienced feelings of embarrassment or discomfort.

Among the offline stories the stage at which perceived risk occurred in the consumption cycle varied. Pre-purchase search and purchase evaluation proved to be very challenging phases in the decision process. Participants usually bought the product for the very first time and went through an intensive information search. They felt overwhelmed, confused, and daunted by the variety of product choice and embarrassed and uncomfortable because they had to contact somebody else for advice. As argued by Mitchell and Boustani (1994) risk perception increases rather than decreases in these phases, and only declines with a satisfactory purchase. However, similar to the online purchase situations, our participants often remained uncertain until the product was used. This delay in risk reduction was even stronger when the product was a gift for somebody else.

Psycho-social risk was one of the most important characteristics of these offline purchases, especially for men (as illustrated in Carl's story about buying lingerie as a Christmas gift). Women seemed to be faced with three sources of perceived risk: psycho-social risk and financial risk (associated with the purchase of gifts and services; or clothes for important social events such as a dress for a 21st birthday party in the U.K.) and also technological risk (where they felt they lacked the requisite expertise to make the purchase and feared the embarrassment of either showing ignorance or making the wrong purchase).

Conflict Relievers: Strategies and Tactics. Finally, the strategies and tactics used for coping with the conflicts differed between the two channels; and varied between men and women in the offline channel (Figure 4.2, box 4). It was notable that consumers experienced greater conflicts in the earlier stages of the consumption process (pre-purchase and purchase stage) in the offline channel (where approach-avoidance behaviors tended to vary by gender), compared with the online channel where most conflicts were experienced in the final consumption stage. In the online environment, purchases were often completed and the feelings of discomfort were often not resolved until after the product had arrived. Some online respondents resolved their discomfort by declining to purchase or by deciding to purchase offline; or as in Damien's case, combining off-line trial (trying on hockey kits in a sportswear shop) with purchasing online.

Word-of-mouth was an important strategy which online consumers adopted to relieve their perceived risk, which particularly derived from their lack of self-confidence about purchasing online (Mitchell & Boustani, 1994, p. 61). Online customers also described abandoning the purchase, when the stress proved to be overwhelming (e.g., Michaela's story about perceived financial risk, below).

Among the offline shoppers, the overwhelming reaction by female customers was to talk to staff; and they often sought assurance that the store's returns policy would allow the goods to be taken back to the shop if they proved unsuitable (e.g., Dorothea's story, below). Men, in contrast, tended to avoid talking to staff and this was often accompanied by the action of leaving the store without making a purchase (cf. Andreas' story, below).

Interactions Amongst Components Leading to Multidimensionality of Conflicts

The chart (Figure 4.2) suggests a neat linear flow of conflict experiences in the two shopping channels. However, our participants' stories illustrate the importance of the interrelationships between environment, product and consumer features in generating sources of conflict (Figure 4.1); and how difficult it is to separate these out into constructs which are independent of one another. We use examples drawn from our participants' stories to show the *interactions* amongst the three components identified in Figure 4.1; we thereby demonstrate the importance of examining the *combination* of environmental with product (or service) and personal factors when investigating AP-AV conflicts that face shoppers in online and offline shopping channels.

'Other-Oriented' Conflict, Outer Directed Behavior (Type 1; Purchasing a Product for Someone Else, e.g., Gift). Mark and Carl were both faced with psycho-social risk when buying lingerie as a gift for their girlfriends. Carl's story was outlined briefly above. Mark's experiences were very similar (especially as he did not have experience of buying his own underwear):

> The first time that I bought lingerie for my girlfriend was pretty embarrassing as I had never purchased a good like this before. . . . The purchase was embarrassing because this was a new purchasing experience for me, and also because I felt uncomfortable in the ladies section of the shop. . . . The most embarrassing part was browsing as this makes it look as though you are really engaging with the product and purchase but you don't want to give that impression as who wants to look like a connoisseur of lingerie!!! I tried to ignore everyone within the section of the store, and look mature, (even though I was really embarrassed, and I wanted to leave the store as quickly as possible). This purchase has now got easier since I have adopted using the Internet. (Mark, U.K. male offline shopper).

Both men felt embarrassment about the product (lingerie), and this was reinforced by the public arena of the ladies' section of the department store where they were both surrounded by fellow customers and sales assistants. Carl described taking the lingerie to the sales till, and being served by a woman sales assistant, as almost the worst part of his experience. In both cases the approach-avoidance conflict involved their desire to purchase a gift for their girlfriend (engage), and this proved to be stronger than their desire to escape from the shop and avoid further embarrassment. However in terms of the approach-avoidance behaviors, Mark's longer term solution was to 'escape' from the offline channel (the department store) to the anonymity of the Internet for subsequent purchases. Note here the importance of learned drives and learned responses. Carl and Mark's stories illustrate very neatly the social punishments often faced by our informants, particularly in *other-oriented situations* such as gift giving, where informants were faced by the emotional sanction of their significant other if they failed to complete the purchase of the present. Maher (1962, p. 289) identified how informants might continue to exhibit symptoms of conflict but might nevertheless stay in the situation until they reached their goal: "Sequential stages in this kind of conflict would therefore consist of (1) approach response; (2) equilibrium and conflict responses, including attempts to escape unless this would bring punishment [. . .] (3) occurrence of the consummatory response when the goal is reached."

Michaela's online story also captures the interaction between the product and the environment. However in her case she decided against purchasing a very special gift as a second anniversary present for her boyfriend, because her fear of divulging her financial details via e-Bay proved stronger than her desire to surprise her boyfriend by obtaining a very rare Arsenal football shirt.

> I wanted to surprise my boyfriend with this really special shirt. It was the first time I was buying anything online [e-Bay] . . . because I REALLY

REALLY wanted this shirt I decided to start to bid. The price was o.k. . . . I did feel comfortable with the website, the user interface, design, and navigation. . . . however, I felt that I didn't exactly trust the individual sellers and I was also afraid about my payment details, . . . However, the urge to buy this shirt was stronger and even if I felt uncomfortable I did go on with the bidding and I finally won the shirt!!! But, I immediately then decided to draw back. I didn't give my payment details or anything because I found that my fear and the risk I was taking was bigger than my desire to give this shirt as a present. I did resolve the conflict I was feeling as I decided not to give my payment details (Michaela, U.K. female offline shopper).

In Michaela's story the approach-avoidance conflict resulted in avoidance behavior, so she was involved in a flight rather than fight conflict, and chose to escape rather than to engage.

'Other-Oriented' Conflict, Outer Directed Behavior (Type 2: Purchasing a Product on Behalf of Someone Else).   In these stories when respondents were buying goods for someone else, they all felt the clear need and drive to make these purchases. However, all their stories were linked to emotional responses (e.g., fear of embarrassment), social risk, and uncertainty. For example, Rich's story about purchasing condoms for a friend (described in part above) showed the importance of the social context, and how his friends (peer reference group) invested the product purchase (of condoms) with significant meaning, which lead to Rich's feelings of mortification. Helga's story illustrates this mixture of feelings (embarrassment, discomfort) evoked by the combination of the nature of the product (buying a Kamasutra book), her social surroundings (e.g., her boyfriend and fellow customers) and the environment in the shop (well lit and very public):

Imagine my brother, organizing a birthday present for his best friend's 20th Birthday. It is Saturday afternoon and . . . they need a KAMASU-TRA BOOK (as sort of a joke) . . . his sister is in the local shopping mall in Vorarlberg (a detail important to know, as nobody stays anonymously in Vorarlberg forever) anyways, why not call her to buy it for him! . . . There is a . . . medium sized bookshop called "Das Buch" in the shopping centre. It has an open front, so that everyone can see inside . . . . I felt a slight discomfort searching for a book like this but the thing I absolutely hated was asking the shop assistant where I could find it. . . . my boyfriend was with me . . . I could feel the people at my back grinning!!! Ahhhh, a young couple enjoying their sex lives, looking for some excitement, ha, ha . . . So I finally stood there in the, for my taste far too long, queue in front of the cash desk awaiting the payment of a cheeky little book. (Helga, Austrian female offline customer).

'Self-oriented' conflict, inner directed behavior. Many of our respondents' stories were about making purchases for themselves. In the offline situations,
the sources of discomfort and anxiety which led to the potential approach-
avoidance conflicts included lack of experience because it was a first time
purchase; lack of knowledge (knowledge uncertainty); the product itself and
often the variety of choice (choice uncertainty); time pressure; and the sales
staff (and sometimes the discomfort with the social surroundings extended
to fellow shoppers, a classic example of the importance of one's fellow customers in a service environment). These aspects are all illustrated in Dorothea's story about buying an MP3 player:

> there are many different brands and models, this decision turned out to
> be very difficult . . . In the beginning I searched for some general informa-
> tion on the Internet. Then I also went to various electric shops to inform
> me about price and features of some of the players . . . . after considering
> everything I went to Saturn (a big electric shop in Austria) and found an
> adequate model. . . . The shop itself is very big and the product lines are
> tagged very well. But the atmosphere wasn't very comfortable as I felt a
> little bit observed by the cameras, shop assistants and other clients. I was
> there on my own . . . Before I bought the player I got counseled shortly by
> an assistant but this guy was quite unfriendly and I was annoyed about
> waiting quite long for this consultation (which was even more bad than
> good) (Dorothea, Austrian female offline customer).

Andreas' story is very similar to Damien's story (described above) except
that he wanted to purchase quite a complex technical product (a digital
recorder) offline from a chain store where the staff were not experts, and
could only offer Andreas information which he could read for himself from
the packaging:

> I went to a Saturn shop and asked for information about . . . advantages
> and disadvantages of a digital recorder in comparison with an analogical
> one. . . . the staff . . . were . . . without profound knowledge about the prod-
> ucts they were supposed to sell. . . . I felt completely unsure about what to
> buy, taking that the prices of these products are relatively high. . . . When
> I requested more specific information about the different models (range of
> microphone, noise filter function, separate folder recording, AVR func-
> tion, or possibility of adding accessories) the staff was not available for
> answering and had to ask each other to give me the proper answer. The sit-
> uation was very uncomfortable because more customers were waiting and
> it was taking very long for me to decide . . . In the end, I bought nothing
> and left the shop only with many brochures from the different trademarks.
> I studied them at home, phoned directly the manufacturer and got from

them the technical information I did not get from the retailer (Andreas, Austrian male offline shopper).

Often the variety of products and information proved overwhelming, as in Dorothea's story; but sometimes the level of product information was inadequate or insufficient, as in the case of Andreas above. Andreas' story (like Michaela's earlier) showed that the approach-avoidance conflict was not always resolved by positive approach behaviors (i.e. engage/stay and make the purchase) but by negative avoidance behaviors, as Andreas chose to escape, and left without making a purchase—thus representing a lost sale for this retailer.

In the online situations, the overwhelming issues which aroused shoppers' discomfort and anxiety related to financial security vis-à-vis the payment options; and concerns about the product itself, often related to quality (which could have been ascertained via touch). Our participants also expressed concerns about delivery reliability and the rules for registration. Yvonne's account is typical of the online stories which we collected about purchasing tickets. In Damien's online story, choice uncertainty and knowledge uncertainty were both present—and both strongly linked to perceived risk; and he adopted a classic tactic for dealing with the conflict, particularly the difficulties of evaluating different brands of hockey kits for upper body protection (described above). He reduced the conflict by combining online (for search and purchasing) with offline (for evaluating the product).

> I simply didn't want to spend so much money on very important protective equipment, which I had never tried on. [In the end] I resolved the discomfort I felt by going to a shop where I could try the kit on, then I bought the kit online (using the same shop's website). Much cheaper that way. (Damien, UK male online shopper).

It was clear that apart from the financial risk for Damien, the strongest sense of risk was associated with whether the hockey kit which he wanted to buy would fit him when it arrived. As for most online shoppers, this conflict and uncertainty could not be easily resolved until the *final* consumption stage when the goods arrived. The conflict reliever in terms of perceived risk which Damien used was to combine offline trial (he went to a local sports shop and tried on the hockey kits) with online purchase. This option was not open to many of the other online purchasers. Their online stories also indicated that the stage at which feelings of perceived risk are strongest is usually towards the end of the purchase cycle just before the goods are received. This sense of perceived risk related to knowledge uncertainty. At that point they had ordered their goods and spent their money but were nervous about whether the tickets would arrive; and if the tickets didn't arrive, how would they chase up the missing tickets without an easy way of contacting the suppliers? Contact information on websites was often limited: telephone numbers could be difficult to trace or expensive to contact; and repeated email requests for information often went unanswered. Tying these results back to perceived risk levels and their impact on self confidence, we clearly see the inverse relationship between specific self confidence and perceived risk confirmed (Bell, 1967, cited in Mitchell & Boustani, 1994, p. 61). Lack of confidence was a recurring theme throughout the online stories, most notably lack of confidence with the channel itself (and its related systems) rather than product-related risk. However, this is true for the online shops that were used for the first time. Participants reported that when they used the online shop again for a second time, then they felt more comfortable with the procedures.

Perceived risk was more usually, but not exclusively, associated with choice uncertainty related to the product rather than the channel, illustrating the links between knowledge uncertainty, choice uncertainty, and perceived risk (Mitchell & Boustani, 1994, p. 57).

Discussion

Current research neglect of the interaction between the retail setting (offline or online), the nature of the product or service, and the consumer's characteristics and predisposition in generating approach-avoidance conflicts, represents a significant gap in our understanding of shopping behavior, and particularly how approach-avoidance conflicts might influence shoppers' preferences for either brick and mortar or virtual shopping environments.

Our findings indicated that approach and avoidance are not necessarily bipolar opposites but separate (if often interdependent) unipolar constructs. Our findings support Babin et al.'s (1998) argument "that positive and negative affects are often but not always unipolar rather than bipolar dimensions . . . one cannot, consequently consider negative affect as simply the opposite of positive effect" (cited in Maxwell & Kover, 2003, p. 554). Our findings also link with Gray's (1990) identification of two different neurobiological motivational systems: "the behavioral activation system (BAS) [approach-related behavior] and the behavioral inhibition system (BIS) [avoidance-related behavior] . . . [which can be] conceived as being generally orthogonal and each related to one broad affective quality: BAS is thought to be related to the experience of PA [positive arousal], and BIS is thought to be related to the experience of NA [negative arousal]" (cited in Updegraff, Gable, & Taylor, 2004, p. 497). Gray's research provides further evidence of different and separate constructs of approach and avoidance, supporting our initial findings. Our stories demonstrate that shoppers can experience both approach and avoidance motivational behaviors at the same time.

Our findings represent an extension of Donovan et al.'s (Donovan et al., 1994, p. 284) work which showed how the M-R (Mehrabian & Russell, 1974) model (essentially Stimulus-Organism-Response) related "features of the environment (S) to approach-avoidance behaviors (R) within the environment, mediated by the individual's emotional states (O) aroused by the environment". Our findings also confirm earlier work on consumer ambivalence (Otnes et al., 1997, p. 80) about the effect of mixed emotions on consumers' experiences, which often resulted "directly from interactions in, or structural features of, the marketplace" pointing to the importance of the interplay between 'internal and external components' notably between emotions and the enactment of "various social roles—each characterized by norms or counternorms that govern role behavior" (Otnes et al., 1997, p. 82).

Donovan et al. (1994, p. 291) demonstrated "that shoppers' emotional states within the store predict actual purchase behavior—not just attitudes or intentions. Moreover, the contribution to emotional variables to store behavior is independent of cognitive variables such as perceptions of quality and price". Donovan et al. (1982) thereby drew an important distinction between emotions and cognitions, which was a distinction we also found confirmed in our dataset. Our findings also showed how emotions can also predict non-purchase behavior (e.g., embarrassment; frustration) illustrated by Andreas who escaped from the shop; and by Michaela who did not purchase. We could see clearly in our stories how emotions drive decisions to purchase as much as cognitive variables, and this was particularly true of the offline stories where social setting was often very important as a contextual or environmental influence on purchase approach avoidance behavior (engage or escape).

Consumer approach-avoidance behaviors can be potentially linked to two different end states: desired or undesired (Higgins, Roney, Crowe, & Hymes, 1994). We compared shoppers' experiences in offline and online settings and elicited their emotional states (arousal and pleasure) and their intentions about how they would behave in a store; and the strategies and tactics which they adopted as potential sources for relieving the conflict(s). A range of conflicts were identified. Drawing on the results from the study we confirm earlier findings that responses to store environments involve both approach and avoidance behaviors (Donovan & Rossiter, 1982, p. 37). We also extended these findings by showing that they are applicable to online environments. For instance, Donovan and Rossiter (1994) distinguished four aspects of AP-AV in an offline retail environment. The AP aspects included the desire to stay in the store (or remain online); to explore the store (or browse the web pages and/or surf the Web site); to communicate with others (or collect online views about goods and services, e.g., Damien's homework about the hockey kit); and the degree of enhancement of and satisfaction with the shopping performance (or with navigating the Web site and purchasing online). The AV aspects include the desire to get out of the store (or to exit the website), to avoid the store (or the Web site in the future) and the communication in a store (or avoid further online communication), and the hindrance of performance (or frustration of navigating the Web site). Alongside the behavioral responses we identified similar emotional states induced by both offline and online environments, i.e., pleasure-displeasure (PL), and arousal-non arousal (AR) (Van Kenhove & Desrumaux, 1997).

Elliot and Thrash (2002, p. 815) propose that "achievement and affiliation arguably represent the two most central domains;" and Donovan and Rossiter's earlier experiment (1982) demonstrated the important role of affiliation in understanding the role of arousal in in-store settings. Donovan and Rossiter (1982, p. 50) demonstrated that arousal was a "key mediator of intentions to spend time in the store" as well as a "positive relationship between arousal and affiliation. The implication of the arousal-affiliation relationship is that more aroused shoppers will be more likely to interact with other people in the store" and that in-store stimuli such as bright lights and rock music may increase arousal. However, our findings also showed the importance of the negative aspects of arousal (as opposed to non arousal), i.e., when the feelings generated by the environment included anxiety, frustration, and embarrassment, and the in-store stimuli (such as the bright lights) reinforced the desire to flee (avoid) rather than stay. This was amply illustrated by Carl's and Mark's stories about buying lingerie for their girlfriends. Their stories also showed the negative side of affiliation, i.e., the desire to minimize contact with the store personnel. This means that in our dataset negative arousal could potentially be linked to rejection of affiliation, which is in contrast to the arousal-affiliation finding identified by Donovan and Rossiter (1982, p. 50). Our findings allow us to offer a counter comparison to Donovan and Rossiter (1982) as our stories showed negative aspects of arousal (embarrassment; frustration; anxiety) which could be aligned with non-affiliative feelings, i.e., desire not to interact with store personnel (cf. Carl and Mark); and desire to minimize interaction with significant others (e.g., friends and peers) in the environment (cf. Helga's purchase of a sex manual).

Conceptualization

From our findings we propose a conceptualization (Figure 4.3) which captures the multi-dimensional aspects of approach-avoidance conflicts. The framework models the relationships between the components of approach-avoidance conflicts which are stimulated by some combination of the environment (physical and information rate); the product (risk perception and product involvement); the reference group (e.g., friends/family; salespeople); and psychological influences (e.g., goal orientation and risk disposition), linked to approach-avoidance behaviors.

Conflicts Caused by Situation Including Physical Aspects and Information Rate. In line with Baker's (1986) framework we identified the situational aspects linked to ambient, design, and social factors in offline settings. In the online setting the ambient and design factors were also present within the context of the Web site. Information rate was important in generating arousal, confirming Mehrabian and Russell's observation (1974) about environmental cues, and our data showed how conflict was often experienced because of the novelty and complexity associated with online shopping. This also links to overload, one of the antecedents of consumer ambivalence where consumers feel "overwhelmed or ill-prepared during the purchasing process and the sheer volume of purchasing decisions to be made" (Otnes et al., 1997, p. 87). In online shopping channels, the sheer volume of decisions related to the need for a series of decisions whilst navigating the Web site.

Conflicts Caused by Product (Risk Perception, Involvement). From the offline data, the nature of the product/service itself generated approach/avoidance conflicts (thoughts, behaviors)—partly linked to psycho-social risk and impression management (e.g., embarrassment cf. condoms, pregnancy test, lingerie); fear of failure (buying the wrong product as a present); and demonstrating a lack of expertise/experience about the product itself. From the online data, the nature of the product or service did not, in itself, seem to generate/stimulate such avoidance conflicts—in fact, it was often the key approach stimulus (e.g., desperate to get hold of a ticket for a sold out concert; keen to get a good deal on tickets or hotel accommodation or costs for a trip).

Conflicts Caused by Reference Groups and Social Context. The importance of the social surroundings (indicated by earlier research, e.g., Mehrabian & Russell, 1974) was clearly evident in the offline data which we had collected. In terms of online experiences, social influences in terms of word-of-mouth and potential social embarrassment caused by not being able to surf the Net and effectively complete online purchases also emerged as clear themes in the dataset. The social factors were present in the form of word-of-mouth, e.g., what others said about the Web site or the procedures for purchasing online. Word-of-mouth was an important strategy that online consumers adopted to relieve their perceived risk, which particularly derived from their lack of self-confidence about purchasing online (Bell 1967, cited in Mitchell & Boustani, 1994, p. 61).

Conflicts Caused by Psychological Influence (Goal Orientation, Risk Disposition). Following Mehrabian and Russell's (1974) earlier work on pleasure and arousal, these psychological factors were clearly present in the stories that our informants told. Many described their feelings in considerable detail and also their attitudes to risk emerged quite clearly. Online experiences in comparison to offline situations, however, were described with more enthusiasm and the respective arousal level seemed to be higher.

This conceptualization (Figure 4.3) identifies firstly, the different sources of conflict with which consumers are faced; and secondly, consumers' preferred risk reduction strategies in relation to environmental, product-related, and psychological factors in approach-avoidance conflicts. There are important implications for managerial strategies as a more refined understanding of the source and nature of approach-avoidance conflicts will help retail managers identify effective ways in which to help consumers manage the

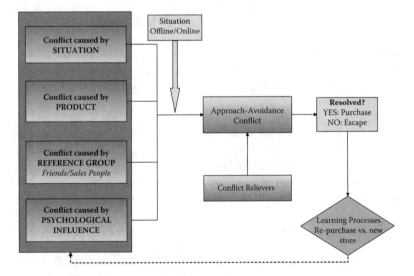

Figure 4.3.
Conceptualization of approach-avoidance conflicts.

different perceived risks (most notably in retail settings, both offline and online) that might lead to breaking off the purchase. How shoppers deal with these conflicts, and shoppers' strategies for reducing risk, could inform how retailers develop risk reduction/management strategies for their respective shoppers, and thereby allow retailers to achieve significant competitive advantage in their respective retailing domains. This model will also contribute to our theoretical understanding of approach-avoidance conflicts in the field of consumer behavior, for instance in terms of motivations and drives in relation to the adoption and diffusion of new products and services (such as innovations in offline and online retail offerings); as well as our understanding of the interaction of different motivations within symbolic consumption, and its associated positive and negative drives (e.g., tastes, distastes, and possible future selves including the negative self).

Conclusion

There is significant literature about approach-avoidance in psychology. Donovan and Rossiter (1982) identified the importance of *affect* or store-induced *pleasure* as an important influence on approach-avoidance behaviors within stores; and thus the relevance of considering emotional affect alongside cognitive factors in shopping behavior. Our purpose was to identify the potential contribution of the approach-avoidance conflict model from psychology (e.g., Miller, 1944, 1964) for understanding shoppers' approach-avoidance behaviors in different retail environments (virtual versus brick and mortar). Donovan et al. (1982, p. 292) called for future research to examine "the relationship between merchandising and atmosphere effects," we went further than this and examined interrelationships between three key components of shopping experience.

Very few studies have tried to systematically examine approach-avoidance conflicts (and the subsequent approach-avoidance shopper behavior) in relation to the complex *interaction* between the individual (e.g., consumers' feelings of arousal and emotions; cognition), the environment (offline or online) *and* the nature of the product or service to be purchased. Donovan et al. (1982) also only studied one type of offline channel (discount department stores) whilst we studied a range of offline and online shopping outlets (from department stores; specialist stores, e.g., bookshops; corner shops; as well as a range of online outlets).

In view of this gap in consumer research, our starting point was a small-scale empirical study, and our goal was to identify and conceptualize the key aspects of approach-avoidance conflicts. In the offline setting, approach-avoidance conflicts were linked to different aspects of the purchase experience, both the product and the retail outlet. In the online setting, approach-avoidance conflicts were largely linked to the retail outlet (purchasing online) rather than to the product. The 'fight or flight' conflicts that individuals typically confront in other areas of their lives, were paralleled by the approach-avoidance conflicts experienced by individuals when they are shopping (whether online or offline); and the pattern of approach-avoidance behaviors could be broadly classified into 'engage or escape'. We found many examples of approach-avoidance conflicts and behaviors in our dataset.

From our analysis we proposed that there were two main categories of approach-avoidance conflicts. The approach-avoidance conflicts were either *other-oriented* (type 1 and type 2) or *self-oriented* in terms of the needs to be met by purchasing the product or service itself. However the conundrum regularly faced by consumers in *other-oriented* situations was how to reconcile conflicting needs or wants, such as their need to satisfy another party (e.g., a girlfriend; family member or friend) by making the purchase whilst meeting personal needs (e.g., avoid embarrassment; avoid psycho-social risk). In the *self-oriented* situations, our respondents were faced with reconciling their need for a product or service with their need to feel comfortable making the purchase (i.e., reducing complexity in choice and decision-making; reducing financial risk; managing performance risk, whether the product would be 'fit for purpose' if purchased online).

Dawson et al. (1990) pointed out the importance of assessing the feeling states brought to the store as well as the feeling states induced by the store, as explored in Donovan et al.'s earlier work (1982) when examining purchase behaviors. This would seem to be equally true of online as well as offline shopping experiences. There were hints of this in the stories, but further study (e.g., observation and interview) would be required to elicit the feelings that online consumers brought to their experiences of shopping online. This would be supported by Updegraff et al.'s (2004) finding that past negative emotional experiences may be 'chronically salient sources' for subsequent experiences, and could be important for further study of approach-avoidance conflicts in online and offline channels.

How consumers deal with these conflicts and their strategies for reducing risks will be of significant interest to offline and online retailers. Brick and mortar and virtual retailers could develop different risk reduction strategies for their respective shoppers and thereby achieve significant competitive advantage in their respective retailing domains.

This was a small scale study which examined respondents from a restricted age range and with the same educational status. However it provided the opportunity to extend theory-building in the area of approach-avoidance conflicts and behaviors amongst consumers. We identified the multi-dimensional aspects of approach and avoidance behavior for consumer behaviors and goals; as well as the fact that approach-avoidance behaviors are driven by different motives and emotions, and therefore are not bipolar but rather individual and independent unipolar dimensions. The application of approach-avoidance theory to shopper behavior will potentially contribute to our understanding of consumer ambivalence by extending research into "mundane consumption scenarios" (Otnes et al., 1997); the relationship between desired and undesired end states (Hogg & Banister, 2001); distastes and the negative self (Banister & Hogg, 2004); and also into other fields of social science such as psychology or educational science (Finset, Steine, Haugli, Steen, & Laerum, 2002; Johnson & Busemeyer, 2001; Smith, Duda, Allen, & Hall, 2002; Van Kenhove & Desrumaux, 1997). This study has shown how important it is to consider the combination of emotional and cognitive reactions in consumers' responses to the different types of retail environment (offline or online); this represents a largely untapped area of research and points to the importance of adopting research strategies that elicit the processes, as well as the outcomes, of consumers' shopping experiences.

References

Babin, B. J., Darden, W. R., & Babin, L. A. (1998). Negative emotions in marketing research: Affect or artifact? *Journal of Business Research, 42*(3), 271–285.

Baker, J. (1986). The role of the environment in marketing services: The consumer perspective. In J. A. Czepeil, C. A. Congram, & J. Shanahan (Eds.), *The services challenge: Integrating for competitive advantage* (pp. 79–84). Chicago, IL: American Marketing Association.

Baker, J., Levy, M., & Grewal, D. (1992). An experimental approach to making retail store environmental decisions. *Journal of Retailing, 68*(4), 445.

Banister, E. N., & Hogg, M. K. (2004). Negative symbolic consumption and consumers' dive for self-esteem: The case of the fashion industry. *European Journal of Marketing, 38*(7), 850–868.

Bell, G. D. (1967). Self-confidence and persuasion in car buying. *Journal of Marketing Research, IV*, 46–52.

Bem, S. L. (1993). *The lenses of gender: Transforming the debate on sexual inequality.* New Haven, CT: Yale University Press.

Chen, Z., & Dubinsky, A. J. (2003). A conceptual model of perceived customer value in e-commerce: A preliminary investigation. *Psychology & Marketing, 20*(4), 323–347.

Chiang, K.-P., & Dholakia, R. R. (2003). Factors driving consumer intention to shop online: An empirical investigation. *Journal of Consumer Psychology, 13*(1 & 2), 177–183.

Dawson, S., Bloch, P. H., & Ridgway, N. M. (1990). Shopping motives, emotional states, and retail outcomes. *Journal of Retailing, 66*(4), 408–427.

Day, G. S., Deighton, J., Narayandas, D., Gummesson, E., Hunt, S. D., Prahalad, C. K., et al. (2004). Invited commentaries on "Evolving to a new dominant logic for marketing". *Journal of Marketing, 68*(1), 18–27.

Dennis, C., Harris, L., & Sandhu, B. (2002). From bricks to clicks: Understanding the e-consumer. *Qualitative Market Research, 5*(4), 281–290.

Donovan, R. J., & Rossiter, J. R. (1982). Store atmosphere: An environmental psychology approach. *Journal of Retailing, 58*(1), 34–57.

Donovan, R. J., Rossiter, J. R., Marcoolyn, G., & Nesdale, A. (1994). Store atmosphere and purchasing behavior. *Journal of Retailing, 70*(3), 283–294.

Elliot, A. J., & Thrash, T. M. (2002). Approach-avoidance motivation in personality: Approach and avoidance temperaments and goals. *Journal of Personality and Social Psychology, 82*(5), 804–818.

Finset, A., Steine, S., Haugli, L., Steen, E., & Laerum, E. (2002). The brief approach/ avoidance coping questionnaire: Development and validation. *Psychology, Health & Medicine, 7*(1), 75–85.

Fischer, E. (2002). *Panel comments: Gender, marketing and consumer behavior.* Paper presented at the ACR, Paris.

Fischer, E., & Arnold, S. J. (1994). Sex, gender identity, gender role attitudes, and consumer behavior. *Psychology & Marketing, 11*(2), 163–182.

Flanagan, J. C. (1954). The critical incident technique. *Psychological Bulletin, 51*(4), 327–358.

Forsythe, S. M., & Shi, B. (2003). Consumer patronage and risk perceptions in Internet shopping. *Journal of Business Research, 56*(11), 867–875.

Freed, A. F. (1996). Language and gender in an experimental setting. In V. L. Bergvall, J. M. Bing & A. F. Freed (Eds.), *Rethinking language and gender research: Theory and practice* (pp. 55–76). London: Longman.

Gray, J. A. (1990). Brain systems that mediate both emotion and cognition. *Cognition and Emotion, 4*, 269–288.

Higgins, E. T., Roney, C. J. R., Crowe, E., & Hymes, C. (1994). Ideal versus ought predilections for approach and avoidance: Distinct self-regulatory systems. *Journal of Personality and Social Psychology, 66*(2), 276–286.

Hogg, M. K., & Banister, E. N. (2001). Dislikes, distastes and the undesired Self: Conceptualizing and exploring the role of the undesired end state in consumer experience. *Journal of Marketing Management, 17*(1–2), 73–104.

Hopkinson, G. C., & Hogarth-Scott, S. (2002). 'What happened was . . . .' Broadening the agenda from storied research. *Journal of Marketing Management, 17,* 27–47.

Hopkinson, G. C., & Hogg, M. K. (2006). Stories: how they are used and produced in market(ing) research. In R. W. Belk (Ed.), *Handbook of qualitative research methods in marketing* (pp. 156–174). Northampton, MA : Edward Elgar.

Hughes, N., & Hogg, M. K. (2006). *Problematizing gendered interpretations of collecting behaviour.* Paper presented at the ACR Gender Conference, Edinburgh.

Johnson, J. G., & Busemeyer, J. R. (2001). Multiple-stage decision-making: The effect of planning horizon length on dynamic consistency. *Theory and Decision, 51,* 217–246.

Joines, J. L., Scherer, C. W., & Scheufele, D. A. (2003). Exploring motivations for consumer Web use and their implications for e-commerce. *The Journal of Consumer Marketing, 20*(2/3), 90.

Kaplan, L. B., Szybillo, G. J., & Jacoby, J. (1974). Components of perceived risk in product purchase: A cross-validation. *Journal of Applied Psychology, 59*(3), 287–291.

Korgaonkar, P. K., & Wolin, L. D. (1999). A multivariate analysis of Web usage. *Journal of Advertising Research, 39*(2), 53–68.

Kwak, H., Fox, R. J., & Zinkhan, G. M. (2002). What products can be successfully promoted and sold via the Internet. *Journal of Advertising Research, January/ February,* 23–38.

Lee, P.-M. (2004). Behavioral model of online purchasers in e-commerce enviroment. *Electronic Commerce Research, 4,* 75–85.

Maher, B. A. (1962). The application of the approach-avoidance conflict model to social behavior. *Conflict resolution, VIII*(3), 287–291.

Maxwell, S., & Kover, A. (2003). Negative affect: The dark side of retailing. *Journal of Business Research, 56,* 553–559.

McCarthy, R. V., & Aronson, J. E. (2000). Activating consumer response: A model for Web site design strategy. *The Journal of Computer Information Systems, 41*(2), 2–8.

Mehrabian, A., & Russell, J. A. (1974). *An approach to environmental psychology.* Cambridge, MA: MIT Press.

Miles, M. B., & Huberman, A. M. (1994). *Qualitative data analysis: An Expanded Sourcebook* (2nd ed.). Thousand Oaks, CA: Sage.

Miller, N. E. (1944). Experimental studies of conflict. In J. M. Hunt (Ed.), *Personality and the behavior disorders* (pp. 431–465).

Miller, N. E. (1964). On the functions of theory. In F. H. Sanford (Ed.), *Research in perception, learning, and conflict* (pp. 97–103). Belmont, CA: Wadsworth.

Mitchell, V.-W. (1999). Consumer perceived risk: conceptualisations and models. *European Journal of Marketing, 33*(1/2), 163–195.

Mitchell, V.-W., & Boustani, P. (1994). A preliminary investigation into pre- and post-purchase risk perception and reduction. *European Journal of Marketing, 28*(1), 56–71.

Monsuwe, T. P. Y., Dellaert, B. G. C., & Ruyter, K. D. (2004). What drives consumers to shop online? A literature review. *International Journal of Service Industry Management, 15*(1), 102–121.

Otnes, C., Lowrey, T. M., & Shrum, L. J. (1997). Toward an understanding of consumer ambivalence. *Journal of Consumer Research, 24*(1), 80–93.

Palmer, J. W. (2002). Web site usability, design, and performance metrics. *Information Systems Research, 13*(2), 151–167.

Shim, S., Eastlick, M. A., Lotz, S. L., & Warrington, P. (2001). An online prepurchase intentions model: The role of intention to search. *Journal of Retailing, 77*, 397–416.

Sinkovics, R. R., & Penz, E. (2005). Empowerment of SME websites-Development of a web-empowerment scale and preliminary evidence. *Journal of International Entrepreneurship, 3*(4), 303–315.

Smith, M., Duda, J., Allen, J., & Hall, H. (2002). Contemporary measures of approach and avoidance goal orientations: Similarities and differences. *British Journal of Educational Psychology, 72*, 155–190.

Sobh, R., Lee, C., & Vaughan, G. (2006, 15–17 June). *Feedback valence and consumer motivation: The moderating effects of positive and negative reference values in self-regulation.* Paper presented at the ACR-Asia Pacific, Sydney, Australia.

Stone, R. N., & Gronhaug, K. (1993). Perceived risk: Further considerations for the marketing dis. *European Journal of Marketing, 27*(3), 39.

Teo, T. S. H., & Yeong, Y. D. (2003). Assessing the customer decision process in the digital marketplace. *Omega, 31*(5), 349–363.

Updegraff, J. A., Gable, S. L., & Taylor, S. E. (2004). What makes experiences satisfying? The interaction of approach-avoidance motivations and emotions in well-being. *Journal of Personality and Social Psychology, 86*(3), 496–504.

Van Kenhove, P., & Desrumaux, P. (1997). The relationship between emotional states and approach or avoidance responses in a retail environment. *The International Review of Retail, Distribution and Consumer Research, 7*(4), 351–368.

Vargo, S. L., & Lusch, R. F. (2004). Evolving to a new dominant logic for marketing. *Journal of Marketing, 68*(1), 1–17.

Wang, Y.-S., & Tang, T.-I. (2003). Assessing customer perceptions of website service quality in digital marketing environments. *Journal of End User Computing, 15*(3), 14–31.

Wolfinbarger, M., & Gilly, M. C. (2001). Shopping online for freedom, control, and fun. *California Management Review, 43*(2), 34–55.

II

NEW FINDINGS IN RETAILING STRATEGY

THE ART OF MARKETING

Sumire Crader
Waseda University, Tokyo, Japan

Judith Lynne Zaichkowsky
Simon Fraser University, Vancouver, Canada

Sensory experiences are immediate, powerful, and capable of changing our lives profoundly, but they are not used to their full extent in branding initiatives at the store level, in product development, packaging design, and advertising. This, despite the well-documented evidence illustrating the effect of the five senses on consumer behavior. [Gobé, 2001, pp. 68–69]

*D*OCTORAL STUDENTS IN MARKETING often study the philosophy of marketing, where a major question on comprehensive exams is "Is Marketing an art or a science?" Now the answer to that question is both, but of course the question is debated and the answer of emphasis depends on your positional argument and supportive examples given. Those with a traditional cognitive and historic Kotler analytic perspective may argue for science. Here the emphasis is on data, strategy, positioning, research, and reasoning.

Those with an emotional, creative, irrational, joyful, and perhaps cultural orientation will view and argue for a higher art form of marketing. In truth, both science and art are needed for successful marketing. It is like the battle of the sexes or saying civilization is male or female. We need both to survive, but men and women have complementary skills and resources to contribute.

Without either sex, civilization will not survive. Similarly, without art, marketing will not survive.

Consumers of today do not purchase commodity items purely based on functionality in order to satisfy their need recognition. Instead, shopping is now the modern form of entertainment through which consumers seek both stimulation and relaxation (Cox, Cox, & Anderson, 2005). Retail stores are the museums and churches of worship of the 21st century. Rob Kozinet provides an insight to these phenomena in the first chapter of this volume. The world's greatest architects are now building shops whereas decades ago they were building museums or corporate headquarters. Just as museums have found that exhibits are no longer enough, stores have found that brands are no longer enough. To keep the products fresh and in the public eye, the shop now has to be the destination, a *museum of product* (Heathcote, 2003).

But the store also has to be a theater—a microcosm of urban life, branding, advertising, and media which draws people in and squeezes the credit cards out of their wallets as they are lifted on a cloud of desire to want to belong to this perfect mini-world and take home a souvenir (Heathcote, 2003). That is to say, consumers are looking beyond the basic functions of a product to look at the brand aesthetics or design when making a purchase decision (Schmitt & Simonson, 1997). Any retailer that wants to compete effectively in this consumer era must be able to appeal to sophisticated buyers that demand more than the brand, product, or service. Thus, marketing needs to be like art to distinguish itself from the visual clutter of the modern world and provoke the senses of shoppers in order to activate their emotions.

For too long, art has not been given the prominence it deserves in marketing. The reason for this may be that most consumers are not conscious of the effect sensory experiences have on their purchasing behavior. Thus, even with market research, marketers may not be made aware of these factors (Gobé, 2001). However, art and its sensory aspects affect consumers so profoundly that marketers cannot afford to ignore their impact on consumer behavior. A recent study has even shown the health benefits of art, where viewing and discussing art led to positive attitudes, increased creativity, lowered blood pressure, and even relieved constipation (The Globe and Mail, 2005). Such positive impacts on the attitude and well-being of consumers can help marketers to actively engage their customer base.

The activation of emotion is important because decision making is aided by positive emotions. "When feeling in control, consumers not only feel higher levels of pleasure and arousal, they also increase their level of involvement, which is a central cognitive variable in their attitudes toward the store" (Chebat & Robicheaux, 2001, p. 87). One of the first studies of shopping centers and emotions felt by customers was carried out by Donovan and Rossiter

(1982). They found that flowing water, such as waterfalls and fountains, had an extremely calming effect on individuals who were agitated, and at the same time elevated the mood of individuals who were feeling low. A casual stroll through most shopping malls will demonstrate this effect.

Some emotions that marketers should strive to activate are (1) well-being; (2) happiness; (3) order; and (4) control. Such emotions can be activated through the senses of taste, hearing, smell, vision, and touch and can all be under control of the retailer.

A Brief Review of Senses as Applied to Retailing

The application of aesthetic qualities to various aspects of the store environment is especially useful in distinguishing products and drawing interest when consumers are not actively seeking information about the products, as is most often the case. Retailers should encourage consumers to connect with the merchandise at the sensual level of touching, seeing, smelling, hearing, and in some cases, tasting. This ability to communicate with all of the senses is the strong point of retailers and should be used to build customer loyalty.

> Over recent years consumers have grown cautious about the messages they are told by companies through traditional media and now they want to know as much information as they can before they will commit to making a purchase. Part of this information is the physicality of a product. The best way to achieve this is to put customer and product together in the same room and allow the human senses to make their own interpretations. (Fulberg, 2003)

Taste. Our taste receptors obviously contribute to our experience of many products. Specialized companies called "flavor houses" keep busy developing new concoctions to please the changing palates of consumers. Taste preferences are also related to culture. This literature will not be reviewed here as it is only tangentially related to retail marketing and art through in-store sampling.

Hearing. So-called "functional music" is played in stores, shopping malls, and offices to either relax or stimulate consumers. Work by Milliman (1982; 1986) varied the tempos of music in supermarkets, restaurants, or stores and found that consumers would unknowingly change their behavior in the retail environment, whether it be ordering more drinks, or buying more or less groceries.

While it is well known that the tempos of songs affect the speed with which consumers react to their environment, another aspect is the familiarity of the music. Consumer's time perception tends to be negatively affected when they are encountered with music they are not comfortable with. Research shows that shoppers felt they had spent more time in environments when the music being played was not of their taste (Yalch & Spangenberg, 1988). For an in-depth review of this literature one is directed to the chapter "Sound Retailing: A Review of Experimental Evidence on the Effects of Music on Shopping Behavior" in this volume by David Allan.

Smell. Odors can stir emotions or create a calming feeling. They can invoke memories or relieve stress. This is because fragrance is processed by the limbic system, the most primitive part of the brain and the place where immediate emotions are experienced. Therefore if a retailer is able to create a connection between a particular scent and the brand or product, any time this scent is present in the consumer's daily life, they will remember the store and the positive emotions tied to their previous experiences with it. Some of our responses to scents result from early associations that call up good or bad feelings, and that explains why businesses are exploring connections among smell, memory, and mood (Scholder Ellen & Fitzgerald Bone, 1998).

There are three dimensions of scent that should be considered. These are the affective nature (e.g., pleasantness), intensity, and its arousing nature (Mattila & Wirtz, 2001). Also, scent can be either ambient or nonambient. Ambient scent can be useful in retail environments where the merchandise themselves do not emit any kind of scent. The presence of pleasant ambient scent increases the likelihood of a positive response, even if the scent itself has nothing to do with the product. This is because pleasant scents trigger pleasant emotions that create a positive appeal for the shopper.

While it is important to choose music that appeals to the target market and complements the brand message, it is also important to make sure that the scent and music are congruent with each other. Mattila and Wirtz (2001) found that the congruence of the arousal level of ambient scent and background music enhanced the consumer evaluation of the shopping experience. When using high arousal music, the scent should also be highly arousing and vice versa. By using both scent and music to complement the other atmospheric elements, marketers will be able to create a carefully controlled store environment that gives customers a pleasant shopping experience.

A great deal of research on the effect of odor finds shifts in consumer's behavior and preferences depending upon the scent in the retail environment (for a review, see Spangenberg, Crowley, & Henderson, 1996). We also find differences between men and women here on what triggers their most pleasurable sensation (Wilkie, 1995). Furthermore we find consumers are not aware of any scent present so this change is happening below their conscious awareness.

Vision. Vision is the main component of the Art of Marketing. It allows one to "consume" marketing because the visual aspect of a product is what a consumer first connects to when shopping (Bloch, Brunel, & Arnold, 2003). This sensory experience forms the consumer's mental images, impressions, and emotions; and determines whether the product will acquire more than a passing glance from its potential buyer. This first glance may be all a marketer has to establish a connection to the consumer. Battles between brands occur in this visual domain, compelling marketers to acquire intimate knowledge of visual consumption processes in order to achieve success in today's market (Schroeder, 2002).

The ability of art to shift preferences of everyday products was investigated by Hagtvedt and Patrick (2006). Their results showed that when an everyday soap dispenser had paintings imprinted on it, it was greatly preferred over those that had non-art images, which were equally decorative. According to their art infusion theory, art not only influences evaluations of unrelated objects positively, it also has a capacity to elicit higher-order sensibility about the nature of life.

An integral part of visual consumption is visual aesthetics. Through visual aesthetics, marketers can distinguish products to create recognition, influence product comprehension and evaluation through image, and form consumer/ product relationships (Bloch, Brunel, & Arnold 2003). Through these advantages, aesthetic marketing delivers tangible values such as: (1) customer loyalty; (2) premium pricing and strong brands; (3) the ability to focus consumers' attention and cut through information clutter; (4) strong logos and brands that lead to protection from competitive attacks; and (5) less time and money spent on creating layouts or messages and less time spent on redesign (Schmitt & Simonson, 1997).

Key elements in visual aesthetics are color, contrast, context, and gestalt. These elements can be used by marketers to create an artistic environment which will stimulate the attention and interest of consumers, in a manner consistent with the brand image.

Color. Scientists and philosophers have been talking about the meanings of colors since the time of Socrates, in the fifth century B.C., but it took Sir Isaac Newton in the early 17th century to shine light through a prism and reveal the color spectrum. We now know that perceptions of a color depend on both its physical wavelength and how the mind responds to that stimulus.

Therefore in-store lighting can be the single most effective factor in increasing the overall sense of satisfaction because it supports "convenience, comfort, and favorable emotional reactions" (Summers & Hebert, 2001).

At the store level, the colors and the lighting used are crucial to forming the consumer's expectations about the store's characteristics because light affects how color is perceived. Bright fluorescent lighting with vibrant colors would be more appropriate for children's clothing verses a more subdued lighting with darker wood tones for men's clothing. The congruence of consumer's notions of what certain stores should look like and the actual store design help customers to feel "right" in a store (Pile, 1995).

Colors may even influence our emotions more directly. Evidence suggests that some colors (particularly red) create feelings of arousal and stimulate appetite, and others (such as blue) are more relaxing. Products presented against a backdrop of blue in advertisements are better liked than when a red background is used, and cross-cultural research indicates a consistent preference for blue all around the world (Chattopadhyay, Gorn, & Darke, 1999; Bellizzi & Hite, 1992; Crowley, 1993).

Some reactions to color come from learned associations. Orange implies economy, pink is a feminine color, and brown is a masculine color. In addition, the color black is associated with power. On a corporate identity level, color is key to brand and store identification. For example, Starbucks is green and 7-Eleven is orange, yellow, and green.

Other reactions to color are due to biological and cultural differences. Women tend to be drawn toward brighter tones and they are more sensitive to subtle shadings and patterns. Some scientists attribute this to biology, since females see color better than males do, and men are anywhere from 10–20 times more likely to be color blind, depending upon the exact color and lighting. Age also influences our responsiveness to color. As we get older, our eyes mature and our vision takes on a yellow cast. Colors look duller to older people, so they prefer white and other bright tones (Faubert, 2002). This helps to explain why mature consumers are much more likely to choose a white car—Lexus, which sells heavily in this market, makes 60 percent of its vehicles in white (Solomon, 2006). Therefore retail environments frequented by those aging boomers better have great lighting and brighter colors to make their customers feel younger or at least not be reminded of their aging eyes.

Color's impact on people's moods and emotions are well known. The use of color is crucial in attracting a consumer's attention and creating interest in a product by activating thoughts, memories, and particular modes of perception. Furthermore, this arousal prompts an increase in the ability to process information (Gobé, 2001).

Contrast.   Contrast is achieved through manipulations of background color, size, and shelf orientation. For example when displaying black dresses, one may put them on mannequins against a white wall with a splash of yellow to stimulate the senses. That way the black will appear interesting, stand out, and attract the eye (see Exhibit 5.1).

Exhibit 5.1.
The black and white check floor with yellow sunflowers draws the eye.
The result is an artistic display for otherwise difficult to see black dresses.

Contrast gives emphasis through drawing the eyes of a viewer. Used successfully, it can allow a brand to cut through visual noise and reach out to the consumer. Though too little contrast creates blandness that is boring for the shopper, too much contrast can lead to an uncomfortable environment. The level of contrast that is appropriate will depend on the target market. Older clientele may want a soothing environment, while younger consumers may thrive off of an environment that stimulates multiple senses. Also, contrast can be useful in signaling changes such as sales, new seasons, or new products. The effective use of contrast will allow the store to keep a consistent brand image without seeming stagnant.

There are many research opportunities here, as the authors could find no published work on the principles of contrast as applied to the retail setting. Contrasting colors, sizes, and shapes would seem to be most applicable to creating art in the retail environment to both relax and stimulate customers.

Context.   Context adds meaning to an object or image. The choice of congruence or contrast between the context and the focal point can create completely different meanings for the viewer. Congruent context can create a unified "story" of the brand that adds richness to the brand message. Meanwhile, a contrasting context can create surprise or humor that can capture the attention of shoppers. For example, in Exhibit 5.2 there is a doll whose head is severed from its body and in-between the head and body there are about a hundred different toys displayed. The context is a contrast and creates surprise for the shopper.

The use of both congruence and contrast will create a store environment that holds the shopper's interest so that they will be more receptive to a richly textured communication about the brand and products. For example, selling luggage against a backdrop of an exotic vacation scene may be more eye catching than just piling the luggage against a bare wall. Selling fragrance in the lingerie department works because the context of sexual allure may be congruent between the products. Selling fragrance in the shoe department would not work because the products are not used in context.

Gestalt.   Gestalt is a concept that the whole is greater than a sum of its parts. It is related to the design concept of unity where the parts are organized so that they interact in a mutually supportive fashion (Veryzer, 1993). When parts of a design do not support each other, the resulting lack of coherence distracts or interferes with the perception of the object or display. This concept should aid in the choice of contrast, color, and context. Each of these elements should work together to create a good Gestalt. Even slight changes in these "underlying dimensions or their interactions can cause massive changes in the Gestalt" (Schmitt & Simonson, 1997). Though marketers

Exhibit 5.2.
This toy display in the center of Galleries Lafayette,
Paris is an example of contrasting context.

should never allow the store environment to get stale, they must be conscious of how any change they make to components of the store will affect the entire perception or Gestalt.

An example might be a retail display showing china with furniture, with the table linens, with the candles, with the stemware, and with the silver—all combined to provide good Gestalt. Each may be thought of as a different product, but they all go together to create a whole or unified 'unit' of use (Exhibit 5.3).

Touch. When a consumer's attention is captured through visual and other sensory cues, there will be behavioral responses such as "moving closer to the object, extended viewing of its appearance, touching of its surface, and ultimately its acquisition" (Bloch et al., 2003). It is easy to see that this need to touch is primal when observing the behavior of small children. Touching is quite literally a way to connect to the outside world and this tendency can be used richly in a retail store environment to increase sales.

Exhibit 5.3.
Many items that are sold separately in different areas of the store should be combined to form a Gestalt of product use.

Moods are stimulated or relaxed on the basis of different sensations reaching the skin. Cashmere sweaters evoke a quite different response than boiled wool. The softness of touch is apparent and inviting. To allow this freedom of touch, the store and product layout should be designed to be experienced, felt, and unfolded (Gobé, 2001). Though packaging needs may prevent a product from being accessible, the retailer should find a way around that to give the customers a chance to play with the products. This can happen with any product from a luxury automobile to toilet paper. People browsing through auto dealerships are always encouraged to sit behind the wheel of the car on display. Britain's Asda grocery chain removed the wrapping from several brands of toilet tissue in its stores so that shoppers could feel and compare textures. The result, the retailer says, was soaring sales for its own in-store brand, resulting in a 50 percent increase in shelf space for the line (Ellison & White, 2000).

Research has shown that people who touch products are more likely to make impulse purchases, and point-of-purchase signs that encourage such touching stimulated sales (Lempert, 2002). This is because touching allows a shopper to "take possession" of an item and can help fulfill the need for instant gratification. This sensation can create an exciting emotional connection to the product and create pleasure for the shoppers. In the picture below (Exhibit 5.4), the shopper is compelled to stop and touch the flowers to see if they are real, thereby being drawn to the store front and the door. The next thought she may have is to step inside the store and further examine the merchandise.

Apple has done a great job of this with their open store layout that gives a customer a chance to try out all of their products. Casual browsers may be turned into serious shoppers through the heightened emotional response to the touching and playing with the products. Apple even goes a step further and gives lectures on how to utilize their products, thus creating an interactive environment that allows for personal interaction between the merchandise and the end user. This gives the shoppers an opportunity to really get to know the product without the pressure of having to ask special permission from the salespeople. Thus, a casual shopper whose interest is piqued is given a chance to become a serious consumer by having an environment that allows the emotional side of the shopper to take over.

New research is starting to identify the important role the *haptic* sense (touch) plays in consumer behavior. Haptic senses appear to moderate the relationship between product experience and judgment confidence; confirming the common-sense notion that we're more sure about what we perceive when we can touch it (Citrin, Stern, Spangenberg, & Clark, 2003). Their study found that individuals who scored high on a "Need for Touch" (NFT) scale were especially influenced by this dimension. Those with a high need for touch responded positively to such statements as: (1) when walking through

Exhibit 5.4.
The opportunity to touch should be front and center of
a retail environment because it encourages shoppers
to stop and examine the merchandise.

stores, I can't help touching all kinds of products; (2) touching products can be fun; and (3) I feel more comfortable purchasing a product after physically examining it (Peck & Childers, 2003).

Applications to Packaging

Studies have found that many in store decisions are made in only a few seconds and only after looking at one or two packages (Arnold, 2003; Sway, 2005). With such a short time to make a decision, it is obvious that the consumer is not making a rational decision, but a decision based on first impressions. This shows the high importance of having packaging that grabs consumers' attention and evokes their emotions.

Packaging can refer to the wrap of the individual product or the shopping bag or box with the name, logo, or visual identity of the store. Part of packaging is the product range, because this communicates what kind of store the shopper is at and differentiates against competitors. In order to appeal to emotions, package designers use color to influence the buying decision. As we know, human reaction to color is emotional rather than rational and is a great way to directly appeal to the senses. This ability to appeal to the senses makes packaging one of the most important point-of-sale merchandising tools (Lempert, 2002). Thus, packaging must go beyond just functional aspects and instead focus on the aesthetic ability to appeal to a shopper. This appeal should capture the shopper's interest so that the product makes it into consideration for the buying decision (Garber, Burke, & Jones, 2000).

With strong packaging, products with little advertising support can still attract the consumer's attention in a way that connects them to the product and ultimately leads to a purchase. Sometimes the package is so important that it is used over and over for other goods that do not relate to the package. One of the authors was in Coin, a small Italian department store in Milan, where she witnessed a customer buying several cosmetic products. The customer had brought her own box, a Hermés box. The clerk put the creams in the box and tied the signature brown Hermés ribbon around it. This was a gift, to which the package had no relation to the contents.

Hence packages themselves can be thought of as having value which may elevate the value of the contents of the package. Smart retailers know that customers save their little decorated shopping bags to reuse as gift bags or even use as lunch bags. In fact, packaging has become so desirable as a symbol, that fake luxury store shopping bags are being sold on the Internet.

Another thing to consider is how to keep the product range and packaging relevant and interesting. It may serve a store well to have several different designer shopping bags which the customer "collects" and thinks of them as pieces of art. The marketer must be aware of the customer's desire for variety and new-ness and keep their store and brand fresh in the consumer's mind. "Retailers that do not update their stores on a regular basis run the risk of appearing out-of-touch with the customer, and if a refurbishment program is left for too long, the change required to modernise the store may be so extensive that the retailer runs the risk of alienating the customers who remain" (Varley, 2005).

Applications to Window Displays

A study by Cox, Cox, and Anderson (2003) found that a big source of shop-ping enjoyment for women was recreational browsing or window browsing. This enjoyable activity can be channeled to create sales opportunities by using the window as a salesperson. Retailers should work to create a store environment in which customers are brought inside through window dis-plays and a store layout that encourages customers to meander through the store, touching and playing with merchandise. This has the potential to change a "just looking" passerby into an engaged shopper.

Making the window display a work of art will stop the shopper and entice him or her to spend time examining the merchandise closely to determine how the merchandise becomes the art form. The following two pictures (Exhibit 5.5) are of the same shop window, one week apart. The store sells high-end china. In the first picture you see the china resting on a bed of wooden spoons and in the second week, different china is resting on bamboo pieces. Both window displays capture attention by the art form and gestalt of the background spoons and bamboo.

The store window also serves the dual purpose of reinforcing the inten-tions of a purposeful customer (Pile, 1995). The signs, displays, lighting, and advertising should reassure loyal shoppers that the store environment they have felt a connection to before is still there for them to enjoy. Though the window display should be changed with frequency to keep up-to-date with changing fashions and seasons, there should always be a foundation of con-sistency that transmits the brand and store message.

Cases in point: KaDeWe, Anthropologie, and Gio Moretti's Jeans Room and Art

KaDeWe (Kaufaus des Westens) is the major department store in downtown Berlin which exemplifies the full-stop entertainment shopping experience.

Exhibit 5.5.
Creating unique works of art in your store window is a
sure way to attract attention to everyday products.

The average time shoppers spend in the store is three hours. A big draw is the huge specialty food floor interspersed among gourmet lunch counters on the seventh floor. Here shoppers can lunch on champagne and lobster, buy vintage wine and specialty coffees from all over the world, and pick out their own fresh water fish from live tanks. Groceries and wine orders are delivered to one's car or home. There is no need to carry items with you in the store. In fact lugging groceries would take away from the urge to spend freely on other consumer goods on the way back to street level. Once the shopper is stimulated and relaxed by the food floor experience, the stroll down the escalator invites a one-store shopping experience for anything and everything one might need or want, from batteries to luxury furs.

Local and international brands are carefully displayed for the shopper. Aisles are not crowded and the merchandise takes on the feeling of art exhibits through aspects such as color-coded displays of men's shirts. Entertainment can pop up at any turn. At Christmas, minstrels stroll though the store with a parade of singers and costumed characters. Children are encouraged to meet and greet the parade. A different event may unfold on each floor. While luxury brands can be purchased at the *KaDeWe*, it remains a place where local German brands can thrive and every shopper can find what they can afford.

An example of a small specialty store centered around a unique consumer lifestyle is *Anthroplogie* found in New York City. This store is unique because they have had great success in the absence of advertising and because their merchandising strategy "does not highlight product so much as set a mood and create context" (LaBarre, 2002). *Anthropologie* does not specialize in a product category, but instead, caters to every need of a very specific customer. It does so through creating stores that carry a wide assortment of product categories from around the globe in a layout that blurs the boundary between the displays and merchandise.

The store itself has a unified feel that uses aesthetics to create a Gestalt that manages to bring together dishware and furniture with clothing. There are no straight aisles and shoppers meander through the various products that are put together to create a story that appeals to the modern, high-income women to which they cater. *Anthropologie* is a good example of a "lifestyle retailer" that "provides a product and service combination for a group of consumers whose needs are determined by particular values, attitudes, and choices made about how their money and time is spent" (Varley, 2005, p. 20).

Jeans Room and Art is where fashion and contemporary art meet at *Gio Moretti's* in Milan. This is a mental and physical space where one discovers the artistic experience and the freedom of luxury. Pieces of modern art and the specific U.S.A. creativity of extraordinary brands of jeans are brought together. Here we no longer speak of "shopping." We now speak of purchases that pay for themselves, of discoveries for our personal allure, and also for making our spaces magnificent for participating in the discovery of new artists. The store is meant to access a mentality that no longer separates fashion from aesthetic sensitivity.

This concept is not new as restaurants and hair salons all around the world have been using their shops as art galleries for up and coming local artists for years. What is new is that the store is not selling a service where customers are committed to spend one to two hours or more at any one visit. Customers are now brought into the retail establishment as much to interact with the art as to purchase the jeans.

Summary

In a world full of hectic consumers who are bombarded with marketing information at every turn, many shoppers have become jaded to traditional marketing efforts. To overcome this rational perspective, it is imperative for marketers to appeal directly to the emotions of consumers. The senses are more easily reached than is the mind and are a better approach to capture the attention of consumers. For example, a beautiful window display that emotionally connects to the consumer can overpower a rational explanation of why the product would be beneficial to them.

Once a basic connection is made with the shopper, the store environment should create a sense of pleasantness for the shopper that helps communicate the brand and store message. This should keep the shopper lingering in the store, touching and playing with the merchandise. This source of instant gratification aids the shopper in envisioning themselves purchasing and taking home the product. Once they have taken possession of the items in their minds, it is only a matter of time before they make the purchase to fulfill this desire. Thus, the more a marketer is able to involve a consumer in their product, the more likely they are able to sell the product to them.

Another benefit to creating this product involvement is that it can serve as a countervailing force to price consciousness (Lichtenstein, Bloch, & Black, 1988). The sensitive topic of price is thus avoided and the basic consideration is switched to value. Even with premium pricing, aesthetic products and store environments that activate the emotions of consumers are able to give more value to consumers than having a cheap price for unpleasant goods or store locations.

These lessons are especially valuable for brick-and-mortar retailers because this is where they can have significant competitive advantage over competing marketing channels. Though the Internet and other such channels can give the opportunity to shop at any time of the day, it cannot go beyond visual and audio stimuli. In this, they are missing the much deeper connection that other senses can create. Also, they can not have complete control over the other senses of the customer. Only in a retail location can a carefully orchestrated environment fully immerse a customer into the shopping world of the marketer's choosing. All components of this environment, to every last detail, should come together to guide the shopper into making a purchasing decision while communicating the brand message to create a lasting loyalty to the store.

References

Arnold, C. (2003). For great visual messages, know the store. *Marketing News,* June 13, 15.

Bellizzi, J., & Hite, R. E. (1992). Environmental color, consumer feelings, and purchase likelihood. *Psychology & Marketing, 9,* 347–63.

Bloch, P., Brunel F. F., & Arnold, T. J. (2003). Individual differences in the centrality of visual product aesthetics: Concept and measurement. *Journal of Consumer Research, 29,* 551–565.

Chattopadhyay, A., Gorn, G. J., & Darke, P. R. (1999). *Roses are red and violets are blue—everywhere? Cultural universals and differences in color preference among consumers and marketing managers.* Unpublished manuscript, University of British Columbia, Canada.

Chebat, J. C., & Robicheaux, R. (2001). The interplay of emotions and cognitions of consumers in the retail environment. *Journal of Business Research, 54*(2), 87–88.

Citrin, A. V., Stern, D. E., Spangenberg, E. R., & Clark, M. J. (2003). Consumer need for tactile input an internet retailing challenge. *Journal of Business Research, 56,* 915–922.

Cox, A. D., Cox, D., & Anderson R. D. (2005). Reassessing the pleasures of store shopping. *Journal of Business Research, 58,* 250–259.

Crowley, A. E. (1993). The two-dimensional impact of color on shopping. *Marketing Letters, 4* (January), 59–69.

Donovan, R. J., & Rossiter, J. R. (1982). Store atmosphere: An environmental psychology approach. *Journal of Retailing, 58*(1), 34–58.

Ellison, S., & White, E. (2000). 'Sensory' marketers say the way to reach shoppers is the nose. *Advertising,* (November 24), 1–3.

Faubert, J. (2002). Visual perception and aging. *Canadian Journal of Experimental Psychology*, 56(3), 164–76.

Fulberg, P. (2003). Using sonic branding in the retail environment—An easy and effective way to create consumer brand loyalty while enhancing the in-store experience. *Journal of Consumer Behaviour, 3*, 193–198.

Garber, J. L., Jr., Burke, R. R., & Jones, J. M. (2000). *The role of package color in consumer purchase consideration and choice.* Cambridge, MA: Marketing Science Institute.

Gobé, M. (2001). *Emotional branding: The new paradigm for connecting brands to people.* New York: Allworth Press.

Hagtvedt, H., & Patrick, V. M. (2006). Art infusion: How the presence of art affects the perception and evaluation of non-art products. In D. Grewal, M. Levy, & R. Krishman (Eds.), *Proceedings of the American Association of Marketing Educators Meeting* (pp. 357–358). Chicago: American Marketing Association.

Heathcote, E. (2003). The theatrical art of high consumption. *Financial Times,* September 16, 14.

LaBarre, P. (2002). Sophisticated sell. *Fast Company Magazine,* December, (65), 93.

Lempert, P. (2002). *Being the shopper: Understanding the buyer's choice.* New York: Wiley.

Lichtenstein, D. R., Bloch, P. H., & Black, W. C. (1988). Correlates of price acceptability. *Journal of Consumer Research,* (September), 273–289.

Mattila, A. S., & Wirtz, J. (2001). Congruency of scent and music as a driver of in-store evaluations and behavior. *Journal of Retailing, 77*(2), 289–293.

Milliman, R. E. (1982). Using background music to affect the behavior of supermarket shoppers. *Journal of Consumer Research, 46*(Summer), 86–91.

Milliman, R. E. (1986). The influence of background music on the behavior of restaurant patrons. *Journal of Consumer Research, 13*(September), 286–289.

Peck, J., & Childers, T. L. (2003). Individual differences in haptic information processing: The "Need for Touch" scale. *Journal of Consumer Research, 30*(3), 430–442.

Pile, J. F. (1995). *Interior design.* 2nd Edition. New York: Prentice Hall, Inc.

Schmitt, B., & Simonson, A. (1997). *Marketing aesthetics: The strategic management of brands, identity, and image.* New York: The Free Press.

Scholder Ellen, P., & Fitzgerald Bone, P. (1998). Does it matter if it smells? Olfactory stimuli as advertising executional cues. *Journal of Advertising, 27*(Winter), 29–40.

Schroeder, J. E. (2002). *Visual consumption.* New York: Routledge.

Social Studies. (2005, October 19). *The Globe and Mail*, p. A20.

Solomon, M. (2006). *Consumer behavior: Buying, having, and being*, 7th edition. Upper Saddle River, NJ: Prentice Hall.

Spangenberg, E. R., Crowley, A. E., & Henderson, P. W. (1996). Improving the store environment: Do olfactory cues affect evaluations and behaviors? *Journal of Marketing, 60*(April): 67–80.

Summers, T. A., & Hebert, P. R. (2001). Shedding some light on store atmospherics influence of illumination on consumer behavior. *Journal of Business Research, 54*(2), 145–150.

Sway, R. (2005). Four critical seconds. *Display & Design Ideas*, November, Vol. 17 Issue 11, 3–3, 1/2p, 1c.

Varley, R. (2005). Store image as the key differentiator. *European Retail Digest, 46*, Summer, 18–21.

Veryzer, R. W. (1993). Aesthetic Response and the influence of design principles on product preferences. In L. McAllister and M. L. Rothschild (Eds.), *Advances in consumer research* (Vol. 20, pp. 224–228). Provo, UT: Association for Consumer Research.

Wilkie, M. (1995). Scent of a market. *American Demographics*, (August), 40–49.

Yalch, R. F., & Spangenberg, E. (1988). An environmental psychological study of foreground and background music as retail atmospheric factors. In A. W. Walle (Ed.), *AMA Educators' Conference Proceedings* (pp. 106–110). Chicago: IL: American Marketing Association.

6

CONSUMER TRUST IN MULTIPLE CHANNELS: NEW EVIDENCE AND DIRECTIONS FOR FUTURE RESEARCH*

Ray L. Benedicktus, III
Michael K. Brady
Peter R. Darke
Florida State University

Clay M. Voorhees
Michigan State University

MULTI-CHANNEL RETAILING: TRENDS AND ISSUES

Many traditional retailers are expanding their retail operations to the Internet in an effort to improve customer service and increase sales. Leading retailers such as Barnes and Noble, Target, Staples, and scores of others quickly embraced the benefits of multi-channel retailing. In fact, 95 percent of retailers are now trying to implement some form of multi-channel marketing (Direct Marketing Association, 2005). As multi-channel marketing is becoming the norm, retailers must provide a consistent customer experience that allows consumers to shop using the channel with which they are most comfortable. Moreover, successful and strategic channel integration allows a firm to increase the number and variety of its consumer purchases, deliver a

* The authors would like to thank the Social Science and Humanities Research Council of Canada for their financial support in the form of a research grant.

unified brand experience for prospective and existing customers across multiple media, strengthen customer relationships via additional interactions, create a more robust database by collecting unique data from each channel, and enhance marketing campaign successes with regards to ROI and customer lifetime value. Customers who buy from two or more channels are thought to be more valuable, have lower attrition rates, and buy a wider range of products (Stone, Hobbs, & Khaleeli, 2002).

The synergies available via multi-channel retailing are certainly encouraging; however, retailers are faced with the challenge of simultaneously maintaining their offline identity and establishing their brand online. In making this transition, gaining consumer trust is a critical success factor. In fact, it is now believed that, "price does not rule the web; trust does" (Reichheld & Schefter, 2000, p. 107). To formulate successful Internet marketing strategies, firms require a comprehensive understanding of how trust is developed and how trust affects online consumer behavior (Bart, Shankar, Sultan, & Urban, 2005). Such an understanding is particularly important for multi-channel firms that may not fully realize the challenges of operating in an unfamiliar channel. Although offline retailing studies may offer some insight on developing consumer trust, virtual exchanges pose unique challenges for trust development and therefore some brick-and-mortar lessons may need to be applied differently on the Internet.

Specifically, widespread fraud on the Internet has reduced consumers' general trust in online retailers. Recent polls from Fraud Watch International (2006) indicate that 31 percent of online buyers have lost money to online fraud and over 80 percent think that they are likely to become a victim at some point in the future. Although auction fraud is the most common complaint (62.7 percent), non-delivery of merchandise from retailer websites represents approximately 16 percent of the $183 million problem and yields a median loss of $410 per victim. The Internet Crime Complaint Center (IC3, 2005) reports that Internet complaints are increasing, with 231,493 complaints reported in 2005, up 11.6 percent from 2004. The National Consumers League (NCL, 2001) identified specific concerns that consumers have when shopping online. About 43 percent of consumers worry about security of credit card information, 22 percent fear abuse of personal information, and approximately 33 percent have had a problem with an online purchase.

As devious e-commerce activity continues to rise, both multi-channel and Internet retailers must gain a better understanding of the factors that affect consumer trust. This is critical because these trust evaluations are the method by which consumers categorize virtuous and fraudulent Internet vendors. In an effort to provide new insight into the process of developing trust online, this chapter discusses recent research findings that suggest specific trust building strategies for both etailers and clicks-and-mortar retailers.

Consumer Trust

Trust is known to be an essential component of exchange (Nooteboom, Burger, & Noorderhaven, 1997) and a central factor in consumer purchase decisions (Chaudhuri & Holbrook, 2001; Gefen, 2000; Reichheld & Schefter, 2000). Additionally, trust is a key component of relationship development, as it allows exchange partners to concentrate on the long-term benefits of the relationship (Ganesan, 1994; Morgan & Hunt, 1994; Reichheld, 1994). Schurr and Ozanne (1985) show that a seller's trustworthiness leads to improved buyer-seller relationships, including more cooperation between parties. Furthermore, trust has significant effects on different stages of customer loyalty (Harris & Goode, 2004).

Researchers in marketing define trusting beliefs as "confidence in an exchange partner's reliability and integrity" (Morgan & Hunt, 1994, p. 23). A related perspective offers that trust is a behavior and is at its highest when the truster not only believes the trust target to be credible, but when the truster is willing to rely on the exchange partner, particularly when the exchange partner has the ability to exploit the vulnerability of the truster (Moorman, Deshpandé, & Zaltman, 1993; Rousseau, Sitkin, Burt, & Camerer, 1998). Given that consumers are highly vulnerable to exploitation on the Internet, trust is likely to be a primary driver of online purchase behavior.

Recent Findings

Recent research suggests many determinants of consumer trust on the Internet. These can generally be classified into: (1) Web site design characteristics, (2) the transparency and makeup of guarantees and privacy and security policies, (3) information cues regarding the firm itself, and (4) characteristics of the customer. Perhaps the largest single undertaking with regards to building trust is the work of Bart, Shankar, Sultan, and Urban (2005), that investigates determinants of trust in all of the aforementioned classes. These researchers show that privacy, navigation and presentation, brand strength, availability of advice, order fulfillment, and absence of Web site errors are all determinants of online trust. Bart et al. (2005) also identify consumer characteristics that evoke trust for specific Web site categories (e.g., expertise for financial services Web sites, shopping experience for portal sites, entertainment for computer sites, and familiarity with the Web site for automobile, travel, and etailer Web sites).

Aiken and Boush (2006) demonstrate that outside certifications, which are frequently used to communicate security, serve as more powerful trust signals than both perceived Web site investment and objective source ratings (e.g., *Consumer Reports* ratings). Specifically, the external certifications or "trustmarks" are found to have such a large impact on affective, cognitive, and behavioral trust dimensions, that two additional trust cues (Web investment and objective source ratings) explained very little additional variance. However, other research calls into question the generalizability of these findings. For example, Bart et al. (2005) report that the explanatory power of security is so basic that its influence is reduced to insignificance in their study due to the dominant effects of other factors. Belander, Hiller, and Smith (2002) found that consumers value specific security features more than seals or statements.

Few studies to date have identified trust cues that are capable of combating purchase risk and/or generalized suspicion. An exception is Schlosser, White, and Lloyd (2006), who show that for purchases of home accessories, Web site investment communicates a firm's ability and thus affects ability-related trusting beliefs regardless of purchase risk. The use of a combination of trust cues (brand familiarity and consensus information concerning the past experiences of other customers) has also been shown to attenuate the negative effects of consumer suspicion (Benedicktus, Brady, Darke, & Voorhees, 2007).

Other notable research has identified several Web site characteristics that boost Web site credibility, including real world feel, ease of use, product selection, information quality, and timeliness (Fogg et al., 2001; Shankar, Urban, & Sultan, 2002; Urban, Sultan, & Qualls, 2000). Additionally, several studies suggest that online trust is an important mediator leading to consumer purchase intentions (Jarvenpaa, Tractinsky, & Vitale, 2000; Schlosser, White, & Lloyd, 2004; Yoon, 2002). Trust is suggested to mediate the effects of brand strength, brand familiarity, order fulfillment, Web site investment, consensus information, and physical store presence, as well as many Web site characteristics on purchase intentions (Bart et al., 2005; Benedicktus et al., 2007; Schlosser et al., 2006). Table 6.1 summarizes the more recent findings discussed above.

Recent studies differentiate offline and online trust and suggest that online trust resides within the Web site or related technologies (Seiders, Voss, Grewal, & Godfrey, 2005). However, these investigations are focused on giving companies a deeper understanding of Web site characteristics that

Table 6.1 Building Trust Online, Recent Findings

Source	Determinant	Effect Size
Aiken & Boush (2006)[a] — *Results vary across trust dimensions*	Third party certification	.23–.31
	Privacy and security	.27–.53
	Multiple trust signals	ns–.18
	Trust undermines	–.47
	C's Internet experience	ns–sig., but not reported
Bart et al. (2005) — *Results vary across Web site categories*	Privacy	.15
	Navigation and Presentation[b]	.17
	Brand Strength[b]	.26
	Advice[b]	.16
	Absence of errors	.18
	Order fulfillment[b]	.03
	C's familiarity with website	.11
	C's online savvy/expertise	.09
	C's Internet shopping experience	.08
	C's entertainment/chat experience	.04
Benedicktus et al. (2007) –*Results vary across trust dimensions*	Physical store presence[b]	.02–.03
	Brand familiarity[a]	.03–.09
	Consensus information[b]	.06–.28
	Suspicion*Brand interaction	ns
	Suspicion*Consensus interaction	.03–.04
	Suspicion*Brand*Consensus[c]	sig., but not reported
Schlosser, White, & Lloyd (2006) –*Results vary for browsers and searchers*	Perceived web site investment[b]	.27–.43
	Privacy statement (strong vs. weak)	sig., but not reported
	Privacy statement (mere presence)	ns
	Risk*Web investment interaction[c]	ns

[a]Mediation of trust on purchase/behavioral intentions not reported.
[b]Trust mediates relationship between factor and purchase/behavioral intentions.
[c]Negative effects of first factor were mitigated by the other respective factor(s).

influence consumer trust judgments (Belanger, Hiller, & Smith, 2002). In contrast, few papers include frameworks that propose effects for specific attributes of multi-channel firms. Although many researchers have included brand manipulations or measures, consensus information and the availability of a physical channel are largely unexplored firm-related factors.

In the subsequent sections of this chapter, we (1) briefly summarize what we know about the power of brand and how this knowledge might lead to future research, (2) discuss the pervasive availability and consumers' use of consensus information when making online trust judgments, (3) offer theoretical support and initial empirical evidence suggesting the presence of physical stores builds trust for some firms, and (4) discuss sources of generalized distrust along with suggestions for reducing its negative effects.

Firm Related Trust Cues

Broad Positive Effects of Brand

Brand name is used frequently as a basis for making choice judgments (Adaval, 2003). Additionally, consumers have a tendency to favor retailers with which they are most familiar (Quelch & Klein, 1996). For example, consumers use the name of well-established brands as a heuristic cue to reduce uncertainty in purchase decisions (Wernerfelt, 1988). In addition to reducing risk, brands communicate many associations that lead to consumer trust (Aaker, 1991; Ambler, 1997; Keller, 1993). For example, brands serve as signals of quality in uncertain buying situations and in the absence of human touch (Bart et al., 2005; Erdem, Swait, & Valenzuela, 2006; Montgomery & Wernerfelt, 1992). Given that a large percentage of online transactions are one-time purchases and devoid of human interaction, the trust cues associated with brand names are of great benefit to firms marketing their products and services on the Internet. Degeratu, Rangaswamy, and Wu (2000) show that brands provide greater comfort to consumers making online purchases than for traditional purchases. Many researchers have shown that firms with familiar brand names are more trusted than relatively unknown firms (Hoeffler & Keller, 2003; Kania, 2001; Ottaway, Bruneau, & Evans, 2003; Wernerfelt, 1988; Yoon, 2002).

Brand names are cues that remind consumers of specific brand associations. In the present context, brand names are particularly important because they are highly associated with a firm's level of operations (e.g., size of company, market position, distribution channels used by the firm) in the minds of consumers. The brand name carries with it certain attributes; namely, familiarity or awareness, associations, feelings of loyalty, and quality perceptions (Aaker, 1991). In addition, affective attitudes toward a particular brand can transfer to the attributes of a product even if little or no information regarding the specific attribute is available. For example, a consumer shopping for a complex electronics product may have little knowledge of the product's reliability or quality, but such consumers are likely to make inferences regarding these traits based on brand associations in memory. Additionally, familiarity with a brand can reduce the consumer's need to engage in an extensive search for brand related information, freeing up both cognitive capacity and time needed to evaluate other aspects of the purchase decision, such as comparing attributes across or within products. Brand related factors are also likely to reduce involvement in processing other information, affect attitude strength, and increase purchase behavior.

Beyond Branding

With respect to firm related factors, it is imperative that our knowledge of multi-channel trust should extend beyond the effects of brand factors alone (i.e., brand equity, familiarity, strength, etc.). Although it is commonly accepted that brand factors will have strong, positive effects on trust and purchase intentions, branding strategies are not always available to firms. In particular, developing a trusted brand is costly and time consuming. For these reasons it is important to consider what other elements of marketing strategy might help establish consumer trust online. The following sections discuss the use of consensus information and physical store presence as additional ways in which firms can establish online trust.

Consensus Information

Consumers have remarkable access to information concerning brick-and-mortar, etailer, and hybrid firms via electronic feedback mechanisms. Following transactions, consumers are often asked to rate firms on either single or multiple scale items that measure factors such as the valence of transaction outcomes, elements of the service environment, and employee friendliness/responsiveness. This information is then aggregated and presented to potential customers via online feedback mechanisms (e.g., judysbook.com, ratings.net) through consumer reporting agencies and watchdog organizations (e.g., American Consumer Satisfaction Index, *Consumer Reports*, Better Business Bureau), or in magazine articles and advertising messages (e.g., 73 percent of respondents say . . . , or 9 out of 10 consumers choose . . .).

Consensus information can also be represented either cross-sectionally or as a time series (e.g., monthly for 3 months, annually for 5 years). Although the formats vary from mean and percentage scores to star ratings and histograms, each method is aimed at conveying the consensus of consumer opinion.

Consensus information discloses the estimated proportion of past customers of a firm that are satisfied with the purchase experience, and is based on a consensus of a subset of customers (e.g., product owners, clients) that has similar perceptions regarding the performance of a firm and/or its products. Consensus information provides customers with an account of the performance of firms in their consideration set. This is suggested to result in *indirect* trust wherein a customer is inclined to trust a firm because the firm is known to be trusted by other customers (Bolton, Katok, & Ockenfels, 2004). Thus, consensus information essentially increases consumer trust in virtuous companies and gives buyers a tool for identifying potentially risky transactions.

The most common view in the persuasion literature is that consensus information is processed by consumers in a heuristic manner. In fact, consensus information is one of the primary heuristics used to form opinions (c.f. Chaiken, Liberman, & Eagly, 1989). Consensus information leads to the inference that the majority opinion must be correct, and therefore the consumer should agree with the majority. The fact that consensus information exerts its influence through an informational mechanism, where majority opinion is used to infer the correct judgment (Burnkrant & Cousineau, 1975), suggests that consensus cues are likely to impact online purchases despite the relatively private nature of such transactions.

Recent evidence suggests that consensus information can have rather broad and powerful effects on attitude judgment. In particular, Darke et al. (1998) show that individuals are willing to rely on consensus information in both high and low motivational settings, although the process underlying the effects depends on the level of motivation. Less motivated individuals use consensus information as a simple, mindless heuristic, whereas consensus information biases the thought process involved in judgment when motivation is higher (i.e., thoughts tend to be more consistent with the majority vs. minority opinion). The result is that consensus information actually has stronger effects under high motivation than low motivation. In addition, less motivated consumers are generally insensitive to the size of the sample used to estimate consensus opinion, thereby violating the normative principle suggesting that large samples typically provide more reliable estimates than small samples (Tversky & Kahneman, 1971). In contrast, increased motivation leads to better differentiation between small and large samples, causing individuals to rely on consensus information only when the sample of responses is large.

Overall, there is evidence that consensus information acts as a powerful cue for judgment in other contexts, as well as more specific indications that consumers view a consensus of positive experiences as evidence that a firm can be trusted. More recent evidence shows that consensus information also has powerful effects on purchase intentions, and that these effects are mediated by perceptions of trust. In fact, Benedicktus et al. (2007) show that consensus information has effects on trust and purchase intentions that are comparable to the broad effects of the brand name of the firm. Furthermore, the effects of consensus and brand were additive, suggesting that consensus information was just as important in determining purchase for the brand name firms as it was for the unbranded firms. Other research demonstrates that firms with high consensus information can charge price premiums (Ba & Pavlou, 2002; Reiley, Bryan, Prasad, & Reeves, 2005).

Recent research has also begun to focus on changes in the level of consensus information that occur over time. Consensus information is often broken down according to when the transactions occurred (i.e., within the past 3 months, the last 6 months, and the past year), and the sequence or pattern of this information can therefore vary as a function of time (consensus can increase, decrease, or remain stable). Sequences of consensus information are likely to be evaluated relative to a reference point (Kahneman & Tversky, 1979). This reference point can be part of the immediate sequence under consideration (e.g., the value of consensus for a prior period) or an outside criterion (i.e., memory or perceived norms). Although it is not yet clear which reference points consumers tend to prefer, preliminary evidence suggests that consumers do in fact have preconceived notions of the absolute magnitudes of ideal, typical, and minimally acceptable consensus levels (Benedicktus et al., 2007), as well as ranges for high, moderate, and low levels of consensus (Benedicktus & Andrews, 2006).

It seems likely that the absolute magnitude of a consensus sequence is compared to a reference point in memory and then adjusted based on reference points within the sequence itself. Supporting this proposition, Loewenstein and Prelec (1993) found that people evaluate sequences involving levels of positive and negative outcomes as upward and downward shifts. Moreover, the loss aversion principle of prospect theory suggests that consumers prefer sequences that improve over time relative to those that depict a decline (Ross & Simonson, 1991). Consistent with these findings, improving consensus sequences has been found to convey greater trustworthiness to consumers than sequences that diminish over time (Benedicktus & Andrews, 2006). These findings are supported by earlier work by Matsui, Kakuyama, and Onglatco (1987), who concluded that consumers avoid purchasing from unsatisfying firms, especially when there is information indicating that satisfaction is decreasing over time.

Future Research Directions. Research on recency effects and fluctuations of the quantity of feedback (number of aggregated customer responses) within sequence periods have yet to be investigated. Additionally, differences in the processing and use of consensus information compared to word-of-mouth (WOM) communications also remains uninvestigated. The aggregate nature and source characteristics of consensus information are in part what distinguish it from individual instances of WOM. However, the two forms of information often appear together online. Future research might fruitfully examine the relative weighting of consensus information versus more personal, but objectively less reliable WOM information in purchase decisions.

Physical Store Presence

The nature of the online environment eliminates many cues that customers may use to determine whether a firm can be trusted (Gefen, 2000, 2002; Reichheld & Schefter, 2000). Trust is built when there are frequent interactions between customers and employees (Doney & Cannon, 1997). Specifically, interactions with employees give customers an opportunity to gain confidence in employees' expertise, evaluate employees' intentions, and develop perceptions of employee likeability and similarity. Moreover, trust in the firm's employees is transferable to the organization (Milliman & Fugate, 1988; Strub & Priest, 1976). Doney and Cannon (1997) demonstrated that likeability of a salesperson and the perceived similarity of the salesperson to the customer have a positive impact on buyer trust. However, person-to-person interactions are less frequent in e-commerce transactions than in physical encounters, presenting a challenge for online firms. Recent technological developments may diminish the differences between online and brick-and-mortar interactions. Although customers and employees have limited capacity to communicate face-to-face in online environments, firms are beginning to facilitate direct employee interactions, making prolific use of virtual help desks, private help chat sessions, and most recently audio enabled avatars (i.e., cartoon personalities mimicking human characteristics) (Holzwarth, Janiszewski, & Neumann, 2006).

Even if personal interactions are replicable on the Internet, past research indicates that intangibility increases risk in purchase decisions (De Ruyter, Wetzels, & Kleijnen, 2001; McDougall & Snetsinger, 1990; Zeithaml & Bitner,

2000), creating a need for additional trust cues. Specifically, the intangibility dimension of risk is activated when consumers do not have access to information regarding the true quality of a product and therefore are unable to judge product quality prior to purchase (Fung & Lee, 1999; Laroche, Bergeron, & Goutaland, 2001). Intangibility also has implications for customer redress, as consumers form expectations for complaint resolution based on their ability to return the purchase to a physical store—a method that consumers believe maximizes the chances of a favorable secondary outcome (Quelch & Klein, 1996).

Brick-and-mortar stores provide customers the opportunity to sample products before buying them. Even if the customer chooses not to physically inspect the product, the mere opportunity to do so may enhance perceptions of transparency in the product description, and thereby increase trust (i.e., customers may infer the firm is less likely to convey misleading statements if the product is available for direct inspection). This thinking is supported by a National Consumers League survey wherein 71 percent of respondents believed that it is important to know where an online seller is located (NCL, 2001) and is related to the belief that brick-and-mortar firms can be held accountable for mistakes, thereby reducing uncertainty about the firm's intentions.

In an online environment, firms with physical outlets are thought to be generally favored over purely virtual companies, as the former are thought to be able to transfer trust from brick-and-mortar environments to the Internet (Epstein, 2005; Melewar & Navalekar, 2002; Schoenbachler & Gordon, 2002). Thus, communicating physical channel presence can be an effective trust building strategy for multi-channel firms. Benedicktus et al. (2007) examine this in online interactions. They demonstrate that firms operating in multiple channels are generally more trusted than firms with no physical operations. However, the positive effect of having a physical store in the immediate area is attenuated when the firm is a recognized brand, as well as when consensus information indicated that the firm was trustworthy. These findings suggest that either a recognized brand name or positive consensus information provide sufficient indication of a firm's trustworthiness, regardless of whether the online firm has a physical store presence or not. For this reason, physical store presence is more important for firms with low consensus and lesser-known brands than for firms with a high consensus of satisfactory performance and well-known brands.

Future Research Directions. Theoretically, physical presence affects trusting beliefs via consumer inferences related to tangibility, responsiveness, redress, and stability. However, no empirical evidence exists with respect to the particular explanation(s). Additionally, differences across levels of physical presence have not been investigated. For example, does the mere presence of a physical store (i.e., a physical store that is not locally accessible) signify trustworthiness to the same extent and through the same set of mediating factors as the presence of physical stores in the customers' locale or in other major cities? It is plausible that this is not the case, as the customer is less likely to have equivalent perceptions of tangibility and redress across these firm types. Furthermore, within each level of physical presence, does the number of stores affect perceptions of responsiveness and stability? Answers to these questions would illuminate the true nature of the differences between physical and online channels, as well as help to isolate the essential factors that can transfer trust from traditional retail settings to an online context.

Consumer Suspicion on the Internet

The majority of existing research concerning consumer trust has focused on normal buying conditions; however, it is also important for managers of online businesses to understand the role of trust under sub-optimal conditions, especially when consumers are initially suspicious. There are a number of indications that the high incidence of online fraud has led consumers to become broadly suspicious towards online transactions. Consumers who have directly or indirectly experienced such fraud tend to react by protecting themselves from future deception and adopting an overly suspicious view of online firms in general (Darke & Ritchie, 2007). Given that many consumers are already reluctant to buy products online (Garbarino & Strahilevitz, 2004), it is important that researchers further investigate the question of how to market products to suspicious consumers. We present a brief outline of how generalized distrust affects consumer judgments and summarize recent findings that identify trust cues that are capable of combating such suspicion.

Rotter (1967) suggested specific distrust is based on prior experiences with the same trust target (e.g., bad experiences with Wal-Mart lead to distrust of Wal-Mart in the future), whereas generalized distrust/suspicion is based on past interactions with different sources that are similar to the trust target (e.g., bad experiences with Wal-Mart lead to distrust of other discount retailers). Consistent with the latter, Pollay (1986) proposed that marketing communications rely on a basic norm of honesty and breaking this norm causes individuals not only to distrust the deceptive information source, but also to make generalizations regarding the trustworthiness of marketers as a group.

The suggestion that dishonest marketing practices can lead consumers to become broadly suspicious was empirically supported in recent research by Darke and Ritchie (2007). A series of studies showed that exposure to false advertising increased suspicion and led consumers to adopt more negative attitudes towards products that were subsequently advertised by the same firm (specific suspicion), as well as to products that came from a second, previously unknown advertiser (generalized suspicion). Moreover, the effects of generalized suspicion were robust in that they lasted for at least a 24-hour period, they were observed over a broad range of product categories, and were present regardless of whether the second product was objectively superior or inferior to its competitors. The findings were understood in terms of a persistent defensive bias, where consumers become overly suspicious of marketers in order to avoid being fooled again.

Given that such generalized suspicions are also likely to exist in the context of online shopping, an important question is what factors may be effective in combating these suspicions. Rotter (1967) suggests that specific sources of trust should be considered as more reliable/diagnostic than feelings of generalized distrust. Since both consensus information and brand name provide specific information concerning the trustworthiness of the particular firm, it follows that rational consumers should rely on these cues over more general suspicions relating to past experiences with other firms, thereby buffering any effects of generalized suspicion. However, initial evidence suggests that neither a recognized brand name nor consensus information alone is sufficient to protect firms against generalized suspicion (Benedicktus et al., 2007; Darke & Ritchie, 2003). Instead, consumers seem to need the additional assurance of multiple trust cues to overcome their initial suspicions, as the combination of high consensus and a familiar brand name was effective in combating initial suspicions, despite the fact that neither factor was effective in isolation.

Future Research Directions. The above findings suggest that multiple trust cues are needed to offset the negative effects of generalized suspicion. It is not yet clear, however, if other combinations would be just as effective. For example, Table 6.1 lists several factors with strong positive effects on trust, including availability of advice, Web site investment, and third-party certification. Although each of these factors provides consumers with firm specific evidence, potentially capable of reducing or overcoming the effects of suspicion, it is unlikely that any of the factors alone would be more capable of combating suspicion than multiple cues. However, it is certainly possible that some combination of these factors would prove capable of attenuating the negative effects of suspicion.

Managerial Implications

Consumers at all levels of Internet experience are cautious when making purchases on the Internet (Penn, Doyle, & Sage, 2005; Schlosser, White, & Lloyd, 2006). This caution is generally justified considering the increasing rates of fraudulent activity online (IC3, 2005; NCL, 2006). Awareness of fraudulent activity is likely to create generalized suspicion among consumers who are considering Internet purchases. This suspicion is the consistent theme by which researchers have illustrated the importance of online trust. Uncertainty arising from suspicion represents a psychological cost for consumers. Communicating trustworthiness to consumers increases the firm's value proposition by lowering these psychological costs. Thus, building trust on the Internet is essential for marketing managers.

Many articles have suggested guidelines by which firms should invest their resources to build trust via Web site characteristics. However, with the exception of the brand literature, relatively few works have addressed firm specific trust building mechanisms. The recent results summarized and proposed in this chapter suggest that trust is the mechanism by which Web site design, privacy and security policies, firm related information cues, and customer characteristics affect purchase intentions.

Due to the dominating effects of trust in online transactions, both familiar and unfamiliar retail brands need to actively manage customer perceptions of trust. Results from recent research suggest that the brand strength of familiar firms is not enough to bolster consumer trust under conditions of suspicion and thus all firms should strive to communicate multiple signals that the firm can be trusted in order to offset the negative effects of suspicion online (Benedicktus et al., 2007). This suggests that familiar brands are not immune to competition from relatively unknown firms. Lesser known firms can elevate their position in the customer's consideration set by highlighting firm attributes such as consensus information and other trust cues. These cues may level the playing field for relatively unknown brands at a cost that is far more reasonable than most brand-building initiatives. Thus, firms could benefit from including information related to the firm's positive consensus ratings in communications with customers. For example, Scottrade.com commercials tout the firm's success in satisfying customers. The message not only attracts new customers, but also reminds existing customers that they are clients of a firm with award winning customer service (JD Power, 2005). Furthermore, firms with less than adequate consensus are endangering themselves and must implement strategies for immediate recovery.

Brand managers should ensure that the firm's brand name is central in all communications with consumers, as this factor is perhaps the quintessential trust cue. In addition to the prominence of the brand name, Web sites should remind consumers of the favorable associations they hold for the brand. Lesser-known companies should benefit heavily from brand initiatives as consumers become more familiar with the firm. Managers of familiar and unknown firms can develop trust by reinforcing favorable brand associations.

Moreover, establishing trust is equally critical for both etailers and hybrid firms. Consumers seek evidence that Internet sellers can perform as reliably as firms in traditional markets. Managers of hybrid firms should ensure that information communicating the firm's physical locations is in obvious view for Web site visitors. This may not explicitly demonstrate the firm's ability to deliver on its promises, but such information gives consumers an indication that the firm has integrated its online and physical channels. It is this implied integration that is likely to drive reliability perceptions upward. Pure etailers are at a general disadvantage in this regard. However, etailers may attempt to demonstrate trust by making contact information (i.e., customer service links, e-mail addresses) prominent and available to customers with minimal search (Lohse & Spiller, 1998). The accessibility of such information conveys that the firm is willing to address customer concerns, thus increasing trust via the benevolence dimension (Ganesan, 1994; Shankar et al., 2002). Companies should also take advantage of technological advances that are closing the gaps between physical and online channel interactions.

Conclusion

Trust is one of the most important factors affecting online purchase decisions, as well as purchases in conventional retail settings. This chapter summarizes recent findings and presents both theoretical and empirical justification for three firm related cues by which managers can readily communicate trustworthiness to consumers. It contributes to the branding and information processing literature by illustrating that (1) among firm attributes, brand is a high scope heuristic, (2) consensus information is a powerful enough trust cue to be considered concurrently with brand, (3) preference for firms with a physical store presence can be overcome using alternate trust cues, (4) firms with familiar brand names and adequate consensus are much less vulnerable to the effects of suspicion, and (5) broadly speaking, multiple trust cues may be required to counteract existing consumer suspicions online.

References

Aaker, D. A. (1991). *Managing brand equity.* New York: The Free Press.

Adaval, R. (2003). How good gets better and bad gets worse: Understanding the impact of affect on evaluations of known brands. *Journal of Consumer Research, 30,* 352–367.

Aiken, K. D., & Boush, D. M. (2006). Trustmarks, objective-source ratings, and implied investments in advertising: Investigating online trust and the context-specific nature of internet signals. *Journal of the Academy of Marketing Science, 34,* 308–323.

Ambler, T. (1997). How much brand equity is explained by trust? *Management Decision, 35,* 283–292.

Anderson, R., Kulhavy, R., & Andre, T. (1971). Feedback procedures in programmed instructions. *Journal of Educational Psychology, 62,* 148–156.

Ba, S., & Pavlou, P. A. (2002). Evidence of the effect of trust building technology in electronic markets: Price premiums and buyer behavior. *MIS Quarterly, 26,* 243–268.

Bart, Y., Shankar, V., Sultan, F., & Urban, G. L. (2005). Are the drivers and role of online trust the same for all websites and consumers? A large scale exploratory empirical study. *Journal of Marketing, 69,* 133–152.

Belanger, F., Hiller, J. S., & Smith, W. J. (2002). Trustworthiness in electronic commerce: The role of privacy, security, and site attributes. *Journal of Strategic Information Systems, 11,* 245–270.

Benedicktus, R. L., & Andrews, M. L. (2006). Building trust with consensus information: The effects of valence and sequence direction. *Journal of Interactive Advertising, 6,* 17–29.

Benedicktus, R. L., Brady, M. K., Darke, P. R., & Voorhees, C. M. (2007). *On the development of consumer trust: Reactions to brand, consensus, physical presence, and suspicion.* Working Paper, Florida State University.

Bolton, G. E., Katok, E., & Ockenfels A. (2004). How effective are electronic reputation mechanisms? An experimental investigation. *Management Science, 50,* 1587–1602.

Burnkrant, R. E., & Cousineau, A. (1975). Informational and normative social influence in buyer behavior. *Journal of Consumer Research, 2*(3), 206–215.

Chaiken, S., Liberman, A., & Eagly, A. H. (1989). Heuristic and systematic processing within and beyond the persuasion context. In J. S. Uleman & J. A. Bargh, (Eds.), *Unintended thought,* (pp. 212–252). New York: Guilford Press.

Chaudhuri, A., & Holbrook, M. B. (2001). The chain of effects from brand trust and brand affect to brand performance: The role of brand loyalty. *Journal of Marketing, 65,* 81–93.

Darke, P. R., Chaiken, S., Bohner, G., Einwiller, S., Erb, H. S., & Hazlewood, J. D. (1998). Accuracy motivation, consensus information, and the law of large numbers: Effects on attitude judgment in the absence of argumentation. *Personality and Social Psychology Bulletin, 24,* 1205–1215.

Darke, P. R., & Ritchie, R. B. (2004). One rotten apple spoils the barrel: Advertising deception, defensive processing, and consumer suspicion. In B. E. Kahn & M. F. Luce (Eds.), *Advances in Consumer Research, 31* (pp. 329–332). Toronto, Canada: Association for Consumer Research.

Darke, P. R., & Ritchie, R. B. (2007). The defensive consumer: Advertising deception, defensive processing, and distrust. *Journal of Marketing Research, 44,* 114–127.

De Ruyter, K., Wetzels, M., & Kleijnen, M. (2001). Customer adoption of e-service: An experimental study. *International Journal of Service Industry Management, 12,* 184–207.

Degeratu, A. M., Rangaswamy, A., & Wu, J. (2000). Consumer choice behavior in online and traditional supermarkets: The effects of brand name, price, and other search attributes. *International Journal of Research in Marketing, 17,* 55–78.

Direct Marketing Association. (2005). The DMA 2005 Multichannel Marketing Report. Retrieved August 25, 2006, from http://www.the-dma.org/bookstore

Doney, P. M., & Cannon, J. P. (1997). An examination of the nature of trust in buyer-seller relationships. *Journal of Marketing, 61,* 35–52.

Epstein, M. J. (2005). Implementing successful e-commerce initiatives. *Strategic Finance, 86,* 22–29.

Erdem, T., Swait, J., & Valenzuela, A. (2006). Brands as signals: A cross-country validation study. *Journal of Marketing, 70,* 34–49.

Fogg, B. J., Marshall, J., Laraki, O., Osipovich, A., Varma, C., Fang, N., Paul, J., Rangnekar, A., Shon, J., Swani, P., & Treinen, M. (2001). What makes web sites credible? A report on a large quantitative study. *Association for Computing Machinery: Special Interest Group on Computer-Human Interaction, 3,* 61–67.

Fraud Watch International. (2006). FWI Archived Polls. Retrieved October 28, 2006, from http://www.fraudwatchinternational.com/pollarchive.php

Fung, R. K. K., & Lee, M. K. O. (1999). EC-trust: Exploring the antecedent factors. *Proceedings of the 5th Americas Conference on Information Systems,* Milwaukee, WI, 517–519.

Ganesan, S. (1994). Determinants of long-term orientation in buyer-seller relationships. *Journal of Marketing, 58,* 1–19.

Garbarino, E., & Strahilevitz, M. (2004). Gender differences in the perceived risk of buying online and the effects of receiving a site recommendation. *Journal of Business Research, 57,* 768–775.

Gefen, D. (2000). E-commerce: The role of familiarity and trust. *Omega, 28,* 725–737.

Gefen, D. (2002). Reflections on the dimensions of trust and trustworthiness among online consumers. *Database for Advances in Information Systems, 33,* 38–53.

Harris, L. C., & Goode, M. M. H. (2004). The four levels of loyalty and the pivotal role of trust: A study of online service dynamics. *Journal of Retailing, 80,* 139–158.

Hoeffler, S., & Keller, K. L. (2003). The marketing advantages of strong brands. *Journal of Brand Management, 10,* 421–445.

Holzwarth, M., Janiszewski, C., & Neumann, M. (2006). The influence of avatars on online consumer shopping behavior. *Journal of Marketing, 70,* 19–36.

IC3. (2005). *2005 IC3 Annual Report.* Retrieved October 27, 2006, from: http://www.ic3.gov/media/annualreports.aspx

Jarvenpaa S. L., Tractinsky, N., & Vitale, M. (2000). Consumer trust in an Internet store. *Information Technology and Management Journal, 1,* 45–71.

JD Power. (2005). *JD Power and Associates 2005 online investor satisfaction study.* Retrieved April 18, 2006, from http://consumercenter.jdpower.com

Kahneman, D., & Tversky, A. (1979). Prospect theory: An analysis of decision under risk. *Econometrica, 47,* 263–291.

Kania, D. (2001). *Branding.com.* Chicago: NTC Business Books.

Keller, K. L. (1993). Conceptualizing, measuring, and managing customer-based brand equity. *Journal of Marketing, 57,* 1–22.

Laroche, M., Bergeron, J., & Goutaland, C. (2001). A three-dimensional scale of intangibility. *Journal of Service Research, 4,* 26–38.

Loewenstein, G., & Prelec, D. (1993). Preferences for sequences of outcomes. *Psychological Review, 100,* 91–108.

Lohse, G. L., & Spiller, P. (1998). Electronic shopping. *Communications of the Association for Computing Machinery, 41,* 81–86.

Matsui, T., Kakuyama, T., & Onglatco, M. L. U. (1987). Effects performance in groups. *Journal of Applied Psychology, 72,* 407–415.

McDougall, G. H., & Snetsinger, D. W. (1990). The intangibility of services: Measurement and competitive perspectives. *Journal of Services Marketing, 4*, 27–40.

Melewar, T. C., & Navalekar, A. (2002). Leveraging corporate identity in the digital age. *Marketing Intelligence and Planning, 20*, 96–103.

Milliman, R. E., & Fugate, D. (1988). Using trust transference as a persuasion technique: An empirical field investigation. *Journal of Personal Selling and Sales Management, 8*(2), 1–7.

Montgomery, C. A., & Wernerfelt, B. (1992). Risk reduction and umbrella banding. *Journal of Business, 65*, 31–50.

Moorman, C., Deshpande R., & Zaltman, G. (1993). Factors affecting trust in market research relationships. *Journal of Marketing, 57*, 81–101.

Morgan, R. M., & Hunt, S. D. (1994). The commitment-trust theory of relationship marketing. *Journal of Marketing, 58*, 20–28.

NCL. (2001). *National Consumer League Online Shopping Survey.* Retrieved October 28, 2006 from http://www.nclnet.org/shoppingonline/shoppingsurvey.htm

Nooteboom, B., Burger, H., & Noorderhaven, N. G. (1997). Effects of trust and governance on relational risk. *Academy of Management Journal, 40*, 308–338.

Ottaway, T. A., Bruneau, C. L., & Evans, G. E. (2003). The impact of auction item image and buyer/seller feedback rating on electronic auctions. *Journal of Computer Information* Systems, *43*, 56–60.

Penn, J., Doyle, B., & Sage, A. (2005). *Rebuilding consumers' trust in the Internet.* Retrieved April 16, 2006 from http://www.forrester.com/Research/Document/Excerpt/0,7211,35612,00.html

Pollay, R. W. (1986). The distorted mirror: Reflections on the unintended consequences of advertising. *Journal of Marketing, 50*(2), 18–36.

Quelch, J. A., & Klein, L. R. (1996). The Internet and international marketing. *Sloan Management Review, 37*(3), 60–75.

Reichheld, F. F., & Schefter, P. (2000). E-loyalty: Your secret weapon on the web. *Harvard Business Review, 78*(4), 105–113.

Reichheld, F. F. (1994). Loyalty and the renaissance of marketing. *Marketing Management, 2*(4), 10–21.

Reiley, D., Bryan, D., Prasad, N., & Reeves, D. (2005). *Pennies from E-bay: The determinants of price in online auctions.* Working Paper. Retrieved August 17, 2005, from http://www.u.arizona.edu/~dreiley/papers/PenniesFromEBay.pdf

Ross, W. T., Jr., & Simonson, I. (1991). Evaluations of pairs of experiences: A preference for happy endings. *Journal of Behavioral Decision Making, 4*, 273–282.

Rotter, J. B. (1967). A new scale for the measurement of interpersonal trust. *Journal of Personality, 36,* 651–665.

Rousseau, D., Sitkin, S., Burt, R., & Camerer, C. (1998). Not so different after all: A cross-discipline view of trust. *Academy of Management Review, 23,* 393–404.

Schlosser, A. E., White, T. B., & Lloyd, S. M (2006). Converting web site visitors into buyers: How web site investment increases consumer trusting beliefs and online purchase intentions. *Journal of Marketing, 70,* 133–148.

Schlosser, A. E., White, T. B., & Lloyd, S. M. (2004). Signaling trustworthiness: The influence of character vs. competence perception on online purchase intentions. Presented August 2004 at *American Psychological Association,* Honolulu, HI.

Schoenbachler, D. D., & Gordon, G. L. (2002). Multi-channel shopping: Understanding what drives channel choice. *Journal of Consumer Marketing, 19,* 42–53.

Schurr, P. H., & Ozanne, J. L. (1985). Influences on exchange processes: Buyers' preconceptions of a seller's trustworthiness and bargaining toughness. *Journal of Consumer Research, 11,* 939–953.

Scott, W., & Derlaga, V. J. (1983). A test of Kelley's ANOVA model. *Small Group Behavior, 14,* 50–62.

Seiders, K., Voss, G. B., Grewal, D., & Godfrey, A. L. (2005). Do satisfied customers buy more? Examining moderating influences in a retailing context. *Journal of Marketing, 69*(4), 26–43.

Shankar, V., Urban, G. L., & Sultan, F. (2002). Online trust: A stakeholder perspective, concepts, implications, and future directions. *Journal of Strategic Information Systems, 11,* 325–344.

Stone, M., Hobbs, M., & Khaleeli, M. (2002). Multichannel customer management: The benefits and challenges. *Journal of Database Marketing, 10,* 39–52.

Strub, P. J., & Priest, T. B. (1976). Two patterns of establishing trust: The marijuana user. *Sociological Focus, 9,* 399–411

Tversky, A., & Kahneman, D. (1971). Belief in the law of small numbers. *Psychological Bulletin, 76,* 105–110.

Urban, G. L., Sultan, F., & Qualls, W. J. (2000). Placing trust at the center of your Internet strategy. *MIT Sloan Management Review, 42,* 39–48.

Wernerfelt, B. (1988). Umbrella branding as a signal of new product quality: An example of signaling by posting a bond. *Rand Journal of Economics, 19,* 458–466.

Yoon, S. (2002). The antecedents and consequences of trust in online purchase decisions. *Journal of Interactive Marketing, 16,* 47–63.

Zeithaml, V. A., & Bitner, M. J. (2000). *Services marketing: Integrating customer focus across firms*, New York: McGraw-Hill.

7

EFFECTS OF LICENSING IN RETAIL MARKETS

Najam U. Saqib
Ryerson University

Rajesh V. Manchanda
University of Manitoba

*I*N THIS CHAPTER, we discuss the impact of a brand alliance strategy, licensing, by investigating its effect on consumers' attitudes and their brand evaluations. Brand alliances have increasingly become an effective strategy to leverage a new or unknown brand (Rao, Qu, & Ruekert, 1999; Voss & Gammoh, 2004). Given the inherent advantage of drawing on the success of a well reputed brand, a brand alliance could increase the chances of a new brand's success. Examples of brand alliances in different industries include NutraSweet and Diet Coke, MSNBC, and IBM personal computers and Intel microprocessors, to name a few.

In the current competitive marketing environment, the importance of brand alliance research is also being recognized by academic researchers (Gammoh, Voss, & Chakraborty, 2006; Simonin & Ruth, 1998; Venkatesh, Mahajan, & Muller, 2000). In a recent essay, Keller (2003) suggests that, compared with using a direct marketing program, associating a brand with other brands is an efficient means of building brand knowledge. Past research identifies a variety of brand alliances; for example, an alliance between a new and a reputable brand (Rao & Ruekert, 1994), composite or ingredient brands (Park, June, & Shocker, 1996; Desai & Keller, 2002), or bundles with branded or unbranded components (Venkatesh & Mahajan, 1997).

In this research, we investigate the effect of one such brand alliance strategy, licensing, on consumers' brand evaluations. In doing so, we focus on the alliance between a new and a reputable brand. One way of leveraging brand knowledge or brand equity, particularly for a new brand, is to secure an endorsement by a well-known brand through licensing. Licensing is a form of brand alliance, which contractually enables a firm to use the name, logo, or other facets of another brand to market its own brand for a fixed fee (Keller, 1998). The incentive for the well-known brand is to earn additional profit through a fixed fee, and to increase its market exposure.

The widespread use of licensing is reflected by the total retail sales of licensed products, which was over $70 billion in 2004 (The Licensing Letter, 2005). The Walt Disney Company, a well-known brand name, licenses its Disney characters for an array of products including merchandise (clothing), publishing (books and magazines), and music (CDs and tapes) (Keller, 1998). An example of a relatively lesser known brand licensed by a well-known brand is Mad Catz video game accessories licensed by Warner Brothers Entertainment. Mad Catz also became an official peripherals licensee for Microsoft's Xbox 360 gaming system (www.madcatz.com).

From an academic standpoint, the research on brand alliances is still preliminary. Typically, to predict the impact of a brand alliance, researchers have measured consumers' attitudes and quality perceptions of the co-branded products and have found a relationship between these alliances and consumers' attitudes (Simonin & Ruth, 1998; Rao et al., 1999; Voss & Gammoh, 2004). Interestingly, research specifically investigating the effect of licensing on consumers' attitudes and brand value perceptions is still lacking. Although the sales figures of the licensed products would suggest that licensing improves consumers' quality perceptions, little or no research systematically investigates consumers' quality and value perceptions of licensing. Previous research shows that consumers' ratings of an unknown brand's perceived quality improve when the brand is allied with a well-known brand (Rao et al., 1999; Voss & Gammoh, 2004). A similar result could be reasonably expected in the case where an unknown brand is licensed by a well-known brand, because much like other brand alliances, licensing also conveys the information that a contractual relationship exists between the two brands. In certain licensing alliances, however, only a logo or a licensing disclaimer, for example "licensed by brand X," is used on the packaging or in advertisements of the product with an unknown brand. In other words, the perceived bond between the two brands may not be realized as strongly as it would be with other alliances, which may lead to weaker effects of licensing. An empirical investigation specifically of a licensing alliance would establish whether the effect of licensing is as strong as any other alliance. Thus, in this research, we empirically test the effect of licensing on consumers' attitudes when an unknown brand is licensed by a well-known brand. In two experiments, we compare an unknown brand name that is licensed with the same brand when it is unlicensed. Using a consumers' perspective we propose that consumers' perceived value of a brand alliance through licensing is formed based on their perceived utility of brands involved in the licensing contract and that such a brand alliance generates enhanced quality and value perceptions for the unknown brand.

It is our expectation that the positive affect created by the alliance of a well-known and unknown brand transfers to the unknown brand through the alliance. Simonin and Ruth (1998) called this affect transfer the spillover effect. After empirically investigating consumers' evaluations of a licensing brand alliance, we also compare the effectiveness of licensing with a brand extension; another popular brand leveraging strategy.

The contributions of this work are three-fold: (1) We provide a theoretical explanation for licensing effects; (2) establish the importance of studying the effects of licensing from a customers' standpoint; and (3) investigate the effectiveness of licensing as a strategy by comparing it with a brand extension of a well-known parent brand. In the remainder of this chapter, we provide a brief review of the previous research and theoretical perspectives that we apply in our investigation. In our discussion we also report on two experiments and their results that support our research. We conclude the chapter by discussing some implications for retail and offer future research avenues.

Background Literature

A review of previous research reveals several related papers that provide support for our main proposition about a licensing brand alliance between a well-known and unknown brand. From a firm's point of view the most widely used approach to explain the effects of brand alliances has been the signaling theory approach (Akerlof, 1970; Spence, 1974; Wernerfelt, 1988). Signaling theory emerged from information economics and is based on the assumption that consumers lack product quality information while making a purchasing decision. High-quality product firms send pre-purchase quality signals to consumers to communicate their product quality information and distinguish their products from low quality alternatives. The quality signals may include a reputable brand name, high price, or increased advertising. Assuming firms are rational, consumers look for signals that would be profitable for the high-quality firms (i.e., in the long-run, high-quality products would generate enough profit to justify expenditures on advertising and other quality signals). Moreover, consumers could also punish the firm by withholding future sales if the quality claims turn out to be false (Wernerfelt, 1988). Thus, a signal of quality, such as a reputable brand name, ensures the product quality and enhances consumers' perceived quality of a product (Rao et al., 1999; Voss & Gammoh, 2004).

Rao and Ruekert (1994) posit that if one brand name on a product gives a certain signal of quality, then the presence of a second brand name on the product should result in a signal that is at least as powerful, if not more powerful, than the signal in the case of the single brand name. Thus, brand alliances can serve as quality signals when an individual new or unknown brand is unable to successfully signal quality and needs a quality-perception boost. Furthermore, when the quality of a product is unobservable (i.e., the product is an experience product), a brand alliance with a reputable brand can provide assurance about the true quality of the product. Thus, an unknown brand could send a signal of high quality by entering into an alliance with a well-known, reputable brand. In a brand alliance of a well-known and unknown brand, given that the well-known brand ally makes a substantial investment in building its brand reputation, and also has future profits at stake, logically it should only enter into an alliance with good quality brands. Thus, from a firm's standpoint, a rational consumers' quality perception of an unknown brand should increase when the unknown brand is allied with a well-known brand.

A Consumers' Perspective

The foregoing was a firm's perspective of a brand alliance. In this chapter, we provide a theoretical explanation for licensing's success from a consumers' standpoint. To support our explanation, two different but related theoretical frameworks are applied: information integration theory (Anderson, 1981, 1991), and the anchoring and adjustment heuristic (Tversky & Kahneman, 1974). Information integration theory (Anderson, 1981) proposes that people use prior experience to make sense of information received from a stimulus. Anderson (1991) notes that integration of information is serial. Moreover, the information is evaluated and integrated one piece at a time. Thus, people first interpret and evaluate the information received, and subsequently integrate the information with existing beliefs or attitudes. Anderson (1991) also implies that people generally begin with the more important stimulus to modify their beliefs and judgments. Based on information integration theory, Simonin and Ruth (1998) also propose that consumers' prior attitudes of two brands presented in each other's context, for example in an advertisement, affect consumers' evaluations of the brand alliance, which subsequently affect their attitudes towards each partner brand. Consumers are likely to access salient attitudes linked with the well-known brand first, and then the positive or negative attitudes formed by the well-known brand likely influences their judgments about the unknown brand. Thus, we posit that if an unknown brand is licensed by a well-known brand, pre-existing attitudes of the well-known brand will affect consumers' attitudes of the unknown brand.

As an underlying processing strategy, the anchoring and adjustment heuristic (Tversky & Kahneman, 1974) provides another explanation of consumers' information processing in evaluating a licensing brand alliance. In fact, anchoring and adjustment has been referred to as a special case of serial integration (Anderson, 1991), in which people integrate information by beginning with the first piece of received information and adjusting their evaluation in the direction of the second piece. Thus, we posit that when consumers are exposed to a well-known and an unknown brand in a licensing contract, their evaluations of the unknown brand are adjusted based on the alliance. A basic tenet of anchoring and adjustment, however, is that the adjustments are 'typically insufficient' (Tversky & Kahneman, 1974, p. 1128) in the direction of the first piece of information. Thus in the overall evaluation, consumers' quality perceptions of the unknown brand is likely to be higher with licensing than without licensing. The study of bundle offers and consumers' evaluation of such offers (Yadav, 1994; Gaeth, Levin, Chakraborty & Levin, 1990) also concur with the notion that consumers make insufficient adjustments such that the overall bundle evaluation is biased in the direction of the item evaluated first (i.e., the anchor). Yadav (1994) reports findings of several studies (Carlson, 1990; Davis, Hoch, & Ragsdale, 1986; Joyce & Biddle, 1981; Northcraft & Neal, 1987) that provide evidence consistent with the notion of insufficient adjustment in the direction of the anchor.

Taken together, information integration theory (Anderson, 1981), and the anchoring and adjustment heuristic (Tversky & Kahneman, 1974) provide a plausible theoretical basis for expecting favourable consumers' evaluations of an unknown or new brand licensed by a well-known brand. A two-fold process is expected for this enhanced evaluation. First, a positive attitude congruent with a well-known brand is accessed and activated from memory (Fazio, Powell, & Williams, 1989) due to the well-known brand's salience. Secondly, this attitude affects consumers' evaluations of the licensing alliance, which in turn results in affect transfer to the unknown brand through the alliance as a spillover effect (Simonin & Ruth, 1998). Thus, we propose that a consumer evaluating a product with an unknown brand name will have a higher quality perception and be more willing to buy the product if it is licensed by a well-known brand than if it were not. However, since the anchoring and adjustment perspective argues for insufficient adjustment in the anchor's direction, we also propose that the quality perception of the licensed product will not be as high as that of the well-known brand (the anchor) itself. In the next section, we discuss an empirical study that tests these propositions.

Experiment 1

Method

Procedure. Experiment 1 employed a three cell between subjects design where the factor manipulated was brand name (Nyko, Nyko licensed by Sony, and Sony). The product stimulus was a hand controller for Sony Playstation, the video game console. In each condition, subjects were exposed to an ad showing a controller for Sony Playstation. Before looking at the ad, subjects were provided a cover story that required them to imagine that they were in the market for a video game controller. The picture of the controller, price, and the features were kept identical across ads and conditions, as we were only interested in the brand and the licensing effects. A lesser known brand name 'Nyko' in this product category was selected based on a pretest. In the control condition, the Nyko brand was used without licensing, whereas in the licensing condition it was shown to be officially licensed by Sony. The pretest showed that the participants considered Nyko (when it was officially licensed by Sony) to more reliable and of better quality than when it was presented alone. In the third condition, the controller was shown to be a Sony controller. This method allowed us to test the licensing effect by comparing it with both Nyko, a lesser known brand by itself, and Sony, the well-known brand.

Dependent Variables. Based on previous research in brand effect studies (Dodds, Monroe, & Grewal, 1991), three dependent variables were used including Perceived Quality, Perceived Value, and Willingness-to-Buy. Following Dodds et al. (1991), five items were used for each dependent variable. Reliabilities in each case were high with Cronbach alpha values more than or equal to .80. The items were measured on 7-point Likert scales. The scale items for each dependent variable are provided in appendix A.

Results and Discussion

In support of our first proposition, a main effect of brand was found on Perceived Quality (F (2, 124) = 4.68, $p < .05$), Perceived Value (F (2, 124) = 3.26, $p < .05$), and Willingness-to-Buy (F (2, 124) = 3.78, $p < .05$). The mean difference between the licensing and the control condition was significant for

Perceived Quality (F (1, 83) = 6.59, $p < .05$, Ms = 5.40 versus 4.80). Similar results were found for Perceived Value (F (1, 83) = 4.28, $p < .05$, Ms = 5.32 versus 4.83) and Willingness-to-Buy (F (1, 83) = 4.42, $p < .05$, Ms = 4.98 versus 4.41). Similarly, the mean difference between the Sony and the control condition was found significant for Perceived Quality (F (1, 83) = 6.23, $p < .05$, Ms = 5.32 versus 4.80), Perceived Value (F (1, 83) = 4.75, $p < .05$, Ms = 5.33 versus 4.83,) and Willingness-to-Buy (F (1, 83) = 6.59, $p < .05$, Ms = 5.05 versus 4.41). However an interesting and unexpected result was that the difference between the mean values of all the three dependent variables for 'Sony condition' versus the 'licensing condition' was not significant ($p > .1$). Thus, the second proposition with respect to insufficient adjustment in the anchor's direction is not supported. Table 7.1 provides a summary of means across conditions. On the whole, the results in Experiment 1 support the proposition that licensing by a well-known brand enhances consumers' perception of brand quality, value and their willingness-to-buy.

The unexpected result found in Experiment 1 is interesting, and somewhat counterintuitive. This result implies that for lesser known brands, licensing by a well-known brand in some cases is likely to have as strong of an effect as the well-known brand name by itself. If this is the case, this would be an interesting finding with important strategy implications for unknown or lesser known brands. To test the generalizability of findings of Experiment 1 in licensing and to investigate if a similar effect with respect to a brand extension holds, a comparison of licensing with brand extensions is discussed in Experiment 2. Brand extensions as a brand leveraging strategy could be compared with licensing for both theoretical and managerial reasons. From a theoretical perspective, we expect that similar processing likely leads to consumers' attitudes and affect transfer when a product is either licensed by,

Table 7.1 Study 1: Mean Scores for Dependent Variables

Experimental Condition	Dependent Variable Values		
	Perceived Quality	Perceived Value	Willingness-To-Buy
Control Condition – Nyko	4.80$_a$	4.83$_a$	4.41$_a$
Lincensing Condition – Nyko Licensed by Sony	5.40$_b$	5.32$_b$	4.98$_b$
Sony Condition	5.32$_b$	5.33$_b$	5.05$_b$

Note: For each dependent measure, overall cell means with unlike subscripts are significantly different at $p < .05$.

or enters the marketplace as an extension of, a well-known brand. Specifically, we conjecture that the attitude formation and affect transfer between the licensing alliance and the licensed brand versus a brand extension and the parent brand might be quite similar.

From a managerial standpoint, a brand extension strategy refers to using an established brand name to introduce a new product (Keller, 1998). Considering the financial risk involved in introducing a new product, in millions of dollars according to some estimates (Aaker & Keller, 1990), a brand extension strategy builds on the strength of a current brand name and thus substantially reduces the risk involved in introducing a new product. If licensing leads to similar outcomes for a new brand, this may have important implications as licensing can often be a relatively low risk strategy to leverage a new or unknown brand with a lower cost as compared to making a substantial investment in an ad campaign to establish a brand name.

Comparing Brand Extensions with a Licensing Brand Alliance

The basic motivation behind a brand extension is that existing beliefs about a well-established brand would most likely be used by consumers to make inferences about a new product introduced as an extension of the same brand (Klink & Smith, 2001). The common aspect of the underlying mental information processing related to a brand extension and a licensing brand alliance is the affect transfer or the spillover effect that takes place from the well-known parent brand to its extension, or to an unknown brand through an alliance with a well-known brand. Consumers most likely use their previously formed global affective impressions of a well-known brand (Fishbein & Ajzen, 1975; Wright, 1975) to infer the quality of the extension in the case of a brand extension, or the unknown brand in the case of licensing. Thus, the basic motivation behind a licensing brand alliance and a brand extension strategy is similar with a common element of capitalizing on affect transfer or the spillover effect. Since past research (Aaker & Keller, 1990; Bottomley & Holden, 2001) and industry evidence (e.g., Diet Pepsi, Coke's Mountain Dew, Snickers® ice cream, Tropicana® smoothies, or Apple's iPOD®) show brand extensions to be an effective strategy for introducing a new product, this warrants the comparison of a licensing brand alliance with a brand extension to determine the effectiveness of the former strategy.

Relevant Variables in a Brand Extension Evaluation Model

The seminal article of Aaker and Keller (1990) hypothesized a number of constructs deemed important for consumers in evaluating a brand extension including brand attribute associations, attitude towards original brand, fit between the original and extension product classes, and perceived difficulty of making the extension. Based on a qualitative study of 20 brand extensions involving these constructs, Aaker and Keller (1990) identify a number of key independent variables used in a regression model that estimates consumers' attitudes towards a brand extension. The dependent variable in the model was consumers' attitudes towards the extension. The independent variables identified included QUALITY (the perceived quality of the original brand), the fit variables which included TRANSFER (transfer of skills/assets from original to extension product class), COMPLEMENT (the degree to which the two products are complements), and SUBSTITUTE (the degree to which the two products are substitutes), and finally the variable DIFFICULT (the degree of difficulty involved in making the extension).

Thus, following previous brand extension research (Aaker & Keller 1990; Bottomley & Holden, 2001; Holden & Barwise, 1995; Nijssen & Hartman, 1994; Sundie & Brodie, 1993), we selected key variables to estimate a model of consumers' attitudes towards a brand extension of a well-known brand and compared it with a model of consumers' attitudes towards a licensing brand alliance, including the same variables. Experiment 2 reports the comparison.

Experiment 2

Method

Procedure. Experiment 2 used a questionnaire through which subjects' responses were collected on key variables to estimate two regression models: one using a brand extension of a well-known brand, and the other using a licensing brand alliance. Following the previous brand extension studies (Aaker & Keller, 1990; Bottomley & Holden, 2001), we used QUALITY, TRANSFER, COMPLEMENT, SUBSTITUTE, and DIFFICULT as independent variables. Similarly, the dependent variable in both models was subjects' attitudes towards the products used as stimuli in the questionnaire. The subjects' attitude measure was an average of their perception of the quality and value of the product and their likelihood of purchasing the product. The items used to collect data for all the variables are listed in appendix B. The brand name used for the extension was IBM, and the two products used as extensions were an IBM wireless mouse and an IBM zip disk. For a licensing brand alliance, we used the same lesser known brand Nyko as used in Experiment 1, which was described as officially licensed by Sony. The two products used for the licensing brand alliance were a Nyko wireless controller, and a memory card for Playstation 2—both described as officially licensed by Sony. To maintain credibility in the experiment we could not use IBM as the licensor for this product category, because it could be perceived as less credible that IBM would license wireless controllers or memory cards. On the other hand, Sony has strong presence in this product category with Sony Playstation, making it a more credible licensor. Nevertheless, a pretest showed that both brands (IBM and Sony) enjoyed high quality perceptions. In the cover letter of the questionnaire, subjects were told that we were interested in their opinions as consumers about a few products. On the following page, they were asked to assume that IBM (Nyko) was planning to launch a product "IBM wireless mouse" ("Nyko wireless controller for Playstation 2—officially licensed by Sony"). Subsequently, subjects provided their responses on key variables about that product. Each subject completed a questionnaire including multiple products in a counterbalanced order. Thus, a total of approximately 1,000 observations for the regression models were collected from 335 participants.

In comparing the two models, we used the F-test. The F-test is used to test the hypothesis that regression coefficients are different across data sets (the two data sets in this experiment: one for brand extension and the other for licensing brand alliance). If the F-test approaches significance (i.e., $p > .1$), one could reject the null hypothesis that regression coefficients from the two data sets are different. Thus, we could conclude that the two data sets show similar patterns of relationships between the dependent and independent variables. In performing our analysis, first we estimated two regression models: one for IBM brand extensions, and the second for Nyko licensed products. See Table 7.2 for results. Next, we pooled the observations from two data sets and estimated the full effects model including data specific constants for each independent variable to account for any data specific differences (Bottomley & Holden, 2001; Woolridge, 2003). Table 7.3 provides these results.

Results and Discussion

As shown in Table 7.2, virtually all of the coefficients from the IBM model and the Nyko model are similar except for the coefficient of QUALITY. In both models, the coefficients of TRANSFER, SUSBSTITUTE, and COMPLEMENT are significant. The coefficient of DIFFICULT (beta = 0.034, $t = 1.36$), however, does not reach significance in the IBM model. The mixed result found for the DIFFICULT variable is consistent with previous brand extension studies (for a comparison see Bottomley & Holden [2001] Table 7.1). The only other coefficient that is substantially different across the two models is

Table 7.2 A Regression Model of Attitude Towards a Product

Independent Variables	Nyko-Licensed by Sony		IBM Brand Extension	
	Regression Coefficient	t-value	Regression Coefficient	t-value
TRANSFER	0.147	4.04***	0.122	3.90***
SUBSTITUTE	0.099	2.61**	0.059	2.45*
COMPLEMENT	0.167	4.55***	0.109	4.09***
DIFFICULT	0.094	3.66***	0.034	1.36
QUALITY	0.117	2.65**	0.479	13.95***
Sample Size	499		501	
Adjusted R-Square	0.20		0.44	

$^*p < .05$
$^{**}p < .01$
$^{***}p < .001$

Table 7.3 Pooled Data

Independent Variables	With QUALITY		Without QUALITY	
	Regression Coefficient	t-value	Regression Coefficient	t-value
TRANSFER	0.122	3.59***	0.243	6.89***
SUBSTITUTE	0.059	2.26*	0.092	3.28***
COMPLEMENT	0.109	3.76***	0.183	5.93***
DIFFICULT	0.030	1.26	0.038	1.45
QUALITY	0.479	12.84***		
d	1.050	2.76**	0.179	0.51
dTRANSFER	0.027	0.57	−0.071	−1.43
dSUBSTITUTE	0.032	0.76	−0.001	−0.03
dCOMPLEMENT	0.058	1.28	−0.003	−0.07
dDIFFICULT	0.065	1.91	−0.062	1.69
dQUALITY	−0.363	−6.55***		
	$F(5, 989) = 9.39$		$F(4, 992) = 1.16$	
	$p < 0.001$		$p < 0.325$	
Sample Size	1001		1001	
Adjusted R-Square	0.20		0.32	

$^*p < .05$
$^{**}p < .01$
$^{***}p < .001$

QUALITY (quality of the parent brand), which shows a much stronger effect for IBM (beta = 0.479, t = 13.95) than for Sony (beta = .117, t = 2.65).

In Table 7.3, we report two models after pooling the data from two data sets: one with QUALITY and one without QUALITY. The F-test from the model with QUALITY does not reach significance (F (5, 989) = 9.39, p < .001); however, when we remove the anomalous result of QUALITY the F-test does reach significance (F (4, 992) = 1.16, p < 1) and we can reject the null hypothesis that regression coefficients across the data sets are different. We believe the anomalous result from QUALITY is data set specific and could be attributed to a possibility that IBM might have had a significantly stronger effect for computer accessories than Sony for video game accessories. Our pretest, however, showed that in general these brands were not considered different in quality. In future research, such an anomalous result from QUALITY could be avoided by creating either fictitious brand names (Rao et al., 1999; Simonin & Ruth, 1998), or using various brand names and product categories (and then using aggregate data for analysis), which could also help generalize the results. Except for the QUALITY variable, which also did not reach significance in the Aaker and Keller (1990) study, our results from the F-test suggest that the two data sets (i.e., one from IBM brand extension products, and the other from Nyko products officially licensed by Sony), represent similar data patterns and relationships between dependent and explanatory variables. Thus, this result allows the conclusion that a lesser known brand, in a licensing brand alliance with a well-known brand, receives a similar quality perception boost, as does a brand extension of a well-known brand. Therefore, we could reasonably infer that the strength of affect transfer is similar in both cases. In other words, a similar perceptual mapping between the two brands is likely in consumers' minds when they process the information from either a licensing brand alliance or a brand extension. Thus, licensing of a new or lesser known brand by a well-known brand could enhance consumers' attitudes towards the former similarly as a well-known brand could for its new extension. Some of the implications of this result could be significant for retailers and brand managers. We discuss some of those implications in the next section.

Conclusion

In this chapter, we investigate the effect of licensing on consumers' brand attitudes and perceptions. We discuss the results of two empirical studies which suggest that licensing by a well-known brand enhances consumers' willingness-to-buy and quality perceptions of a new or lesser known brand.

The results of the second experiment indicate that little perceived difference exists in consumers' attitudes towards a brand extension of a well-known brand and a licensed ally of a well-known brand. This important finding helps to explain the phenomenal success of licensed products in many industries. This work identifies licensing as an effective strategy for a new brand to create desirable brand knowledge about its brand and to increase its brand equity. Thus, the research supports the notion that a brand alliance, specifically licensing, may be an efficient strategy for leveraging brand knowledge for a new brand as opposed to making large upfront investments in a direct marketing program (Keller, 2003).

Implications

A licensing brand alliance could be an effective way for a smaller firm to leverage its brand and increase its brand equity. Building or buying a brand could be an expensive proposition for a risk averse firm with limited resources. Licensing provides an efficient means of brand positioning as a better quality brand. Licensing could also provide additional extrinsic product information to facilitate brand evaluations and help consumers choose a product among competing alternatives.

Another implication of this research is that brand managers of well-known brands ought to be careful in selecting the products they license. Our research shows that if a licensed product is a close substitute and/or in direct competition with the well-known brand's own extension, it could potentially result in a loss of sales for its own extension. The possibility of such an outcome increases if the licensed product is perceived as having a similar quality because of licensing, but is offered at a lower price than the well-known brand ally's own extension.

In a study of consumer goods, Alpert, Wilson, and Elliot (1993) found that higher prices alone did not succeed in signaling higher quality. However, higher prices accompanied with premium-quality signals in other elements of the marketing mix did succeed. The authors concluded that since premium pricing strategy alone may not be successful if price is the only marketing variable emphasized, brand managers should therefore think in terms of a premium quality positioning that requires the application of quality cues across the marketing mix. Findings of the current study have implications for those brand managers who face the task of enhancing their brand image without relying too much on high price, and at the same time do not want to lower the price to avoid sending an inferior quality signal and possibly face decreasing revenue. Licensing provides a better route to enhance the brand image without necessarily having to rely exclusively on product price levels.

Implications for Retail

The research discussed in this chapter has a number of implications for retailers. It is commonly known in the industry that lesser known brands offer relatively higher margins than national brands do in order to gain some shelf space. The findings reported in this chapter show that consumers' brand evaluations of licensed products improve as a result of licensing. Thus, retailers may want to consider carrying products that are licensed by well-known national brands to support their bottom line. This research suggests that consumers would be willing to pay a premium for a product that is licensed by a well-known brand. Thus, retailers would be well advised to consider licensed products, even at premium, but reasonable prices.

Given the positive consumer response towards products licensed by well-known brands, highlighting the licensing feature in advertising and promotional materials to gain consumers' attention could be an effective strategy. For example, if a product is licensed by a well-known brand, this feature or disclaimer could be shown prominently on the packaging or in the ad copy. Similarly, within a store, the licensing feature could be used strategically on point-of-sale displays and/or on the shelf space with the help of packaging to catch shoppers' attention. In order to make use of some of these strategies, a retailer may want to consider licensed products available within a product line, while making a decision to place a new product line on the store shelves.

Brand managers of new firms may want to secure licensing for some of their products by well-known brands as a strategy to secure shelf space at major retailers. Major retailers such as Wal-Mart, Best Buy, and Target are often reluctant to provide scarce shelf-space to new brands due to the risk of possible failure of the brand. For retail buyers, licensing of a new brand by a well-known brand could reduce the perceived risk involved in trying out a new brand.

The results of our studies also imply that consumers may perceive products licensed by a well-known brand to have a similar quality to the brand's own extension. This finding has significant implications for emerging brands and smaller or start-up retailers. One of the reasons retailers carry well-known or national brand products is to generate traffic in their store and to keep customers there for longer periods of time. However, from a supply point of view for a start-up retailer, offering national brand products is typically an expensive and high risk strategy. For example, in electronics and most other consumer goods industries, due to the high demand of national brands and their extension products, it is often a struggle for smaller retailers with less purchasing power to keep their shelves stocked around the busy holiday season. Lesser known brand products have a relatively lower demand and greater supply available compared to national brands. If a retailer could find a number of lesser known brand products that are licensed by national brands, greater flexibility and inventory control could be achieved during the holiday season when most retailers generate 40 percent of their annual sales revenue. Although the impact of the national brand licensed products may not be as strong as the national brand products themselves, our results do suggest that it could still be an effective strategy. This approach may help bring and keep customers in the store while addressing the issues related to lack of supply that are the result of an exclusive reliance on national brands.

This study also has some implications for consumers. Price-sensitive consumers could opt for products with lesser known brands that are licensed by well-known brands to avoid paying high prices for national brands. At the same time, the quality is ascertained, at least to some extent, due to the fact that the product is licensed by a well-known brand. Since a product licensed by a high quality brand must maintain its quality, a licensed product may offer a relatively inexpensive alternative without sacrificing too much perceived quality.

Finally, the implications of licensing for retail themes are also enormous. The two studies within this research suggest that affect created by two brand names in a licensing contract significantly influence consumers' attitudes towards the alliance. Major retailers could join with well-known brands in exclusive contracts to differentiate their merchandize and enhance consumer loyalty. For example, JCPenney, the Dallas-based retailer, signed an exclusive contract with the Dallas Cowboys to set up licensed shops in their stores (Ritter, 2002). Similarly, the drug store chain Walgreens signed a deal with Universal Studios, and develops a full line of exclusive merchandise tied to various licensed properties, such as The Land Before Time and Jurassic Park (Desjardins, 2002). It may be difficult for smaller retailers to sign exclusive deals with major brands. However, they could use some of the products licensed by major brands to accomplish the same objective.

Limitations and Future Research

One of the limitations of the studies reported here could be the strong brand effect of both IBM and Sony brands. It is less clear whether similar results could be replicated with a well-known brand such as Compaq, Dell, Panasonic, or Samsung but without as strong of an effect as that of IBM or Sony. Future research should investigate this issue to increase the generalizability of the current research.

A number of other unanswered questions also arise with respect to brand alliances in general and licensing in particular. For example, what are the potential effects on image of the well-known brand, if it licenses lesser known brands, even though the lesser known brands maintain their quality. Brand managers will have to consider the costs and benefits of licensing lesser known brands. The specific question addressed could be whether the royalty fees and additional market exposure is worth the risk of possible damage to the licensor's brand image.

Another avenue for future research could be investigating the selection of appropriate partners for brand alliances. Evidence from the industry shows that not all brand alliances or licensing efforts succeed (Farquhar, 1990); some failures include, for example, when Jack Daniels distillery used its brand for charcoal briquettes, Dunkin Donuts for cereal, Jacuzzi for bath toiletries, Harley Davidson for cigarettes, Adidas for cologne, etc. In selecting an appropriate partner, the issue for the licensor would be protection of its brand image. On the other hand, the issue for the licensee would be ascertaining that the licensor's brand has a perceptual fit with the licensee's brand name, provides a competitive leverage, and benefit transfer. Thus, a number of issues related to licensing and brand alliances could be investigated in future research. In this chapter, our emphasis was on a consumer's perspective; however, the retail implications of licensing suggest that future research in licensing and brand alliances from a manager's perspective could also have a significant impact on brick and mortar retailing.

Appendix A
Description of Scale Items for Dependent Variables in Experiment 1

The following scales were adopted from Dodds et al. (1991):

Perceived Quality Items

1. The likelihood that the product would be reliable is: (very high to very low)
2. The workmanship of the product would be: (very high to very low)
3. This product should be of: (very good quality to very poor quality)
4. The likelihood that this product is dependable is: (very high to very low)
5. This product would seem to be durable (strongly agree to strongly disagree)

Perceived Value Items

1. This product is a: (very good value for the money to very poor value for the money)
2. At the price shown the product is: (very economical to very uneconomical)
3. The product is considered to be a good buy (strongly agree to strongly disagree)
4. The price shown for the product is: (very acceptable to very unacceptable)
5. This product appears to be a bargain (strongly agree to strongly disagree)

Willingness to Buy Items

1. The likelihood of purchasing this product is: (very high to very low)
2. If I were going to buy this product, I would consider buying this model at the price shown (strongly agree to strongly disagree)
3. At the price shown, I would consider buying the product (strongly agree to strongly disagree)
4. The probability that I would consider buying the product is:(very high to very low)
5. My willingness to buy the product is: (very high to very low)

Appendix B
Description of Items for Variables in the Regression Study

Dependent Variables

1. Your overall perception of the quality of an IBM (Nyko – Officially licensed by Sony) (product) is:
2. Your overall perception of the value of an IBM (Nyko – Officially licensed by Sony) (product) is:
3. If you were to buy a (product), the likelihood that you would buy an IBM (Nyko – Officially licensed by Sony) (product) is: ($\alpha = 0.79$)

Independent Variables (IBM)

TRANSFER: Would the people, facilities, and skills used in developing, refining, and making IBM computers be helpful in making an IBM wireless mouse (zip disk)?

SUBSTITUTE: How would you rate the substitutability of a regular wired mouse (zip disk) hooked up to an IBM computer with an IBM wireless mouse (with a hard drive of IBM to save data)?

COMPLEMENT: How would you rate the complementarity of an IBM wireless mouse (using an IBM zip disk) when used with an IBM computer?

DIFFICULT: How difficult do you think it would be to manufacture an IBM wireless mouse (zip disk)?

QUALITY: To me the overall quality of the IBM brand is:

Independent Variables (Nyko – Officially licensed by Sony)

TRANSFER: Would the people, facilities, and skills used in developing, refining, and making "Sony Products" be helpful for Sony to ascertain the quality of Nyko products, and to determine whether or not Nyko products should be licensed?

SUBSTITUTE: How would you rate the substitutability of a Sony Playstation II controller (memory card) with a Nyko wireless controller (memory card) (licensed by Sony) for use with Playstation II?

COMPLEMENT: How would you rate the complementarity of a Nyko wireless controller (memory card) (licensed by Sony) when used with Sony Playstation II?

DIFFICULT: How difficult do you think it would be to manufacture Nyko wireless controllers (memory cards) (licensed by Sony)?

QUALITY: To me the overall quality of the Sony brand is:

References

Akerlof, G. A. (1970). The market for 'Lemons': Quality under uncertainty and the market mechanism. *Quarterly Journal of Economics, 84*, 488–500.

Alpert, F., Wilson, B., & Elliot, M. T. (1993). Price signaling: Does it work? *Journal of Consumer Marketing, 10*, 4–15.

Anderson, N. H. (1981). *Foundations of information integration theory.* New York: Academic Press.

Anderson, N. H. (1991). *Contributions to information integration theory.* Hillsdale, NJ: Lawrence Erlbaum Associates.

Aaker, D., & Keller, K. (1990). Consumer evaluations of brand extensions. *Journal of Marketing, 54*(1), 27–41.

Bottomley, P. A., & Doyle, J. R. (1996). The formation of attitudes towards brand extensions: Testing and generalising Aaker and Keller's model. *International Journal of Research in Marketing, 13*, 365–377.

Bottomley, P. A., & Holden, S. J. S. (2001). Do we really know how consumers evaluate brand extensions? Empirical generalizations based on secondary analysis of eight studies. *Journal of Marketing Research, 38*, 494–500.

Carlson, B. W. (1990). Anchoring and adjustment in judgments under risk. *Journal of Experimental Psychology, 16*, 665–676.

Davis, H. L., Hoch, S. J., & Ragsdale, E. K. E. (1986). An anchoring and adjustment model of spousal predictions. *Journal of Consumer Research, 13*(June), 25–37.

Desai, K. K., & Keller, K. L. (2002). The effects of ingredient branding strategies on host brand extendibility. *Journal of Marketing, 66*, 73–93.

Desjardins, D. (2002). Walgreens signs deal with Universal. *Drug Store News®*, March 25, Deerfield, IL.

Dodds, W., Monroe, K. B., & Grewal, D. (1991). Effects of price, brand, and store information on buyers' product evaluations. *Journal of Marketing Research, 27*, 307–319.

Farquhar, P. (1990). Managing brand equity. *Journal of Advertising Research, 30*, RC-7-RC-12.

Fazio, R. H., Powell, M. C., & Williams, C. J. (1989). The role of attitude accessibility in the attitude-to-behavior process. *Journal of Consumer Research, 16* (December), 280–288.

Fishbein, M., & Ajzen, I. (1975). *Belief, attitude, intention and behavior: An introduction to theory and research.* Reading, MA: Addison-Wesley.

Gaeth, G. J., Levin, I. P., Chakraborty, G., & Levin, A. M. (1990). Consumer evaluation of multi-product bundles: An information integration analysis. *Marketing Letters, 2,* 47–57.

Gammoh, B. S., Voss, K., & Chakraborty, G. (2006). Consumer evaluation of brand alliance signals. *Psychology and Marketing, 23,* 465–486.

Holden, S. J. S., & Barwise, P. (1995). An empirical investigation of what it means to generalize. In M. Bergadaa (Ed.), *Proceedings of the 24th annual conference of the European marketing academy* (pp. 677–1687). Cery Pontoise, France: ESSEC.

Joyce, E., & Biddle, G. C. (1981). Anchoring and adjustment in probabilistic inference in auditing. *Journal of Accounting Research, 19,* 120–145.

Keller, K. L. (1998). *Strategic brand management.* Upper Saddle River, NJ: Prentice Hall.

Keller, K. L. (2003). Brand synthesis: The multidimensionality of brand knowledge. *Journal of Consumer Research, 29*(4), 595–600.

Klink, R. R., & Smith, D. C. (2001). Threats to the external validity of brand extension research. *Journal of Marketing Research, 38,* 326–335.

The Licensing Letter. (2005). *EPM Communication Inc., 9*(1), January.

Northcraft, G. B., & Neale, M. A. (1987). Experts, amateurs, and real estate: An anchoring and adjustment perspective on property pricing decisions. *Organizational Behaviour and Human Decision Processes, 39,* 84–97.

Nijssen, E. J., & Hartman, D. (1994). Consumer evaluations of brand extensions: An integration of previous research. In J. Bloemer, J. Lemmink, & H. Kasper (Ed.), *Proceedings of the 23rd annual conference of the European marketing academy* (pp. 673–683). Maastricht, The Netherlands: European Marketing Academy.

Park, C. W., Sung, Y. J., & Shocker, A. D. (1996). Composite branding alliances: An investigation of extension and feedback effect. *Journal of Marketing Research, 33,* 453–466.

Rao, A., Qu, L., & Ruekert, R. W. (1999). Signaling unobservable product quality through a brand ally. *Journal of Marketing Research, 36,* 258–268.

Rao, A., Qu, L., & Ruekert, R. W. (1994). Brand alliances as signals of product quality. *Sloan Management Review,* (Fall), 87–97.

Ritter, I. (2002). Uncommon Area. *Shopping Center Today.* (September), International Council of Shopping Centres, New York.

Simonin, B. L., & Ruth, J. A. (1998). Is a company known by the company it keeps? Assessing the spillover effects of brand alliances on consumer brand attitudes. *Journal of Marketing Research, 35,* 30–42.

Spence, M. (1973). Job market signalling. *Quarterly Journal of Economics, 87,* 355–374.

Sunde, L., & Brodie, R. J. (1993). Consumer evaluations of brand extensions: Further Empirical Evidence. *International Journal of Research in Marketing, 10,* 47–53.

Tversky, A., & Kahneman, D. (1974). Judgment under uncertainty: Heuristics and biases. *Science, 185,* 1124–1131.

Venkatesh, R., Mahajan, V., & Muller, E. (2000). Dynamic co-marketing alliances: When and why do they succeed or fail? *International Journal of Research in Marketing, 17,* 3–31.

Venkatesh, R., & Mahajan, V. (1997). Products with branded components: An approach for premium pricing and partner selection. *Marketing Science, 16,* 146–165.

Voss, K. E., & Gammoh, B. S. (2004). Building brand through brand alliances: Does a second ally help? *Marketing Letters, 15,* July–October, 147–159.

Wernerfelt, B. (1988). Umbrella branding as a signal of new product quality: An example of signaling by posting a bond. *Rand Journal of Economics, 19,* 458–466.

Wooldridge, J. M. (2003). *Introductory econometrics: A modern approach.* Second edition, Thomson South-Western.

Wright, P. L. (1975). Consumer choice strategies: Simplifying versus optimizing. *Journal of Marketing Research, 11,* 60–67.

Yadav, M. S. (1994). How buyers evaluate product bundles: A model of anchoring and adjustment. *Journal of Consumer Research, 21* (September), 342–353.

III

THE INFLUENCE OF SOCIAL IDENTITY VARIABLES ON SHOPPING BEHAVIOR

8

EXPLORING THE LINK BETWEEN MASCULINITY AND CONSUMPTION

Linda Tuncay
Loyola University Chicago

Cele C. Otnes
University of Illinois at Urbana—Champaign

*D*UE TO A VARIETY of social changes such as the increase in working women, the delay of first marriages, and the rise of single-parent households headed by men, gender roles and consumption patterns have shifted in today's society. However, until very recently, gender and consumption has been largely examined in terms of female shoppers. Recent research highlights the importance of understanding male consumers, especially in regard to their gender identities. Kimmel and Messner (2001) state the importance of studying men as gendered beings, as gender is an organizing force in society. They state, "Rarely, if ever, are men understood through the prism of gender" (p. ix). Male consumers are especially important for consumer behavior because more and more men are delving into the consumption arena, and are even avid consumers of goods and services such as fashion and grooming products. Whereas these goods have traditionally been labeled as too feminine and taboo for heterosexual men, a shift in acceptable notions of masculinity has resulted in a booming demand for such products. In fact, the men's grooming market in the U.S. and Europe will constitute an estimated $38 billion business in 2008 (Market Watch, 2006). Companies such as Shiseido and Inter Parfums have acquired product lines exclusively targeting men, in an effort to capture share in this growing market. Furthermore, a relatively new label, that of "metrosexual," describes the man who spends time and money on his appearance and who is in touch with his feminine side (www.wordspy.com). Although this label may fade from the popular press radar, these new consumption behaviors have persisted and have become part of the lifestyle of even the everyday "Joe" (Kyles, 2005). In fact, a survey called *The Future of Men* conducted by advertising agency Euro RSCG, found that men's views about their own masculinity are changing, and they are increasingly engaging in consumption behavior that traditionally has been considered off-limits. For example, the survey found that 89 percent of men felt good grooming habits are essential for a successful business career, and nearly half felt that getting a manicure was acceptable (www.newswire.ca). The changing landscape of men as avid consumers poses an incredible opportunity for companies to expand their target markets and go after the lucrative male consumer. Thus, the approach taken by marketers to reach these male consumers has now become more important than ever.

But more important than the metrosexual label is the notion that this "new" man is a departure from the tenets of "old" masculinity, and that the boundaries of acceptable consumption behavior for a man has changed. Yet there is little understanding of the interplay between gender identity and consumption with regard to male consumers. With few exceptions, male consumers in general are largely absent from research on consumption (see Belk & Costa, 1998; Holt & Thompson, 2004; Otnes & McGrath, 2001; Peñaloza, 2001; Schouten & McAlexander 1995; Sherry et al., 2004 for exceptions). This chapter seeks to uncover the theoretical underpinnings of how notions of gender influence men's consumption behaviors and provides the opportunity to expand our knowledge in an important but neglected domain in consumer research. In order to understand the link between gender and consumption, a thorough review is needed of how the construct of masculinity has evolved over time and how current notions underlie the contemporary consumption behaviors of men.

Research Questions

Thus, the principal research questions this chapter will explore are (1) How have notions of masculinity evolved over time? (2) How are masculinity and consumption intertwined? (3) Based on past research, what tensions, if any, underlie men's consumption behavior? To explore these questions, we will provide an extensive review of relevant work that examines issues related to gender and consumption. This literature review will detail how masculinity has been defined over time, including the historical, cultural, and temporal aspects. In addition, research on masculine ideals and how masculinity and consumption are related will be highlighted.

Definitions of Masculinity

There is a great deal of confusion as to what it means to be masculine in the 21st century. Although the notions of maleness and masculinity were once synonymous, a new discourse on sex emerged in the early 20th century due in part to the efforts of scientists, mostly in Germany, who explored trans-sexuality (Meyerowitz, 2002). After decades of debate, a person's psychological sex became referred to as gender, whereas sex referred to a person's biological sex. Despite this distinction, masculinity continues to be a nebulous construct. Beynon (2002) states masculinity and femininity are "more amorphous and difficult to define in our society than ever in recent past. . . . What can be said with undeniable certainty is that as we embark upon the 21st century masculinity is being placed under the microscope as never before" (p. 3). Not only is masculinity difficult to define, but some researchers contest the existence of such a construct at all. MacInnes (1998, p. 40) claims that masculinity exists simply as a "fantasy" about how men should behave, a way to help people make sense of their lives. He further argues for the "end of masculinity," and claims that soon the only differences between men and women will be anatomical.

Other researchers note that the construct of masculinity is actually comprised of many masculinities. Cornwall and Lindisfarne (1994) hold that there is no fixed notion of masculinity—rather, it has numerous and indistinct meanings that change over time, depending on the context. Moreover, masculinity is varied in its construction and enactment (both within and outside of the boundaries of the marketplace) and can be dependant on various factors such as historical context, geographic location, class standing, ethnicity, culture, age, marital status, sexuality, and various individual differences (Beynon, 2002). Further, it can be expressed by both men and women (see Halberstam, 1998 for a discussion on female masculinity).

Moreover, masculinity has been defined and researched differently depending upon the worldview or lens of the researcher. Bourke (1996) discusses the five predominant ways to conceptualize masculinity. The *biological perspective* holds that masculinity is equated with maleness whereas the second wave *feminist* perspective focuses on the notion of power differentials between men and women and emphasizes the oppression of women. In the feminist tradition, researchers have noted that the study of masculinity is not contrary to feminist research. In fact, Fischer and Gainer (1994) state that if feminism research focuses solely on women, there is a risk of reinforcing the notion that men are the "norm." Therefore, because gender is a relational process, it is necessary to study both masculinity and femininity as they develop in relation to one another.

In addition to the biological and feminist research traditions, the perspective of *socialization* asserts that masculinity is a result of the appropriate socialization of men. In fact, the tradition of socialization conceptualizes masculinity as a Goffmanesque presentation. This term is named after Erwin Goffman's (1971) conceptualization that individuals (in this case, boys) are actors following a scripted role in their performances on how to be men. In fact, as boys learn to become men, they also realize that particular gendered performances are more valorized than others. Goffman (1963) states that society deems one type of masculinity ideal, against which all other forms are measured:

> In an important sense there is only one complete unblushing male in America: a young, married, white, urban, northern, heterosexual, Protestant father of college education, fully employed, of good complexion, weight, and height, and a recent record in sports. Every American male tends to look out upon the world from this perspective, this constituting one sense in which one can speak of a common value system in America. Any male who fails to qualify in any one of these ways is likely to view himself—during moments at least—as unworthy, incomplete, and inferior. (p. 128)

Whereas notions of white masculinity dominate societal norms, so does the construct of heterosexual masculinity. Recent scholars have observed an interesting interplay between the homosexual and heterosexual men's aesthetic appearances as members of both groups seemingly strive to take on outward characteristics stereotyped as appropriate for the other. For example, Forrest (1994) discusses the relationship between sexuality and masculinity by describing the "butch shift," where young gay men portray themselves, through their clothing and sporting activities, as heterosexual men. Moreover, other gay men may embrace hyper-masculinity by exaggerating macho behaviors. While the gay subculture has long engaged in consumption in order to construct an attractive physical appearance (Kates, 2002), heterosexual men, especially since the 1980s, have sought out this "look" through an interest in clothes and fashion. The most recent exemplar of a focus on appearance can be observed through the metrosexual.

In addition to the view that men engage in various performances of gender, the *psychoanalytical* perspective discusses the notion that masculinities vary and are shaped as a result of varying sociological, historical, and cultural environments. The study of *discourse* holds that masculinity is constructed through discourses, or through a complex system of cultural meanings in society. For example, an extensive amount of past research in masculinity has tackled cultural issues such as race and ethnicity (Irwin, 2003; Wallace,

2002), religion (Boyarin, 1997), sexuality (Forrest, 1994), and class (Holt & Thompson, 2004). In summary, there are a multitude of perspectives to the study of gender. All five of the predominant approaches, as well as other streams not mentioned, have contributed to an enhanced understanding of the construct, albeit from different perspectives. The historical and temporal nature of masculinity will be discussed next.

Masculinity as a Historically Situated Construct

The construct of masculinity is deeply embedded within the historical time period in which a man resides. It is also greatly impacted by a man's stage in life. Beynon (2002) states, "Masculinity is positioned in time in two senses: it changes *around* the individual man and *for him* as he ages" (p. 17). For example, Tuncay (2006a) found that Generation X men, who may be in a transition period between the bachelor life and marriage, often expressed a sometimes conflicting desire for pursuing attractive women as well as a need to someday build a family in their conceptualizations of masculinity. Thus, masculinity can be experienced differently at various stages in a man's life. In addition to the temporal nature of masculinity, historical context also impacts a man's experience. If we examine this construct throughout American history, it is evident that masculinity and the position of men in society were once defined by their property ownership. By the 1930s (with its peak in the 1950s), a man's role in society was to be the breadwinner for his wife and children and thus, earn respectability in the community. Work and masculinity were closely connected in a cultural discourse that was reiterated by government and business. For example, Suzik (2001) details the Civilian Conservation Corps created by Franklin D. Roosevelt in response to the increasing number of young men who were unemployed during the Great Depression. The popularity of this organization, which claimed to "build better men" through hard work, as well as its substantial support by the government, clearly signaled societal beliefs that boys became men through work (Suzik, 2001). Even private businesses during that time, such as General Motors in conjunction with the Fisher Body Craftman's Guild, actively recruited students from the Boy Scouts, YMCA, and public schools to participate in elaborate engineering contests, in hopes of training men to work in technology fields (Oldenziel, 2001). These examples illustrate the societal belief that the road to manliness through self-control, self-reliance, and being a productive worker was firmly entrenched in social life (Register, 2001). It is also interesting to note that while middle-class men performed the role of the breadwinner, working-class men performed "rough masculinity." This type of masculinity can be characterized by drinking and rowdiness, while at the same time gaining respect as men by garnering wages equivalent to middle-class earnings (Meyer, 2001).

Although the prevailing notions of masculinity in the early 20th century were rooted in the role of financial provider, an alternate type of masculinity was evident as well. This "new" type of masculinity in the 1920s and 30s is best described by the Peter Pan philosophy where men were in an endless pursuit of play and personal satisfaction through the consumption of goods (Register, 2001). This new masculinity later evolved into what became known in the 1950s and 1960s as the Playboy. Unlike the role of provider, this new man was self-indulgent, consumption-driven, and backlashed against domestic notions (Osgerby, 2001). This consumption-driven masculinity can be seen in more contemporary times with the Wall Street "yuppie" lifestyle in the 1980s and the metrosexual of today. Beynon (2002) notes that the last 50 years have marked a shift in masculinity due to its fragmented nature. Thus, while certain ideals were salient throughout history, the last five decades have shown a great deal of variety in the masculine roles that men can assume.

Contemporary Themes of Masculinity

The notions of masculinity continue to evolve even in today's society. So what is the current "new man?" Beynon (2002) claims that while masculinity has undoubtedly changed in the 1980s, 1990s, and beyond, there are no clear definitions of the new man. But while what it means to be masculine is an ill-defined construct, there are certain themes in contemporary masculinity that can be noted. These include "telemasculinity" and "buddydom." Fiske (1987) defines telemasculinity as the enactment of masculinity through action, adventure, competition, aggression, and consumption of "male toys" such as cars and guns.

In addition, Beynon (2002) discusses notions of "buddydom" where masculinity is celebrated through relationships between men. A popular arena where this "buddydom" is played out is in the domain of sports. By engaging in athletic activities, men can build comradeship, enact the role of hero, and courageously overcome hurdles and stiff competition. Sabo (1992) states that the cultural space of sports is where men determine their place in the pecking order and where boys learn that pain is sometimes more important than pleasure in defining their manhood. In a similar vein, Messner (1992) claims that sports is a marker of masculinity and provides self-esteem in men who excel in this arena by clearly distinguishing the "others" who do not achieve this status and who are thus wrought with uncertainty. Consumer researchers have also looked at the context of sports in relation to masculinity. Fischer and Gainer (1994) attempted to understand how athletic activities, or a form of consumption that had clear divisions between men and women, may shape and reinforce men's socially defined gender roles. The authors echo past researchers in that sports is a primary socializing experience that shapes and reinforces a sense of masculinity and provides authenticity. The authors found a clear link between sport and masculinity and explained that informants defined a range of masculinities in regard to sports. For example, biking holds a different meaning of masculinity versus the more aggressive sport of boxing. In fact, past researchers have also empirically found similar themes of adventure and athleticism as a part of masculinity (e.g., Harris, 1995; Tuncay, 2006b.) While athleticism and adventure have been associated with the "new" man, other themes of masculinity have emerged over time. The ever-changing content of gender roles will be discussed in more detail in the next section.

The Cultural Ideals and Norms of Masculinity

Past gender research has discussed the gender role norms and ideals that exist in today's society (see, e.g., Brannon, 1976; Harris, 1995; Lindsey, 1997). Harris (1995) empirically researched the messages that American men are faced with by their peers, family, and the media, and developed a typology of gender role norms. This typology details 24 norms, or standards for how men should behave. These norms detail various prescriptions such as the norm of Control, or the idea that men should always be in control of their lives and the norm of the Nature Lover, or the idea that men should commune with nature. Mangan (2003) reflects on this list of male gender role norms.

> The list seems to contradict itself at several points. For example, it pinpoints the contradictory messages that a man should be [a] "Faithful Husband" and "Playboy." Clearly, it is virtually impossible to fulfill both roles at the same time: how, then, can these contradictions be negotiated? By choosing the one and ignoring the other? Or by understanding the two as successive: the man sows his wild oats early in life, then settles down? Or as part of an evolutionary development from an old-fashioned model of masculinity, which is being superseded by a more modern (and domesticated) one? Some men will successfully negotiate the contradictions within the gender scheme; for others the existence of apparently contradictory messages will be a source of long-standing confusion. Perhaps the most important aspects of gender ideology are less to do with the messages themselves, than with what men do with them once they have heard them. (p. 209)

Thus, tensions seem inherent in the prescriptions that are set forth for men on how they should enact their masculinity. These tensions will be explored in more detail later in this chapter. While Harris (1995) has detailed gender role norms, Brannon (1976) conceptualized the ideals of masculinity. He describes four ideals which include No Sissy Stuff, or the anti-feminine norm; The Big Wheel, the notion that money makes the man; The Sturdy Oak, typifying toughness; and Give 'Em Hell, which emphasizes aggression and violence. Lindsey (1997) notes another ideal and modernized the typology by describing the Macho Man, or a man who seeks sexual pursuits. While past gender research has delved into the content of ideal masculinity, little research has provided an updated view from the perspective of male consumers. However, Tuncay (2006b) conducted an in-depth study on men's conceptualizations of masculinity in advertising and formulates a typology of masculine ideals that exist in advertising among Generation X men. The ideals salient in today's advertising is especially important because it illuminates the cultural values that society holds (see for example Schroeder & Zwick's, 2004 discussion on representations of masculinity in advertising). Tuncay (2006b) details eight masculine ideals that emerged from the informants' expressions of masculinity, including ideals such as the Attractive Man, which highlights the importance of appearance for today's man. Although it is important to gain an understanding of the content of conceptions of masculinity, it is also vital to understand how masculinity is enacted in the marketplace.

Marketplace Masculinity

As men shift from a largely production role in society to an increased participation in consumption, the links between masculinity and the marketplace continue to grow. Beynon (2002) describes this type of "new" man as one who is both narcissist and materialist. Indeed, past research has detailed the firm link between material objects and expressions of masculinity (see, e.g., Tuncay, 2006a discussion of conceptions of masculinity among metrosexuals).

The Gendered Self and Product/Brand Congruity.   Research in the 1970s and 1980s explored the congruity between the gendered self and product preference and brand choice. Sirgy (1985) explains that consumers seek products that are congruent with their self-concepts. Some research has found this congruity effect with regard to the gendered self (Bellizzi & Milner, 1991; Fry, 1971; Vitz & Johnston, 1965; Worth, Smith, & Mackie, 1992). That is, individuals prefer goods or spokespeople that match their sense of masculinity and femininity. On the other hand, other researchers have found weak support for the congruence between the gendered self and consumer behavior variables (Gentry & Doering, 1977; Gentry, Doering, & O'Brien, 1978; Kahle & Homer, 1985; Schmitt, LeClerc, & Dube-Rioux, 1988). These disparate findings may be due to the fact that sex and gender have not been uniformly conceptualized in the past literature. While these studies take an important first step in understanding the link between the self and consumption of gendered products, they do not provide a holistic picture of the interplay between broader gender ideologies and the motivation to consume gendered goods. To understand these linkages, we turn to a review of research that takes an in-depth qualitative or multi-method approach to understanding this issue.

Gender Roles, Shopping, and Consumption Behavior. Several important studies have made inroads into the link between gender and consumption. Fischer and Arnold (1990) point to research by Scanzoni and Szinovacz (1980) which holds that people with more traditional gender role attitudes conform to norms that prescribe involvement in gender traditional activities and prohibit involvement in less traditional activities. Thus, men with more traditional gender role attitudes may be likely to avoid involvement in shopping, which is often labeled as a woman's domain. To this point, Fischer and Arnold (1990) find gender role attitudes moderate involvement in the traditionally feminine domain of Christmas gift shopping. Simply put, men whom the authors define as egalitarian bought more for recipients and spent more time shopping than traditional men.

Other researchers also compare the ways men and women shop. Underhill (1999) claims gender differences do exist in the domain of shopping. He found that in contrast to women, men move faster through the store, spend less time browsing, and do not typically ask questions. In addition, he holds that men prefer eye-catching displays, technology, gadgets, and obtaining information firsthand from written materials. Despite some research which indicates men and women shop differently, Otnes and McGrath (2001) found that myths still exist on how men shop. They found in their study of male shoppers that some men did indeed enjoy shopping and even purchased "feminine" goods such as crystal. Holt and Thompson (2004) also examined men and the everyday consumption of goods and found evidence of non-stereotypical male consumption behavior. These two studies will be discussed at greater length later in this chapter. In addition to the important research on gender and consumption, some researchers have also examined expressions of masculinity in retail settings. In Chapter 1 of this book, Kozinets discusses the emergence of experiential retail in today's marketplace. Consumer researchers have investigated experiential consumption in the context of retail venues largely targeting male consumers, such as Nike Town (Sherry, 1998) and ESPN Zone (Sherry et al., 2004). The authors discuss enactments of masculinity, including a heightened sense of competition, violence, achievement, and risky behavior, as consumers played out their sports fantasies.

Literature Synthesis

With regard to the literature on gender and consumption, the research offers mixed support for the notion of gender role congruity, which may be due to variance in the measurement of gender constructs over time. Further, few studies have investigated the link between gender ideology and consumption from an in-depth qualitative perspective, especially with regard to male consumers. Even influential research in the area of shopping, such as Miller's (1998) in-depth study of shopping among residents in a London neighborhood, does not address how gender influences the shopping discourse, although Miller acknowledges that with regard to shopping, "there is an important component of gender that is foundational to this ritual practice" (p. 9). Thus, men in general are seldom viewed as consumers or through the lens of gender. The research that does exist suggests the multifaceted and layered nature of male consumption. Future research should explore these issues due to its importance for marketing practitioners and advertisers, and also to build our theoretical knowledge in this neglected area of study.

Moreover, because notions of masculinity have shifted over time and culminated in the fragmented masculinities of today, there are a multitude of possible tensions in the marketplace. Whereas certain masculine ideals have prevailed at certain points throughout history, it is clear that today's man may choose from a myriad of masculine performances. Although this diversity may seem appealing to some, it is also wrought with uncertainty, which may explain the tensions that some male consumers experience in the marketplace. These tensions will be discussed in the next section.

Tensions Within Masculinity and Consumption

It is clear from past research that men are often confronted with a fragmented and sometimes conflicting notion of what it means to be a man in today's society. This tension can be seen in men's consumption patterns as well. With the salience of gender role transcendence (as discussed by Otnes & McGrath, 2001), men are pushing the boundaries of acceptable behavior. While this behavior is pleasurable for some consumers, others seem to experience some anxiety. In fact, three recent consumer behavior studies allude to tensions experienced by male consumers in the marketplace (Holt & Thompson, 2004; Otnes & McGrath, 2001; Tuncay & Otnes, 2006).

One of the tensions that definitions of masculinity create is a tension between heterosexuality and homosexuality. Past research has identified that the fear of being labeled homosexual is a key component of hegemonic masculinity, or the dominant form of masculinity in society (Kimmel, 1994). Moreover, Sender (2004) points to theorist Eve Kosofisky Sedgwick, who claims that the homosexual/heterosexual distinction is the "primary organizing principle [in society] in the 20th century" (p. 143). Thus, it is no surprise that male consumers, such as the metrosexual informants in the study by Tuncay and Otnes (2006), were highly concerned about maintaining that distinction. Informants in that study worried that their metrosexual behaviors, or the consumption of fashion and grooming products, would lead them to be branded as a homosexual. They employed two distinct strategies while shopping to apparently deflect this perception. The first is what they call "proactive censoring," where informants are quick to point out the boundaries of the clothes and grooming products among the offerings in the marketplace, by labeling certain objects as either too gay or too feminine. Although such censoring often emanates from the informants themselves, in some cases the men ask others if items are "too gay," or rely on visual cues in the retail store to help them decide whether an item is appropriate. In this way, informants employ both companions and strangers in the marketplace (McGrath & Otnes, 1995) as information sources, in order to help them navigate shifting gender boundaries. The second strategy the informants employed was what we called "masking," or actions that consumers take to hide or deemphasize the consumption behavior they display to others. Goffman (1971) alludes to a concept similar to masking in his discussion of the presentation of self. He notes how misrepresentation, or a "discrepancy between fostered appearance and reality," can occur when the performer is not "authorized to give the performance" (p. 59).

Another tension identified by past research is between conforming to society's expectations of what it means to be a man and the desire to break away from the constraints of this conformity. For example, Holt and Thompson (2004) observe that some men reject traditional masculine gender roles when engaging in everyday consumption behavior. One of their informants decries his peers who accept typically "macho" behaviors such as adhering to the breadwinner role and engaging in sports and hunting activities. This informant seeks to highlight his feminine values in an attempt to reject more traditional notions of masculinity. More broadly, Holt and

Thompson (2004) find their male informants manage such tensions by constructing an identity of the "man-of-action hero," that both embodies rugged individualism and adheres to collective interests.

Related to men's tendencies to break away from stereotypical masculine behavior, Otnes and McGrath (2001) dispel myths about "typical" male shopping behavior. They discuss three common stereotypes of male shopping behavior, including the "Fear of the Feminine" stereotype, which holds that men seek to avoid products associated with the feminine sphere. Despite commonly held perceptions of male shopping behavior, Otnes and McGrath (2001) found contradictory evidence. For example, some men engage in long shopping trips, visit "feminine" shops, and even purchase "feminine" goods such as crystal and china. The authors contribute to a theory on male shopping behavior and explain:

> The emergence of non-stereotypical male shopping behavior stems from the following: (1) transcendence of the masculine gender role; (2) an achievement orientation that is nevertheless paradoxically entrenched in aspects of the male gender role; (3) "feminine" shopping behavior and (4) achievement outcomes that relate to specific types of success. (p. 131)

According to the authors, several achievement outcomes underlie male shopping, including professional success, sexual success, and shopping success. Moreover, this tenet of achievement is both culturally embedded in traditional ideals of masculinity and often has been cited as a motivation for men's consumption behavior (Csikszentmihayli & Rochberg-Halton, 1981). In this manner, men shop to "win" (Otnes & McGrath, 2001). Thus, it appears that men manage the tension of engaging in a traditionally feminine space by adhering to the ethic of achievement.

In summary, past research has shown that men are often confronted with conflicting and unattainable notions of masculinity. These notions manifest in the shopping and consumption behaviors of male consumers and create both pleasurable and anxiety-provoking tensions. Past research (e.g., Holt & Thompson, 2004; Otnes & McGrath, 2001; Tuncay & Otnes, 2006) illuminates particular tensions experienced by men in the marketplace. These tensions lead to various outcomes in consumers' lives such as proactive censoring, masking behavior, construction of new identities, and achievement outcomes. Future research should explore the multitude of tensions male consumers feel and how they cope with these tensions in the marketplace. By investigating these issues, marketers can begin to understand how they can effectively and ethically manage these tensions.

Potential Theoretical and Managerial Contributions

This chapter offers a comprehensive review of the literature on masculinity and consumption. First, by understanding how notions of masculinity have evolved over time, we can begin to gain a holistic and temporally situated understanding of how men experience their sense of masculinity. With this enhanced knowledge, we can shed light on the tensions inherent in men's gender roles and begin to understand the influence of gender ideology on consumption behavior. This review illuminates the fact that men experience various pleasurable and anxiety-provoking tensions in their masculinity-consumption dialectic. These tensions lead men to pursue various strategies in the marketplace, in order to either embrace these tensions, or to ease any dissonance that emanate from them.

In addition to the potential theoretical contributions of this review, this research also has significant implications for marketers. Male consumers in general are largely under-researched, even though they constitute a large and viable market. By understanding the mechanisms through which gender influences men as they engage in consumption, marketers can effectively develop ad campaigns, retail settings, and new products that attract these consumers. Marketers can seek to understand and minimize tensions that cause consumers anxiety and enhance tensions that cause pleasure. In this manner, marketers can more effectively target their customers, as well as minimize anxiety in consumers.

In conclusion, we hope this review demonstrates the importance of aiming research efforts at the male consumer, because it is clear that the activity of publicly embracing shopping as a means of identity construction has become highly salient to men's lives. As a result, understanding the male shopper should be high on the priority list of both academics and practitioners.

References

Belk, R. W., & Costa, J. A. (1998). The mountain man myth: A contemporary consuming fantasy. *Journal of Consumer Research, 25*, 218–240.

Bellizzi, J., & Milner, L. (1991). Gender positioning of a traditionally male-dominant product. *Journal of Advertising Research, 31*, 72–79.

Beynon, J. (2002). *Masculinities and culture.* Philadelphia: Open University Press.

Bourke, J. (1996). *Dismembering the male: Men's bodies, Britain and the great war.* London: Reaktion.

Boyarin, D. (1997). *Unheroic conduct: The rise of heterosexuality and the invention of the Jewish man*. London: University of California Press.

Brannon, R. (1976). The male sex role: Our culture's blueprint of manhood and what it's done for us lately. In D. David & R. Brannon (Eds.), *The 49% majority*. Reading, MA: Addison-Wesley.

Cornwall, A., & Lindisfarne, N. (1994). *Dislocating masculinity: Comparative ethnographies*. London: Routledge.

Csikszentmihayli, M., & Rochberg-Halton, E. (1981). *The meaning of things: Domestic symbols and the self*. Cambridge, MA: Cambridge University Press.

Fischer, E., & Arnold, S. J. (1990). More than a labor of love: Gender roles and Christmas gift shopping. *Journal of Consumer Research, 17*, 333–345.

Fischer, E., & Gainer, B. (1994). Masculinity and the consumption of organized sports. In J. Arnold Costa (Ed.), *Gender issues in consumer behavior* (pp. 84–103). Thousand Oaks, CA: Sage Publications.

Fiske, J. (1987). *Television culture*. London: Methuen.

Forrest, D. (1994). 'We're here, we're queer and we're not going shopping:' Changing gay male identities in contemporary Britain. In A. Cornwall & N. Lindisfarne (Eds.), *Dislocating masculinity: Comparative ethnographies*. London: Routledge.

Fry, J. N. (1971). Personality variables and cigarette brand choice. *Journal of Marketing Research, 8*, 298–304.

Gentry, J., & Doering, M. (1977). Masculinity-femininity related to consumer choice. In K. Hunt (Ed.), *Advances in consumer research, 5*, Ann Arbor, MI: 423–437.

Gentry, J., Doering, M., & O'Brien, T. (1978). Masculinity and femininity factors in product perception and self-image. In K. Hunt (Ed.), *Advances in consumer research, 5*, Ann Arbor, MI: 326–332.

Goffman, E. (1963). *Stigma: Notes on the management of spoiled identity*. Englewood Cliffs, NJ: Prentice-Hall.

Goffman, E. (1971). *The presentation of the self in everyday life*. Garden City, NY: DoubleDay & Company, Inc.

Halberstam, J. (1998). *Female masculinity*. Durham, NC: Duke University.

Harris, I. (1995). *Messages men hear: Constructing masculinities*. London: Taylor & Francis.

Holt, D. B., & Thompson, C. J. (2004). Man-of-action heroes: The pursuit of heroic masculinity in everyday consumption. *Journal of Consumer Research, 31*, 425–440.

Irwin, R. (2003). *Mexican masculinities*. Minneapolis: University of Minnesota Press.

Kahle, L., & Homer, P. (1985). Androgyny and midday mastication: Do real men eat quiche? In E. Hirschman & M. Holbrook (Eds.), *Advances in consumer research, 12*, Ann Arbor, MI: 242–246.

Kates, S. (2002). The protean quality of subcultural consumption: An ethnographic account of gay consumers. *Journal of Consumer Research, 29*, 383–399.

Kimmel, M. (1994). Masculinity as homophobia. In H. Bod & M. Kaufman (Eds.), *Theorizing masculinities.* 119–141.

Kimmel, M., & Messner, M. (2001). *Men's lives.* Needham Heights, MA: Pearson Education Company.

Kyles, K. (2005). Now serving: Beefcake. *Red Eye,* November 15, 6–7.

Lindsey, L. L. (1997). *Gender roles.* Upper Saddle River, NJ: Prentice-Hall.

MacInnes, J. (1998). *The end of masculinity.* Buckingham: Open University Press.

Mangan, M. (2003). *Staging masculinities: History, gender, performance.* New York: Palgrave Macmillian.

MarketWatch (2006). Trading up opportunities in male grooming: How to profit by going beyond the "metrosexual" myth. Retrieved September 1, 2006 from www.datamonitor.com

McGrath, M. A., & Otnes, C. C. (1995). Unacquainted influencers: When strangers interact in retail settings. *Journal of Business Research, 32*, 261–272.

Messner, M. (1992). *Power at play.* Boston: Beacon.

Metrosexuality. (n.d.) Retrieved December 6, 2005, from www.wordspy.com *Metrosexuals: The future of men?* (n.d.) Retrieved June 2003, from www.newswire.ca

Meyer, S. (2001). Work, play, power: Masculine culture on the automotive shop floor, 1930–1960. In R. Horowitz (Ed.), *Boys and their toys* (pp. 13–32). New York: Routledge.

Meyerowitz, J. (2002). *How sex changed.* Cambridge, MA: Harvard University Press.

Miller, D. (1998). *A theory of shopping.* Ithaca, NY: Cornell University Press.

Oldenziel, R. (2001). Boys and their toys: The Fisher Body Craftman's Guild, 1930–1968, and the making of a male technical domain. In Roger Horowitz (Ed.), *Boys and their toys* (pp. 139–168). New York: Routledge.

Osgerby, B. (2001). *Playboys in paradise.* New York: Oxford International Publishers.

Otnes, C. C., & McGrath, M. A. (2001). Perceptions and realities of male shopping behavior. *Journal of Retailing, 77*, 111–137.

Peñaloza, L. (2001). Consuming the American West: Animating cultural meaning and memory at a stock show and rodeo. *Journal of Consumer Research, 28*, 369–399.

Register, W. (2001). Everyday Peter Pans: Work, manhood, and consumption in urban America, 1900–1930. In R. Horowitz, (Ed.), *Boys and their toys* (pp. 199–228). New York: Routledge.

Sabo, D. (1992). Pigskin, patriarchy, and pain. In M. Kimmel & M. Messner (Eds.), *Men's lives* (pp. 347–361). New York: Macmillian.

Scanzoni, J., & Szinovacz, M. (1980). *Family decision making: A developmental sex-role model*. Beverly Hills, CA: Sage.

Schmitt, B., LeClerc, F., & Dube-Rioux, L. (1988). Sex typing and gender schema theory. *Journal of Consumer Research, 15*, 122–128.

Schroeder, J., & Zwick, D. (2004). Mirrors of masculinity: Representation and identity in advertising images. *Consumption, Markets and Culture, 7*, 21–52.

Schouten, J. W., & McAlexander, J. H. (1995), Subcultures of consumption: An ethnography of new bikers. *Journal of Consumer Research, 22*, 43–61.

Sender, K. (2004). *Business, not politics, the making of the gay market*. New York: Columbia University Press.

Sherry, J. F., Jr. (1998). The soul of the company store: Nike Town Chicago and the emplaced brandscape. In J. F. Sherry, Jr. (Ed.), *Servicescapes: The concept of place in contemporary markets* (pp. 109–146). Lincolnwood, IL: NTC Business Book.

Sherry, J. F., Jr., Kozinets, R. V., Duhachek, A., DeBerry-Spence, B., Nuttavuthisit, K. & Storm, D. (2004). Gendered behavior in a male preserve: Role playing at ESPN Zone in Chicago. *Journal of Consumer Psychology, 14*, 151–158.

Sirgy, J. M. (1985). Using self-congruity and ideal congruity to predict purchase motivation. *Journal of Business Research, 13*, 195–206.

Suzik, J. R. (2001). Building better men: The CCC boy and the changing social ideal of manliness. In R. Horowitz (Ed.), *Boys and their toys* (pp. 111–138). New York: Routledge.

Tuncay, L. (2006a). Conceptualizations of masculinity among a "new" breed of male consumers. In L. Stevens & J. Borgerson (Eds.), *Eight conference proceedings for gender, marketing, and consumer behavior* (pp. 312–326).

Tuncay, L. (2006b). Men's responses to depictions of ideal masculinity in advertising. In G. Fitzsimmons & V. Morwitz (Eds.), *Advances in Consumer Research, 33*, 64.

Tuncay, L., & C. C. Otnes. (2006). Exploring the link between the "new masculinity" and consumption: Underlying tensions and shopping behavior. *Working paper*.

Underhill, P. (1999). *Why we buy—The science of shopping*. New York: Simon & Schuster.

Vitz, P., & Johnston, D. (1965). Masculinity of smokers and the masculinity of cigarette images. *Journal of Applied Psychology, 49,* 155–159.

Wallace, M. (2002). *Constructing the black masculine.* Durham, NC: Duke University.

Worth, L. T., Smith, J., & Mackie, D. M. (1992). Gender schematicity and preference for gender-typed products. *Psychology & Marketing, 9,* 17–30.

9

ASSESSING PERCEIVED DISCRIMINATION IN "BRICK AND MORTAR" RETAIL SETTINGS USING A POWER-RESPONSIBILITY EQUILIBRIUM FRAMEWORK

Jerome D. Williams
University of Texas at Austin

May O. Lwin
Nanyang Technological University

Anne-Marie G. Hakstian
Salem State College

Velma A. R. Gooding
University of Texas at Austin

*A*CCORDING TO FEDERAL COURT cases filed from 1990 to 2002, people of color have reported negative retail shopping experiences based on allegations of being followed around in stores, being accused of and detained for shoplifting based on race, not being allowed to write checks in stores located in ethnic neighborhoods, and being subject to racial slurs by retail employees (Harris, Henderson, & Williams, 2005). These experiences and the outcomes of both state court cases and state civil rights agency cases suggest that consumers may have concerns about what responses to marketplace discrimination can balance the possible inadequate protection by retail establishments and by the government as power-holders. Unfortunately, very little research has been conducted on marketplace discrimination to help retailers better understand how they can effectively respond to the changing multicultural marketplace climate, and particularly to issues related to marketplace discrimination. In this chapter we propose the use of the Power-Responsibility Equilibrium framework as a conceptual model to address this need. The model allows the integration of the hitherto unstudied triad of: (1) retailer/marketer business policies and actions toward marketplace discrimination; (2) government regulation and public policies toward marketplace discrimination; and (3) consumer responses to marketplace discrimination. At this phase, we merely propose the framework and its various components and suggest how it can be applied in assessing marketplace discrimination. An empirical study to test the model will be the next phase of this research.

We begin this discussion by establishing why there is a need for research on marketplace discrimination in retail settings, followed by background on understanding terminology differences between consumer racial profiling (CRP) and marketplace discrimination. We next give a brief overview of some of the recent studies on consumer discrimination. Finally, we introduce the Power-Responsibility Equilibrium (PRE) model framework and discuss the various components and how they apply to retail discrimination.

The Need for Research on Perceived Discrimination in Retail Settings

According to the Selig Center report on the multicultural economy and multicultural purchasing power, consumers of color comprise approximately one third of the U.S. population and wield over a trillion dollars of purchasing power (Humphreys, 2004). The Selig report also estimates that in 2009, the combined buying power of the three racial groups of African Americans, Asians, and Native Americans will be more than triple its 1990 level of $456 billion, and exceed $1.5 trillion. For the ethnic group of Hispanics, who can be of any racial group, the Selig report notes that the growth in the Hispanic population and purchasing power is reshaping the retail landscape. Hispanics' economic clout will rise from $222 billion in 1990 to $992 billion in 2009, a percentage gain of 347.1 percent that is substantially greater than the 148.5 percent increase in non-Hispanic buying power. Over this 19-year period, the percentage gains in multicultural buying power of all multicultural target markets will grow much faster than the white market.

For "brick and mortar" retailers, these demographic changes and growth in multicultural purchasing power are particularly important. For example, according to the 2003 National Shopping Behavior Study from Meridian, a Troy, Michigan-based strategic marketing communications agency, ethnic minority consumers are becoming more important to department store retailers (Henderson, 2004). In the most recent Meridian study, 11 percent of Caucasians, 15 percent of Hispanics, and 18 percent of African Americans reported spending the most at a department store. Data from the study indicates that the African American and Hispanic consumer groups now account for 25–30 percent of department store sales. According to the report, the significant changes in the shopping behavior of these consumer groups and their purchasing motivations will require department store management to make meaningful changes to their strategies to effectively serve their new customers. These trends are particularly important for department store retailers because in the four year history of the National Shopping Behavior Study, the percentage of consumers naming department stores as the place they spend the most has declined from 15 percent to 11 percent, but the percentage of Hispanics and African Americans who identify department stores as the place where they spend the most money continues to outpace the percentage of Caucasians.

However, there is mounting evidence that "brick and mortar" retailers have failed to provide a "welcoming" shopping environment for consumers of color. For example, Williams and Snuggs (1997) conducted a mail survey of 1,000 households and found that 86 percent of African Americans felt that they were treated differently in retail stores based on their race, compared to 34 percent of whites. Also, according to a more recent Gallup Poll Social Audit Series on black/white Relations in the United States (Henderson, 2001), 35 percent of blacks say they are treated less fairly than whites in neighborhood shops, 46 percent say they are treated less fairly in stores downtown or in malls, and 39 percent say they are treated unfairly in restaurants, bars, and theaters. This poll also indicated that 27 percent of all black respondents, and 41 percent of black males between 18 and 34 years of age, felt that they were treated unfairly in the last 30 days in a store where they shop. Since 1990, the popular press has reported numerous accounts of marketplace discrimination against consumers of color. In a general press article on the new face of retail racism in America (Knickerbocker, 2000), the following incidents are noted:

- In the Washington area, KayBee Toys has been charged in a federal civil rights suit with refusing to accept personal checks at stores in predominately black neighborhoods. The Equal Rights Center, a civil rights organization in Washington that filed the suit, called this "an overt example of consumer racism."

- The U.S. Justice Department recently charged the Adam's Mark Hotel chain with a pattern of discrimination, including overcharging black guests for inferior rooms while subjecting them to stricter security requirements.
- Florida officials charged a Miami restaurant owner with automatically adding a service charge to bills of black customers but not to those of white patrons.
- In Boston, city councilor Gareth Saunders filed a complaint against a taxi service for refusing to pick him up at his home in a predominately black neighborhood, black actor Danny Glover was refused taxi service in New York.

Retailers that remain insensitive to multicultural market segments run the risk of alienating these segments and, as a result, suffering severe economic consequences. The following few examples highlight how firms have been subjected to a significant negative financial impact as a result of their lack of sensitivity to diverse market segments:

- Sales at Yvonne Elibe's Dearborn, Mich., Treasure Cache fell more than 50 percent following an incident involving marketplace discrimination (Bean, 2001).
- After a landmark discrimination case, Denny's conducted a poll of potential customers and found that close to 50 percent of African Americans said they would never come to Denny's (Bean, 2003).
- Texaco lost a billion dollars in stock value in 48 hours during the period when they were sued by African American plaintiffs for systematic discrimination and the *New York Times* reported on tape-recorded conversations by Texaco executives denigrating African American employees (Bean, 2003).

Also, it should be noted why retail discrimination research may be more important for "brick and mortar" versus online retailers. Currently the majority of blacks (60 percent) and Hispanics (68 percent) do not use the Internet (National Telecommunications and Information Administration, 2002). Lwin and Williams (2004) suggest that as these numbers increase, minority consumers may find fabrication of certain demographic and other descriptive information online to be a convenient mechanism for shielding themselves from the type of discriminatory behavior they might encounter in "brick and mortar" retail environments. One of the main differences between in-store versus online retailing for consumers of color is that online shopping allows consumers to maintain a certain degree of "anonymity" in terms of their racial/ethnic background. When a consumer is in a "brick and mortar" establishment and interacting interpersonally with sales and other store personnel, the consumer's race/ethnicity generally is rather obvious. This lack of racial "anonymity," coupled with the attitudes reported above that a significant percentage of consumers of color feel that they are treated unfairly in stores due to their race, emphasizes the importance of a better understanding of how "brick and mortar" retailers can respond to marketplace discrimination, whether it be real or perceived.

Understanding Terminology: Consumer Racial Profiling vs. Marketplace Discrimination

There is various terminology related to marketplace discrimination that frequently is used in the literature and popular press, e.g., "Shopping While Black" (Gabbidon, 2003), consumer racial profiling (Williams, Henderson and Harris, 2001), consumer discrimination (Harris, 2003), and statistical discrimination (Lee, 2000). When most people hear the term "racial profiling," they generally associate it with the vernacular term "Driving While Black or Brown" (DWB). This typically occurs when law enforcement officers stop, question, investigate, detain, and/or arrest individuals based on their race or ethnicity rather than on probable cause or even a reasonable suspicion that these individuals have engaged in criminal activity. According to a survey by *The Washington Post*, the Henry J. Kaiser Family Foundation, and Harvard University (Morin & Cottman, 2001; Valia, 2001), nearly 4 in 10 blacks—37 percent—said they had been unfairly stopped by police because they were black, including 52 percent of all black men and 25 percent of all black women. The survey notes that blacks are not the only Americans who say they have been the targets of racial or ethnic profiling by law enforcement. One in five Latino and Asian men reported they had been the victims of racially motivated police stops.

For many researchers, "consumer racial profiling" is analogized to law enforcement racial profiling, similar to DWB. When it involves consumers, the phenomenon is commonly referred to as "Shopping While Black or Brown" (SWB). However, it is important to recognize that in a retail context many types of marketplace discrimination do not involve suspecting customers of engaging in criminal activity. In this chapter, we use "marketplace discrimination" as a broader term to capture not only Consumer Racial Profiling (CRP), but other types of discriminatory marketplace situations where consumers do not receive equal treatment for equal dollars. Essentially, whether there is criminal suspicion or not, we are concerned with any type of differential treatment of consumers in the marketplace based on race/ethnicity that constitutes denial of or degradation in the products and/or services offered to the consumer. Our definition of marketplace discrimination also covers consumption experiences beyond shopping in retail stores. For example, the Harris et al. (2005) analysis of federal cases demonstrated that marketplace discrimination frequently occurs in places of public accommodation such as hotels, restaurants, gas stations, and service providers, as well as retail establishments including grocery/food stores, clothing stores, department stores, home improvement stores, and office equipment stores. Furthermore, marketplace discrimination impacts members of minority groups beyond those classified as black/African American, such as Hispanics, Asians, Native and Arab Americans. In fact, since September 11, 2001, there has been heightened interest and concern about CRP as it applies to anyone perceived as Middle Eastern, including South Asians, Latinos, and Jews (Nakao, 2001).

Overview of Marketplace Discrimination Studies

As noted above, research on marketplace discrimination is an emerging field, with very few published studies. Here we report on the studies we could find based on our search of the literature, which includes empirical and conceptual papers, dissertation abstracts, and working papers.

Gabbidon (2003) reviews the recent literature on SWB and examines legal cases where retailers have been accused of engaging in racial profiling in retail establishments. The key questions he attempts to answer are: (1) Which criminological theories are best suited to explain racial profiling? (2) What literature exists regarding racial profiling in the private sector? (3) What types of racial profiling incidents are currently occurring in retail settings? (4) What have been the outcomes of these incidents? and (5) What potential remedies are there for reducing the SWB phenomenon? The study couches racial profiling under the following three criminological perspectives: labeling theory, conflict theory, and the colonial model. He concludes that, like DWB, the issue of SWB requires serious scholarly attention. He also suggests the following as representing viable strategies to reduce such profiling: (1) require clerks and security personnel to receive education on the perils of racial profiling; (2) encourage victims of profiling to sue retailers who engage in these practices; and (3) work with civil rights groups to organize boycotts. He also urges federal officials to increase current levels of funding to study and remedy these discriminatory practices.

Harris et al. (2005) analyzed 81 federal court decisions made between 1990 and 2002 involving customers' allegations of race and/or ethnic discrimination in the marketplace. In their analysis, they categorized the 81 cases into three different dimensions of discrimination and profiling against people of color, namely: (1) level of service (outright denial versus degradation in service); (2) type of discrimination (subtle or overt); and (3) assumption of predisposition to criminality (present or not). They found that as many as 40 percent of the cases they examined involved allegations that customers were treated as criminals. Two thirds of the cases they examined contained allegations of degradation of goods and/or services. Those cases were almost evenly divided between subtle degradation (28 cases or 35 percent of all cases) and overt degradation (26 cases or 32 percent of all cases). Among the cases involving a denial of goods and/or services (one third of all cases), 78 percent contained allegations of overt denial and only 22 percent were subtle denials. Although the cases arose in many different types of retail establishments, a significant number took place in large retail stores (17 cases or 30 percent of all cases). More than one third of these cases (37 percent) arose in bars and/or restaurants.

Using a similar framework to the Harris et al. (2005) study, Williams, Harris, and Henderson (2006a) analyzed federal court decisions involving consumer racial profiling and other marketplace discrimination solely in the State of Illinois, along with state court decisions and complaints brought before the Illinois Human Rights Commission. This "drill-down" approach allowed them to focus on a particular geographic location (i.e., Illinois) and gain some insight as to how the courts and the Human Rights Commission in this location have dealt with marketplace discrimination, and to compare the results to the broader, national Harris et al. (2005) study. Using the three themes of alleged discrimination (subtle or overt), the level of service (degradation or denial), and the existence of criminal suspicion (present or absent), they concluded that real and perceived consumer discrimination remains a problem in the American marketplace, and specifically in Illinois. They also called for further research in order for researchers, marketers, public policy makers, and the law enforcement community to effectively address the issue. The authors also used the same framework to analyze consumer racial profiling and other marketplace discrimination by examining 120 state cases, including 91 state court cases and 29 state civil rights agency cases, involving customers' allegations of race and/or ethnic discrimination (Williams, Harris, & Henderson, 2006b).

Crockett, Grier, and Williams (2003) investigated the perceptions of discrimination among African American men. The participants in this study vividly recollected instances they perceived as discriminatory across a variety of retail settings. The authors surmise that perceived discrimination serves as a self-protective function in accordance with social psychology literature, and provide new insight into this phenomenon by proposing specific problem-focused and emotion-focused coping strategies that are employed in response to perceived discrimination.

Davidson and Schumann (2004) extended the Crockett et al. (2003) study by focusing on the key antecedents of perceived discrimination. In their model they focus on target personal factors, situational factors, and actor personal factors as antecedents to the cognitive personal outcome of perceived discrimination. Continuing this stream of research, Davidson and Schumann (2005), in a working paper, developed a model of perceived discrimination using the Cognitive-Emotive Model of Consumer Complaint Behavior (CEMCCB) developed by Stephens and Gwinner (1998), as a useful framework for organizing the constructs and variables involved in perceptions of discrimination in retail settings. Also, Davidson's (2006) dissertation addresses this topic further and represented the latest extension of their work.

There have been several studies focusing on the psychological aspects of discrimination. For example, Carter, Forsyth, Mazzula, and Williams (2005) explore the psychological and emotional effects of racism for people of color through a phenomenologically-based qualitative investigation. Although their study did not focus primarily on retail settings, they do analyze situations where subjects in their study report situations of consumer racial profiling where they are followed around in stores. The authors' analysis attempts to deconstruct racism through a differentiation between two types of racism, and to argue for a distinction that does not currently exist in the literature. They offer a new paradigm for understanding race-based traumatic stress that involves unpacking racism and distinguishing between racial discrimination and harassment. The results of their exploratory investigation support the contention of numerous scholars who claim that racial discrimination and harassment can result in race-related stress reactions. Also, Wakefield and Hudley (2005) investigated male African American adolescents' thinking about responses to racial discrimination, including scenarios involving experiences of racial discrimination while making a purchase at a department store and shopping at a mall. Results were discussed in terms of the social cognitive variables of self-presentation and perceptions of discrimination.

There are also two working papers as exploratory research that address emotional response to consumer racial profiling. Building on the Harris et al. (2005) study, Bright (2006) explored emotional responses to consumer racial profiling cases. Participants read summaries of actual federal court cases involving consumer allegations of racial/ethnic discrimination in retail settings and then rated how the case made them feel on a variety of emotions. She found that participants responded most vigorously to the overt denial case than to the subtle and degradation cases. This finding is consistent with the premise of aversive racism which reveals itself when there are legitimate non-racist excuses available. That is, people are less disturbed by the more subtle acts of discrimination than they are by more blatant ones. In her working paper, Koplove (2006) also explored emotional responses. Her preliminary findings partially supported the hypothesis that perceived retail discrimination that included levels of blatant criminalization would lead to higher incidences of protracted negative emotions.

In another working paper, Gooding (2006) combined mass communication, marketing, psychology, and sociology literature to understand how consumer racial profiling originates. Gooding suggests that African Americans many times experience CRP because of salespeople's, security guards', or management's prejudice, derived from implicit associations and automatic responses that stem from negative stereotypical media images. She argues that, although these media images were hegemonically constructed over centuries and designed for the masses to build negative mental categories of minorities to preserve a white dominant social structure, negative automatic impressions/responses and CRP policies and practices can be changed with training and relationship building between races. She observed, "If these [stereotypical] associations are left unchecked, they will be allowed to affect a company's bottomline and to leave psychological scars that will remain in the minds of African Americans" (p. 17).

The Power-Responsibility Equilibrium Framework

To examine issues related to the increasing concern over marketplace discrimination by both consumers and retailers, we apply the Power-Responsibility Equilibrium (PRE) framework to increase our understanding of how corporate business policies regarding discrimination and regulatory efforts by the government relate to consumer responses. PRE originates from power relationship studies in the field of sociology and social psychology (Emerson, 1962) and holds that social power and social responsibility should go hand in hand (Laczniak & Murphy, 1993). The more powerful partner in a relationship has the societal obligation to ensure an environment of trust and confidence. According to the theory, if a company chooses a strategy of greater domination and less responsibility, the company will lose in the long run as consumers take defensive action to reduce the firm's power. This framework draws upon a long history of research on theories of power-dependence relations. For example, Emerson (1962) proposed a simple theory of power relations to resolve some of the ambiguities surrounding power and authority in social exchanges, and outlined how the weaker party in a relationship can undertake balancing (i.e., defensive) actions to influence the structure of the power-dependence relationship. Both Laczniak and Murphy (1993) and Caudill and Murphy (2000) theoretically discussed the power-responsibility model in a business context. Shenkar and Ellis (1995) applied the framework to business interactions between organizations and their members, and Vlosky, Wilson, and Vlosky (1997) applied it to the franchisor-franchisee relationship. To our knowledge, the framework has not been applied yet to study the relationship between retailers and their customers.

Applying the PRE Framework to Discrimination in Retail Settings

In a retailing context, we use the PRE framework to advance the notion that consumers will balance perceived deficits in protection against mistreatment in the marketplace (i.e., discrimination in "brick and mortar" retail establishments) by power holders (retailers/businesses and government/regulators) with their own defensive actions. The associations between government regulation, business policy, and consumer behavior are integrated into a triad via a single conceptual base model using the PRE framework.

Based on this framework, consumer concern over marketplace perceived discrimination in the retail environment is the endogenous mediating entity between business policy and regulatory perceptions, and negative responses. Our PRE model allows a system perspective that emphasizes how the responsibility shown by power holders can act as a predictor of potentially damaging consumer actions. Consumer concern over perceived marketplace discrimination, rather than being modeled as a dependent variable to policy, or an independent variable to response behaviors, is proposed as a mediating variable between the policy, regulation, and consumer response behaviors. As studies have shown that concern can play both causal and consequential roles, positioning it as an intermediary allows for an examination in an inclusive context.

In this chapter, we build upon the work of Lwin, Williams, and Wirtz (2007) where they apply PRE to online consumer concern over Internet privacy. Here, we apply the PRE framework to marketplace discrimination rather than privacy concern by proposing that the partners in this exchange context are the corporations and government on the one hand (i.e., the power holders in this exchange that should show responsibility), and the consumer on the other (i.e., the party in this exchange that expects responsible use of power by the other two parties). The consumer, as a less dominant party in this interface, would be motivated to generate balancing actions when the power holders are not viewed to be socially responsible. Similarly, Caudill and Murphy (2000) recommended that the PRE model may be useful for explaining ethical issues in online marketing and for understanding online privacy. A similar perspective appears to be indicated by Gronmo (1987) who suggested that technological factors are likely to strengthen corporate power and weaken the consumer's, hence leading to various kinds of consumer actions (Gronmo, 1987).

In Figure 9.1, we show the major components of our PRE framework when applied to marketplace discrimination. On the left side are the two general

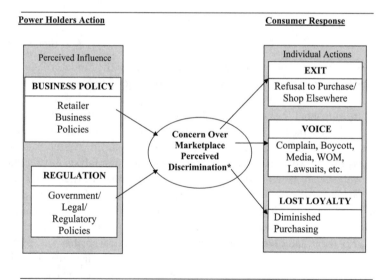

Notes: ☐ Areas that contribute to equilibrium

*Measured using psychological scales, e.g., the Perceived Ethnic Discrimination Questionnaire (Brondolo, et al., 2005), Discrimination Response Index (Wakefield & Hudley, 2005), etc.

Figure 9.1

Power-responsibility equilibrium framework: balancing power holders action and consumer responses due to perceived discrimination in retail settings.

categories of power-yielding influences (the retailer and government). Business Policy is defined as the perceived retailer policy of how the firm exercises its power toward consumers, particularly toward multicultural consumers and situations involving perceived mistreatment based on discrimination. As noted by Laczniak and Murphy (1993), large firms especially have inherent ethical responsibilities based purely on their size and power, and thus should be expected to show social responsibility. Regulation is defined as the perceived regulatory policies of how the various government agencies, the other key power holder, devise and implement laws related to marketplace discrimination. In the middle of the model, the effects of Business Policy and Regulation on consumer behavior are mediated by Concern over Perceived Marketplace Discrimination. On the right side of the model, we show the actions that individual consumers can take to balance the perceived influence of the Power Holders on the left side of the model. The remainder of this section will provide additional background on each of the components in the model.

Business Policy

Retailers represent one of the major Power Holders in the model. When consumers encounter marketplace discrimination, one of the ways they ascertain if the retailer as a Power Holder can be responsive to their concerns is by examining what the corporate policy is concerning treatment of consumers from diverse backgrounds. A company's website is one place where such information should be available. Therefore, as a preliminary step to assess Business Policy, we conducted an exploratory content analysis during 2005 of 57 Web sites of firms based on the 81 cases identified in the Harris et al. (2005) study, where these firms were defendants accused of consumer racial profiling in federal court cases. We found that 35 percent of the sites featured standard practices and codes of conduct with some language associated with CRP, 32 percent had diversity initiatives listed on their websites, and 28 percent indicated on their sites that they had supplier diversity initiatives that support minority businesses. Also, 12 percent of the sites provided news releases and/or articles about diversity issues, CRP case judgments where the firms were victorious, or what they were doing to remedy CRP charges or practices. If one believes the corporate websites, awareness of such Business Policies designed to ensure the fair and equal treatment of customers should reduce concern over marketplace discrimination.

Using the Web site of one firm as an example, in 2001, consumers in 175 cities in 30 states filed a class action lawsuit against Cracker Barrel Old Country Restaurant in which African Americans alleged that they were segregated and forced to sit in the smoking section, or had to wait as white customers were seated quickly, or were not served and were told the restaurant was closing as whites ordered and were served. In 2005, Cracker Barrel's Web site featured a photo of the company's director of outreach (an African American male), a media release about how the company will address claims of discrimination, and strong language used in a new public accommodation policy statement. The policy directed to employees but posted for the public states: "Cracker Barrel's policy of 'Pleasing People' does not include accommodating customer or employee prejudices based on race, or color" (http://www.crackerbarrel.com/).

Regulation

Government regulation represents the other major Power Holder in the model. When consumers encounter marketplace discrimination, one way they ascertain if government regulation can protect them is by examining the various laws concerning consumer racial profiling and marketplace discrimination. Awareness of the laws should reduce consumer concern over marketplace discrimination. We now provide a brief summary of the laws addressing CRP and marketplace discrimination.

Claims of marketplace discrimination can be filed under various state and federal laws. In addition, plaintiffs frequently rely on common law claims. Although these causes of action provide some measure of relief, in most cases, they prevent the racial element of the retailer's conduct from being exposed (Harris, 2003).

Common Law Claims. A typical tort law claim arises when retailers detain customers on suspicion of shoplifting. Under such circumstances, plaintiffs often sue the retailer for false imprisonment and/or assault and battery. Retailers usually defend their conduct as permissible under merchant detention statutes that allow storeowners to protect their goods by detaining and searching "in a reasonable manner shoppers reasonably suspected of shoplifting." Contract law provides another potential common law basis for a marketplace discrimination claim. Racial discrimination of customers arguably violates contract law's duty of good faith and fair dealing. Some legal scholars advocate changes in contract law that would prohibit discrimination in the formation, performance, enforcement, and termination of a contract. While a plaintiff theoretically could bring a marketplace discrimination claim based on the "duty to serve" doctrine, this property law doctrine has become ineffective in protecting individuals from racial discrimination in retail settings. During the eighteenth and nineteenth centuries, "owners of any commercial property that was held open to the public had a duty to serve all patrons." The common law rule has mutated so that it currently immunizes most businesses, except innkeepers and public transportation organizations, from the duty to serve (Harris, 2003).

State Public Accommodations Laws. Forty-five states have enacted legislation prohibiting race discrimination in places of public accommodation. Only Alabama, Georgia, Mississippi, North Carolina, and Texas do not protect people of color when they are treated unfairly in restaurants, hotels, gas stations, and other business establishments. Traditionally, state laws covered places used by travelers such as transport facilities, restaurants, and lodgings, as well as places of entertainment, amusement, or cultural contact. Today, most state statutes treat retail stores as "places of public accommodations" although there is still some variation in terms of the type of establishments that are covered from state to state.

Forty-one states and the District of Columbia have established specific agencies empowered to enforce their public accommodations laws. The role and authority of the civil rights agencies vary from state to state but, in general, they are responsible for educating the public about its rights and the business community about its duties, studying the problem of discrimination, developing policies and procedures, and advising the legislature. Most agencies have the authority to process complaints of discrimination filed by individuals by investigating the complaint, attempting conciliation between the parties, and conducting a hearing whose outcome is subject to judicial review (Harris, 2006).

State public accommodations statutes are underutilized for a variety of reasons. Among them are the meager remedies available to plaintiffs who successfully prove discrimination. In addition, a large number of complaints are conciliated at the agency level so that issues do not reach the courts. Furthermore, a majority of states (29) require individuals to file a claim within 180 days of the alleged discriminatory incident. This relatively short filing deadline precludes individuals from seeking and obtaining redress in some cases.

Federal Laws. Victims of marketplace discrimination have advanced valid claims under the Civil Rights Acts of 1866 and 1964. We briefly describe these two laws and their application to cases of consumer racial profiling and marketplace discrimination. Among its goals, the Civil Rights Act of 1866 was designed to ensure "that a dollar in the hands of a Negro will purchase the same thing as a dollar in the hands of a white man" (Jones v. Alfred H.

Mayer Co., 1968). Plaintiffs who successfully prove intentional discrimination under this act are entitled to both equitable (injunctive) and legal (monetary) relief, including compensatory and punitive damages (Johnson v. Railway Express Agency, 1975). Equitable relief refers to the issuance of a court order prohibiting the defendant from engaging in discriminatory conduct. Section 1981 of the Civil Rights Act of 1866 provides that *"All persons . . . shall have the same right . . . to make and enforce contracts . . . as is enjoyed by white citizens."* The term "make and enforce contracts" includes *"the enjoyment of all benefits, privileges, terms, and conditions of the contractual relationship."* The U.S. Supreme Court has stated that the purpose of Section 1981 was "to remove the impediment of discrimination from a minority citizen's ability to participate fully and equally in the marketplace" (Patterson v. McLean Credit Union, 1989). Similarly, Section 1982 provides that: "All citizens of the United States shall have the same right as is enjoyed by white citizens . . . to purchase personal property." Personal property is any tangible or intangible property that is not real estate. Most courts have narrowly interpreted the scope of Sections 1981 and 1982 by focusing on conduct that prevented the formation of the contract, as opposed to conduct affecting the nature or quality of the contractual relationship. Many federal courts insist that Section 1981 and 1982 plaintiffs must produce evidence that they were denied the opportunity to complete a retail transaction in order to state a valid claim (Harris, 2003). However, in many cases, people of color who are harassed or otherwise treated differently than white customers are not prevented from completing their transaction with the store.

Title II of the Civil Rights Act of 1964 is the federal public accommodations law whose goal is "to ensure that all members of society have equal access to goods and services." It prohibits discrimination in "places of public accommodation" that is, privately-owned institutions that are open to the public (42 U.S.C. §2000a et. seq.). The statute includes in its definition of "places of public accommodation" such commercial establishments as hotels, motels, restaurants, gas stations, theaters, and sports arenas. Title II does not cover most retail stores. This means that the federal public accommodations law allows retail store personnel to discriminate against customers based on their race. There are some exceptions to this rule since the Act does cover retail stores that contain eating establishments as well as eating establishments that are located on the premises of any retail store (Harris, 2006).

Under Title II, an individual is required to notify the appropriate state or local civil rights agency of the alleged discrimination prior to filing suit. Such notification must occur within a certain timeframe established by the state's public accommodations statute, if there is one. Plaintiffs who are not aware of the statutory deadline fail to meet it and their claims are dismissed.

The statute only permits a court to issue equitable or declaratory relief (42 U.S.C. §§ 2000a-3, 2000a-6(b)). As previously noted, equitable relief is non-monetary. Similarly, declaratory relief is a binding adjudication of the rights and status of the litigants even though no relief is awarded. The inability to recover monetary damages for violations of their rights undoubtedly discourages people of color and their lawyers from seeking redress under Title II (Harris, 2006). In sum, current law provides incomplete and inconsistent coverage against race discrimination in retail stores.

Concern Over Perceived Marketplace Discrimination

There have been a number of studies assessing perceived discrimination from a psychological perspective, most of which are described in the above section on an overview of marketplace discrimination studies. Here we briefly discuss some of these same studies but specifically focus on some of the measures and instruments that have been used to test subjects on the perceived discrimination construct. Our emphasis is on understanding some of the research underpinning the middle component of our PRE framework, namely, concern over marketplace perceived discrimination.

In discussing perceived discrimination as a construct, Davidson and Schumann (2005) point out that perceived discrimination is the cognitive appraisal that is triggered by a combination of the target personal factors, situational factors, and agent personal factors. They note that perceived discrimination may evoke one or several emotions including sadness, depression, anxiety, aggression, and anger (Dion, 2001; Mays & Cochran, 2001). Dion contends that perceiving oneself as a target of discrimination is a psychosocial stressor. Such an appraisal is threatening in that "victims impute stable, malevolent motives and intentions to the antagonist(s) and see themselves as a deliberate target of nasty attitudes and behavior by the antagonist(s)" (2001, p. 4). More often than not, targets are unlikely to predict that they will be discriminated against. This unpredictability may serve as an additional source of stress, apart from the appraisal process itself. Studies show that perceived discrimination is correlated with some psychiatric disorders such as depression (Noh & Kaspar, 2003; Mays & Cochran, 2001).

Davidson (2006) points out that there are three perspectives from which the phenomenon of perceived discrimination may be examined—the perspective of the person accused of engaging in the behavior (the actor), the perspective of the person who perceives the action as directed toward him/herself (the target), and the perspective of an observer who is not directly engaged in the encounter (3rd person). Davidson (2006) summarizes social psychology research examining each perspective (actor, target, and observer) and provides key findings from this research. She notes that each of these perspectives may be different even when describing the same event (Shelton & Richeson, 2005).

> People construct rather than simply record their experiences, in that they assign personal, social and cultural meaning to the events and outcomes of their stories thereby giving meaning, relevance and value to experiences that would otherwise just be a sequence of happenings. (Friend & Thompson, 2003, p. 24)

Empirical evidence has found an actor's perceptions of his/her own racial bias to be only weakly correlated to targets' and observers' perceptions of the actor's racial bias (Dovidio, Kawakami, & Gaertner, 2002).

Wakefield and Hudley (2005) developed and tested a Discrimination Response Index (DRI) in a study investigating male African American adolescents' thinking about responses to racial discrimination. They used the DRI to assess responses to scenarios describing students who experienced racial discrimination in various settings, including making a purchase at a department store and shopping at a mall. Two types of scores are derived from the DRI: (1) cross-situational response scores (each response type summed across scenarios); and (2) situation-specific response scores (each response type within each scenario).

In another working paper, Koplove (2006) used the *Perceived Ethnic Discrimination Questionnaire–Community Version* (PEDQ) (Brondolo et al., 2005) in examining emotional responses to marketplace discrimination. Participants related a personal story of a negative retail experience, whether and why/why not they believed this incident was a consequence of their ethnicity, and how they responded to the discriminatory treatment. Then, subjects rated their emotional responses on 13 emotions taken from the PEDQ.

Consumer Action

There have been a number of studies delineating various individual responses to perceived discrimination in general, and perceived marketplace discrimination specifically, particularly in retail settings. We briefly discuss some of this research, the different types of responses, and summarize the three types of responses we proposed for our application of the PRE framework to retail settings.

In developing their model, Davidson and Schumann (2005) discuss coping strategies. They refer to the work of Stephens and Gwinner (1998) that describes coping strategies as the actions one uses to decrease a stressful event. There are three general coping strategies: "problem-focused," "emotion-focused," and "avoidance." Problem-focused strategies are action-oriented strategies aimed at resolving the stress incurred as a result of perceived discrimination. Crockett et al. (2003) identified the following problem-focused strategies: formal complaints, outing, and word-of-mouth. Formal complaints are primarily intended to produce a sense of retribution. Outing refers to the target publicly confronting the actor. Word-of-mouth strategies may serve as a social support mechanism for the target. Davidson and Schumann (2005) suggest that there appear to be two other problem-focused strategies that are applicable for targets of discrimination: going public with the allegations of discrimination to media outlets and seeking legal redress.

The two remaining coping "emotion-focused" and "avoidance" strategies also are discussed by Davidson and Schumann (2005). Emotion-focused strategies are inwardly-directed strategies that are designed to protect the target in the face of perceived harm (Stephens & Gwinner, 1998). While Crockett et al. (2003) identify "non-confrontation" and "internalization" as two emotion-focused strategies for targets of discrimination, Davidson and Schumann (2005) suggest that "non-confrontation" might better fit as an "avoidance" strategy. Internalization results in the target bearing some or all of the psychological responsibility of perceived discrimination. Davidson and Schumann (2005) suggest that an example of "internalization" would be a customer attributing discriminatory treatment as his/her fault for failing to dress appropriately; such a strategy allows the target to maintain a sense of control over his/her well-being. Finally, avoidance coping strategies involve circumventing discrimination by distancing oneself from the situation. As noted above, Davidson and Schumann (2005) would classify Non-confrontation as such a strategy.

In their study, Wakefield and Hudley (2005) point out that understanding the psychological and physical consequences for those who endure ethnic and racial discrimination requires examining how people respond to and cope with such behavior (Krieger & Sidney, 1996; Phinney & Chavira, 1995). They point to the models of adult behavior developed by Feagin and Sikes (Feagin, 1991; Feagin & Sikes, 1994) that postulated four distinct types of responses to discrimination (withdrawal, resigned acceptance, verbal, and physical confrontation). These responses included withdrawing from the situation of discrimination, ignoring the discrimination while continuing the interaction, verbally challenging the discrimination, and physically responding to the discrimination.

Based on the above discussion of research and conceptualization of responses to perceived discrimination, in our PRE framework on the right side of Figure 9.1, we focus on individual consumer responses to heightened concern over perceived marketplace discrimination, e.g., refusing to purchase, shopping elsewhere, complaining, boycotting the store, generating media attention over mistreatment, negative word-of-mouth, filing lawsuits, loss of store loyalty, etc. We group these consumer responses into the three domains of Exit, Voice, and Lost Loyalty. In *Exit, Voice, and Loyalty,* Hirschman (1970), a noted economist, describes a similar set of strategies: (1) exit (leave the store), (2) voice (complain, file a lawsuit, and so forth), and (3) loyalty (accept and continue to purchase from the retailer). Collectively, these strategies are what Emerson (1962) would call in PRE lingo "balancing operations," and are the consequences of a perceived imbalance in the power-dependence relationship.

Conclusion

It seems clear that vestiges of race and ethnic discrimination continue to create vexing problems in the retail sector. It also seems clear that additional research is needed to assist retailers in dealing with these issues. Davidson (2004) notes that the literature shows that *perceived* discrimination is indeed a *real* problem in marketing environments for ethnic minorities. A number of variables that influence perceived discrimination have been well evidenced by social psychologists. However, she points out that there is a need to examine these variables specifically in a marketing context. To address this need, we have presented a Power-Responsibility Equilibrium framework as one approach. We feel that the most significant contribution of this framework is that it gives retailers an opportunity to assess how consumer concern over perceived discrimination can trigger negative consumer responses detrimental to their business. This can occur when consumers feel a need to employ these actions as balancing mechanisms when the perceived influence of business policies and government regulation of the Power Holders heightens consumer concern over perceived marketplace discrimination.

In this chapter we propose the PRE model as a potential conceptual framework to assess consumer response to current marketplace discrimination. For future research, we suggest that the framework be used for empirical studies. For example, the PRE framework could be used in an experimental study employing various scenarios that manipulate different levels of perceived influence by the Power Holders (i.e., Business Policy by retailers and Regulation by government). The scenario approach is similar to that used by other researchers. For example, Wakefield and Hudley (2005) developed five hypothetical scenarios that assessed Feagin's (1991) initial four response types to acts of racial discrimination. Also, Bright (2006) and Koplove (2006), in their exploratory work, used the scenario approach. In a PRE context, scenarios could be based on actual court cases of consumer racial profiling and marketplace discrimination, using the dimensions of discrimination developed by Harris, et al. (2005): (1) the type of discrimination (overt or subtle); (2) the level of service (degradation or denial); and (3) suspicion of criminal treatment (present or not). Based on actual court cases, Table 9.1 provides

Table 9.1 Summaries of Four Types of Cases Based on Actual Marketplace Retail Discrimination Cases

The four types of case classification are based on Harris, et al. (2005).

I. Subtle Degradation

Defendant: Dillard's Department Store

Case: Chapman v. The Higbee Company, 256 F.3d 416 (2001), vacated by 270 F.3d 297 (6th Cir., 2001).

Summary of Case: Chapman is an African-American woman who was shopping at Dillard's. She decided to try on some clothes. As she entered a fitting room that a white woman had just left, Ms. Chapman noticed a "sensor tag" on the floor. She tried on some clothing, decided not to purchase anything, and hung the clothes back on the hangers. She left the fitting room to return the clothing to the racks. A sales assistant then entered the fitting room and noticed the sensor tag on the floor. She notified security. A Dillard security guard then stopped Chapman and directed her back to the fitting room. He and a female manager checked Chapman's purse and her clothing, but nothing was found. Chapman pointed out the white woman she had seen exiting the fitting room before she entered, but the security guard did not detain the white woman. The manager apologized to Chapman and Chapman left the store. Dillard's motion for summary judgment was granted; a panel of the 6th Circuit Court of Appeals affirmed the trial court's decision (2001); the panel's decision was vacated by the 6th Circuit sitting en banc (2001).

II. Overt Degradation

Defendant: J.C. Penney Department store

Case: Lewis v. J.C. Penney, 948 F.Supp. 367 (D.Del. 1996).

Summary of Case: Ms. Lewis, a black woman, and her friend, a white woman, went shopping at a J.C. Penney store with their children, made several purchases, and left the store. As they approached Ms. Lewis' car in the store's parking lot, the store's security guards asked the two women to return to the store for the guards to inspect their bags. The guards conducted the search in the loss prevention office. In her complaint, Ms. Lewis claimed that the search of her bags was completely different from the cursory search of her friend's bag and a simple glance at her receipt despite the fact that she had accumulated far more merchandise than Ms. Lewis. In contrast, after ascertaining that Ms. Lewis' bags contained no stolen merchandise, the guard requested her identification and questioned her about a discrepancy between the name on her charge card and the name on her work identification card. The incident lasted between ten and twenty minutes after which one of the guards apologized to the women. J.C. Penney's motion for summary judgment was granted (1996).

Table 9.1 (Continued)

III. Subtle Denial

Defendant: Ocean Mecca Motel

Case: Murrell v. Ocean Mecca Motel, Inc., 262 F.3d 253 (4th Cir. 2001).

Summary of Case: Mrs. Murrell, a white woman, took her two African American grandsons and their mother on a weekend trip to the beach. She entered a motel's office to inquire about room availability while the remainder of her family stayed in the car. She checked into the motel for two nights and paid the bill in advance with cash. The family then deposited their bags in the room and headed for the outdoor pool. Within a few minutes, the desk clerk appeared at the pool and demanded that they leave immediately. When asked: "Why? What did we do?" the clerk said, "I want you off my premises now!" He did not respond to their repeated requests for an explanation. The clerk attempted to withhold $50 for a room-cleaning charge, but Mrs. Murrell protested that her family had occupied the room for less than ten minutes and eventually received a full refund. Later, the clerk claimed that he was enforcing the four-person room occupancy limit. The Murrell party consisted of four people and the motel's brochure and website stated that all rooms had between five- and seven-person limits.

IV. Overt Denial

Defendant: Wal-Mart Discount Department Store

Case: Cedeno v. Wal-Mart Stores, Inc., 1999 WL 1129638 (E.D. Pa. 1999).

Summary of Case: Plaintiffs, who are Hispanic, were shopping in a Wal-Mart store. One member of the party was accused of shoplifting. During the discussion with the police, Wal-Mart's assistant manager told all four plaintiffs that they were prohibited from returning to the store. As they were leaving, plaintiffs heard the assistant manager say that "Spanish people come here to steal." The following week, two of the plaintiffs returned to the store with other relatives, including children. The assistant manager called the police. The police asked for IDs. No one had any. One of the plaintiffs became angry and the police arrested the three adults in the party. Plaintiffs concede that, although they shopped at Wal-Mart frequently prior to this incident, they had never encountered discriminatory treatment there. The court found that, besides the assistant manager's unfortunate comment, the record presented a straight-forward picture of a retail store responding to incidents of shoplifting, trespassing, and disorderly conduct on its premises. In granting Wal-Mart's motion to dismiss the case, the court stated that the isolated comment was insufficient to convert otherwise reasonable conduct into race-based discrimination.

four categories of case examples by combining the first two dimensions (type of discrimination and level of service) to create the four categories of Subtle Degradation, Overt Degradation, Subtle Denial, and Overt Denial. A case is classified as overt when discrimination is obvious and specific. A case is classified as subtle if the discrimination is ambiguous and nonspecific. A case is classified as degradation when the consumer receives diminution in the level of service and/or product. A case is classified as denial when the consumer is not allowed access to the service and/or product.

We feel that it is critical for people of color to remain vigilant to the remaining vestiges of segregation and discrimination, understand their legal rights, hold Power Holders accountable, and make their voices heard when they encounter marketplace discrimination. We also feel that it is critical for researchers and retailers to better understand consumer responses to marketplace discrimination if they hope to effectively reach all consumers, both majority and minority, cultivate them as customers, and maintain their loyalty. Retail success in the 21st century will only come to those retailers who understand the diversity of the marketplace and what they must do in terms of retail strategies to not only recognize that diversity but value it.

References

Bean, L. (2001, April 18). *Retail racial profiling: Retrain staff to focus on customer service.* Retrieved April 18 from www.DiversityInc.com

Bean, L. (2003, October, November). Legal: What happened to diversity's bad boys Texaco, Denny's, Coca-Cola? *DiversityInc.*, 111–116.

Bright, J. (2006). *Emotional responses to consumer racial profiling cases.* Working Paper, Salem State College Psychology Department, Salem, MA.

Brondolo, E., Kelly, K. P., Coakley, V., Gordon, T., Thompson, S., & Levy, E., (2005). The perceived ethnic discrimination questionnaire: Development and preliminary validation of a community version. *Journal of Applied Social Psychology, 35*(2), 335–365.

Carter, R. T., Forsyth, J. M., Mazzula, S. L., & Williams, B. (2005). Racial discrimination and race-based traumatic stress: An exploratory investigation. In R. T. Carter (Ed.), *Handbook of racial-cultural psychology and counseling: Training and practice,* (Vol. 2), (pp. 447–476). Hoboken, NJ: Wiley.

Caudill, E. M., & Murphy, P. E. (2000, Spring). Consumer online privacy: Legal and ethical issues. *Journal of Public Policy and Marketing, 19*, 7–19.

Crockett, D., Grier, S. A., & Williams, J. A. (2003). Coping with marketplace discrimination: An exploration of the experiences of Black men. *Academy of Marketing Science Review, 4*, 1–21.

Davidson, E. F. (2006). *Shopping while black: A study of perceptions of discrimination in retail settings.* (Doctoral dissertation proposal, University of Tennessee, Department of Marketing, Logistics and Transportation, Knoxville, Tennessee).

Davidson, E. F., & Schumann, D. (2004). Shopping while black: Antecedents of perceived discrimination in retail settings. *Proceedings from the Academy of Marketing Science Cultural Perspectives on Marketing Conference.* Puebla, Mexico.

Davidson, E. F., & Schumann, D. (2005). *Shopping while black: An examination of perceived discrimination in retail settings.* Working Paper. University of Tennessee, Department of Marketing, Logistics and Transportation, Knoxville, Tennessee.

Dion, K. L. (2001). The psychology of perceived prejudice and discrimination. *Canadian Psychology, 43*, 1–10.

Dovidio, J. F., Kawakami, K., & Gaertner, S. L. (2002). Implicit and explicit prejudice and interracial interaction. *Journal of Personality and Social Psychology, 82*(1), 62–68.

Emerson, R. M. (1962). Power-dependence relations. *American Sociological Review, 27*, 31–40.

Feagin, J. R. (1991, February). The continuing significance of race: Antiblack discrimination in public places. *American Sociological Review, 56*, 101–116.

Feagin, J. R., & Sikes, M. P. (1994). *Living with racism: The black middle class experience.* Boston: Beacon Press.

Friend, L. A., & Thompson, S. M. (2003). Identity, ethnicity and gender: Using narratives to understand their meaning in retail shopping encounters. *Consumption, Markets and Culture, 6*(1), 23–41.

Gabbidon, S. L. (2003, August). Racial profiling by store clerks and security personnel in retail establishments. *Journal of Contemporary Criminal Justice, 19*, 345–364.

Gooding, V. A. (2006). *The African-American shopping experience: Relationships between stereotypes, implicit association, automatic response & consumer racial profiling.* Working Paper, University of Texas, School of Advertising, Austin, Texas.

Gronmo, S. (1987). Technology, information and power: A rejoinder. *Journal of Consumer Policy, 10*, 453.

Harris, A. G. (2003). Shopping while black: Applying 42 U.S.C. § 1981 to cases of consumer racial profiling. *Boston College Third World Law Journal, 23*(1), 1–57.

Harris, A. G. (2006). A survey of federal and state public accommodations statutes: Evaluating their effectiveness in cases of retail discrimination. *Virginia Journal of Social Policy and the Law, 13*, 331–394.

Harris, A., Henderson, G. R., & Williams, J. D. (2005). Courting consumers: Assessing consumer racial profiling and other marketplace discrimination. *Journal of Public Policy & Marketing, 24*(1), 163–171.

Henderson, T. P. (2001, June). Perception that some merchants practice racial profiling generates debate. *Stores, 83*(6), 26–32.

Henderson, T. P. (2004, February). Another potential solution. Retrieved February 2004, from http://www.stores.org/archives/chief.asp

Hirschman, A. O. (1970). *Exit, voice, and loyalty.* Cambridge, MA: Harvard University Press.

Humphreys, J. M. (2004). The multicultural economy 2004: America's minority buying power. *Georgia Business and Economic Conditions, 64*(3), Retrieved October 27, 2006, from http://www.selig.uga.edu/forecast/GBEC/GBEC043Q.pdf

Knickerbocker, B. (2000, January 14). New face of racism in America: Retailers denying checks and cab drivers refusing rides in minority. *The Christian Science Monitor,* 1.

Koplove, M. A. (2006). *Criminal treatment and confrontation in retail discrimination.* Working paper. Salem State College Psychology Department, Salem, MA.

Krieger, N., & Sidney, S. (1996). Racial discrimination and blood pressure: The CARDIA study of young black and white adults. *American Journal of Public Health, 86*, 1370–1378.

Laczniak, E. R., & Murphy, P. E. (1993). *Ethical marketing decisions: The higher road.* Boston: Allyn & Bacon.

Lee, J. (2000). The salience of race in everyday life: Black customers' shopping experiences in black and white neighborhoods. *Work and Occupations, 27*(3), 353–376.

Lwin, M. O., & Williams, J. D. (2004). A model integrating the multidimensional developmental theory of privacy and theory of planned behavior to examine fabrication of information online. *Marketing Letters, 14*(4), 257–272.

Lwin, M. O., Williams, J. D., & Wirtz, J. (2004). The effects of consumer concern for personal information privacy on the Internet: A power-responsibility equilibrium model. Working Paper. National University of Singapore.

Mays, V. M., & Cochran, S. D. (2001). Mental health correlates of perceived discrimination among lesbian, gay and bisexual adults in the United States. *American Journal of Public Health, 91*, 1869–1876.

Morin, R., & Cottman, M. H. (2001, June 22). Discrimination's lingering sting: Minorities tell of profiling, other bias. *Washington Post*, p. A1.

Nakao, A. (2001, September 28). Arab Americans caught in profile snare: Detained, denied boarding or kicked off planes for looking Middle Eastern. *The San Francisco Chronicle*, p. A1.

National Telecommunications and Information Administration (NITA). (2002). *A nation online: How Americans are expanding their use of the Internet.* Washington, DC: U.S. Department of Commerce.

Noh, S., & Kaspar, V. (2003, February). Perceived discrimination and depression: Moderating effects of coping, acculturation, and ethnic support. *American Journal of Public Health, 93*(2), 232–238.

Phinney, J. S., & Chavira, V. (1995). Parental ethnic socialization and adolescent coping with problems related to ethnicity. *Journal of Research on Adolescence, 5*, 31–53.

Shelton, J. N., & Richeson, J. A. (2005). Intergroup contact and pluralistic ignorance, *Journal of Personality and Social Psychology, 88*(1), 91–107.

Shenkar, O., & Ellis, S. (1995). Death of the organization man: Temporal relations in strategic alliances. *The International Executive, 37*, 537.

Stephens, N., & Gwinner, K .P. (1998). Why don't some people complain? A cognitive-emotive process model of consumer complaint behavior. *Journal of the Academy of Marketing Science, 26*(3), 172–189.

Valia, M. (2001). Racial profiling, discrimination still prevalent, survey finds. *DiversityInc.com*, Retrieved June 25, 2006, from http://diversityinc.com/

Vlosky, R. P., Wilson, D., & Vlosky, R. (1997). Closing the interorganizational information systems relationship satisfaction gap. *Journal of Marketing Practice, 3*(2), 75.

Wakefield, W. D., & Hudley, C. (2005, Summer). African American male adolescents' preferences in responding to racial discrimination: Effects of ethnic identity and situational influences. *Adolescence, 40*(158), 237–256.

Williams, J. D., Harris, A. G., & Henderson, G. R. (2006a). Equal treatment for equal dollars in Illinois: Assessing consumer racial profiling and other marketplace discrimination. *The Law Enforcement Executive Forum, 5*(7), 83–104.

Williams, J. D., Harris, A. G., & Henderson, G. R. (2006b). States of denial and degradation both subtle and overt: Marketplace discrimination across America. In I. M. Martin, D. W. Stewart, & M. Kamins (Eds.), *Marketing & public policy conference proceedings, 16*, Chicago: American Marketing Association.

Williams, J. D., Henderson, G. R., & Harris, A. (2001, November–December). Consumer racial profiling in retailing: Bigotry goes to market. *The New Crisis, 108,* 22–24.

Williams, J. D., & Snuggs, T. (1997). Survey of attitudes toward customer ethnocentrism and shopping in retail stores: The role of race. In C. Pechmann & S. Ratneshwar (Eds.), *Society for consumer psychology 1997 winter conference proceedings* (pp. 161–162). Postdam, NY: Society for Consumer Psychology.

THIRD-PARTY EFFECTS IN SERVICESCAPE ENVIRONMENTS: INSIGHTS FROM URBAN CONSUMERS IN APARTHEID AND POST-APARTHEID SOUTH AFRICA

Julie A. Ruth

Rutgers University-Camden, School of Business

Crossroad: A place where two or more roads intersect; any center of congregation or activity for a widespread area.

Webster's New World Dictionary, 1988, p. 331

*A*LTHOUGH INTERNET SHOPPING HAS captured the imagination of consumers, retailers, and academics, most of the world's consumers still shop for goods and services in physical rather than virtual settings. Shopping in physical retail environments is an activity that serves not only functional purposes such as obtaining sought-after goods and services, but also provides entertainment and emotional value (Babin, Darden, & Griffin, 1994; Wakefield & Baker, 1998; Arnold & Reynolds, 2003). The retail shopping environment is also a crossroads for a society and her people, as the consumer interacts with salespeople and third parties in the servicescape (Bitner, 1992; Grove & Fisk, 1997; Bloch, Ridgway, & Dawson, 1994; Sherry, 1998). It is this notion of servicescape as crossroads for social activity—and the influence of third parties on the consumer in that environment—that is the subject of this chapter.

Perhaps nowhere in the world is the social milieu of the servicescape more in flux than the Republic of South Africa. For most of the 20th century, and especially during the 1948–1990 time period, the apartheid system of government denied South Africans of color the right to vote, live where they wished, and other freedoms of movement and choice. The apartheid system of laws and customs endorsed and enforced a separation of peoples based on categories that defined the population in terms of race[1]: Africans/Blacks, Coloureds (mixed-race), Indian, or White. For example, with the passage of the *Group Areas Act* in 1950, South Africans of color were forcibly removed from town centers to "locations" or "townships" that were segregated by race. With the *Native Laws Amendment and Pass Act* of 1952, Black South Africans and other people of color[2] were required to carry identification passbooks that stipulated spheres of legal movement (Ross, 1999). These and many other government actions resulted in minority White domination over the Black majority and other people of color, and had numerous effects such as limiting shopping and retail service opportunities by race. Laws and customs further dictated the way in which retail establishments were patronized. Entrances to retail establishments, queues for information or service, and other retail amenities such as toilets were labeled and segregated by race (Ross, 1999).

With the transition to a democratic system of government in 1994, and the adoption of a new constitution acknowledged as one of the most progressive in the world, all South Africans are now in theory free to live, work, and shop where they wish. As a result, South Africa is experiencing significant changes in its political, social, and economic institutions (Sparks, 1995; Boshoff & van Eeden, 2001; Burgess & Harris, 1999). Servicescapes are in great flux, with new patterns of where and how South Africans shop and consume.

Because of heightened attention to race during the 20th century and the entrenched persistence of race-based beliefs and attitudes (Smith, Stones, & Naidoo, 2003), the changing patterns of shopping activity and behavior are likely to make the race of third-party strangers salient to consumers in South African servicescapes. As noted by Fiske (1993), an individual's race is one of the most visually and immediately accessible pieces of information available for use in categorizing people in social contexts. Stereotypes are considered to be social categories that are associated with "beliefs about the characteristics, attributes, and behaviors of certain groups," and are used in making

---

[1] During the apartheid era, South Africans were identified and labeled according to physical traits associated with race such as skin color, hair, eyes, and the like. The term race is still commonly used in South Africa and by South Africans. The term race rather than ethnicity will be used throughout. See also Grier and Deshpandé (2001).

[2] Following Henderson et al. (1999), people of color is a term used to describe non-Whites.

sense of the social world (Hilton & von Hippel, 1996, p. 240). That is, "people use stereotypes to the extent they seem to have explanatory value," giving rise to inferences, evaluations, and in-group/out-group effects (Fiske, 1993, p. 166). Consistent with these notions, Grier and Brumbaugh (2005) found that when evaluating ads, South African consumers were sensitive to the race of individuals depicted in the persuasive communication.

Consumer research has examined third-party or stranger effects in service-scapes but without emphasis on race. Two types of stranger influence have been identified: (1) overt, face-to-face encounters between shopper and third party including, for example, one party seeking or receiving help, admiring another consumer's ability or choice, competing in some way, or expressing complaints about service; and (2) covert, indirect, non-face-to-face encounters such as unobtrusively observing or following another (McGrath & Otnes, 1995; see also Grove & Fisk, 1997). Argo, Dahl, and Manchanda (2005) propose that noninteractive social presence—described as a situation where a social entity is physically present but is not involved or engaged with the shopper—exerts influence through size, proximity, and strength or importance of the other. Argo et al. (2005), for example, found that the "mere presence" of others affects emotions and self-presentation under conditions where a relatively larger number of others are in close proximity.

This study, then, seeks to understand influence arising from consumer observation of salient visible characteristics of third-party shoppers, such as race. Investigating such third-party influence in a society in great flux such as South Africa may provide greater access to perceptions, attitudes, and experiences that might be present but less accessible to shopper-informants in other countries and cultural contexts.

Method

This study was part of a larger one where depth interviews were conducted with 80 South Africans regarding consumption lifestyles in apartheid and post-apartheid times (see Ruth, 2006). Depth interviews were used because of the ease with which informants could relate lifestyle and consumption experiences. Interviews also afforded ample opportunity to probe for a fuller understanding of each informant's current and past life situation and experiences.

The Informants, Interviews, and Interviewers

The research was conducted from 2003–2005 among consumers in large and medium urban centers in South Africa including Cape Town, Port Elizabeth,

Durban, Johannesburg, and Pretoria. Interviews were conducted in community centers, homes, offices, or public places. Each interview lasted between 20 minutes and 2 hours. Informants ranged in age from early 20s to 70s. Interviews were conducted in English and were occasionally augmented with translation assistance to or from Xhosa or Zulu, two of South Africa's 11 official languages. Some informants were recruited by a marketing research firm and received remuneration for their participation; other informants were recruited by the author and received a token of appreciation.

Following McCracken (1988), a guide for interview questions and prompts was developed. Interviews began with conversation to set a friendly tone, put the informant at ease, and elicit background information about the informant's life context such as family and work status, education, and area of residence. Interview topics included current lifestyle, life circumstances during apartheid, and/or a product that had transforming effects. In the course of the interview, nearly every informant self-identified with one of four labels that were, and still are, widely used to refer to an individual's race: Black [B], Coloured [C], Indian [I], or White [W], which account for 79 percent, 9 percent, 3 percent, and 9 percent of the population respectively (Statistics South Africa, 2005). Nearly 50 percent of informants for this study were Black, with a relatively even distribution among other races.

Interviews were conducted by the author (White female, 40s) and a graduate student (African American female, 30s) trained in interview research methods. Informants sometimes referred to the interviewers as American, suggesting an outsider status that likely lessened some presumptions that would have been in place based on race, had the researchers been South African. Rapport was usually quickly established, and informants shared extensive and far-ranging life experiences including fears, courage, hopes, physical suffering, joys, and ethical lapses. Interviews were audiotaped and then transcribed, with the exception of two interviews summarized with field notes.

Analysis

In the course of these interviews, 40 informants related servicescape experiences; texts from these interviews form the data for this study. The analysis is interpretive and involved reading and rereading the text to derive understanding of third-party influence processes and characteristics that distinguish them. Informants are referred to by pseudonyms; the informant's race, gender, and age are provided in brackets. Italicized portions of informants' comments reflect third-party influence.

Interpretation

The interpretation begins with an overview of servicescape environments in apartheid and post-apartheid South Africa, followed by a presentation of five third-party influence processes that stem from sensitivity to race of others in the servicescape.

Shopping and Retail Service Delivery in Apartheid and Post-Apartheid Times

Until the end of apartheid, "the country tended to reflect the shopping needs and aspirations of the [minority] White segment of the population. . . . Most major . . . shopping developments were located in White suburban" areas or town centers (Wiese, 1997, p. 231). The needs and circumstances of the majority of South Africans were largely ignored by formal-sector retailers. South Africans of color were typically served by Black, Coloured, or Indian entrepreneurs operating in their respective race-based townships (Wiese, 1997). Further, shopping in large chain stores was difficult for South Africans of color because of the distance between town centers and townships where people of color were required to live.

Not unlike consumers in Crockett and Wallendorf's (2004) study of Black Milwaukee and the costs associated with outshopping, South Africans of color faced—and still face—economic and other costs associated with travel between townships and shops in town by formal transportation (e.g., public buses) or informal transportation (e.g., unregulated "taxi" vans; see Wiese, 1997). In addition, during apartheid, being in town without one's pass could result in a person of color being jailed, as recalled by Noziga [B, F, 40s]: "My mother-in-law sent my husband to the shop, he didn't carry his pass. He ended up in jail. . . . This guy [who owns the retail shop in town] knows my husband . . . but it was the law" during the apartheid era for people of color to have their passes available for inspection at all times.

With the end of apartheid, South Africans of color are able to—and do—shop in formerly White-dominated servicescapes. In addition, several informants perceived that chain grocery stores such as Pick N Pay and clothing stores such as Pages are now recognizing needs and buying power in Black, Coloured, and Indian communities, and have opened stores closer to or directly in these communities. Still, South African consumers of all races often shop in local retail establishments because of proximity to home or work. Retail establishments in townships frequently were—and still are—informal. Common types of informal retail establishments include: *shabeens*, where township residents gather in modest structures or shacks for drinking and socializing; outdoor or home-based retail enterprises that offer goods like clothing or fruits and vegetables; or convenience store-like *spazas*[3] where consumers buy a limited assortment of grocery items such as milk, bread, a box of tea bags, or even one tea bag. For example, Mary [B, F, 30s] periodically travels from her shack in an informal settlement to a small, nearby grocery to purchase a card that enables her to use electricity—sparingly because of its expense—for chores like ironing or entertainment such as watching TV.

Third-Party Influence Processes

The analysis uncovered five types of processes through which third parties exert influence on consumers in the servicescape through consumers' sensitivity to race-based characteristics. Huston (1983) describes influence as a process by which an individual or group affects or changes the thoughts, actions, or emotions of another. Table 10.1 summarizes the five influence processes uncovered in this study, as well as characteristics distinguishing them including whether the third party is physically present in the servicescape, relationship of the third party and consumer, and level of contact during the episode. Consistent with Grove and Fisk (1997), who observed that third parties can positively or negatively affect a range of consumer behavior, Table 10.1 also addresses effects of these processes on the consumer's servicescape experience.

Gazing upon others from afar in the servicescape.   One of the hallmarks of brick-and-mortar retailing is that the consumer is participating in a physical environment, which is almost always populated by other consumers (Bitner, 1992). While in the process of satisfying functional needs to obtain goods and services, consumers gaze upon unknown third parties in this social milieu. Consistent with the mere presence effect articulated by Latané (1981), the consumer does not interact directly with strangers but rather takes in information about the other from afar. If the observed characteristics of the third party are largely expected, relatively little attention is directed toward such fellow consumers. If third-party characteristics are somewhat unexpected, attention is devoted to them. Thus, influence occurs because the presence of the third party affects the content and direction of the consumer's thoughts (Huston, 1983).

---

[3] Spaza is a Xhosa word meaning "hidden," which "originated at the time when the average spaza had to be hidden from the authorities to avoid fines for selling illegal products or at illegal times" (Wiese, 1997, p. 232).

In South Africa, the race of third parties is often the subject of such consumer attention. For example, in the apartheid era, the *Prohibition of Mixed Marriages Act* of 1949 made interracial marriage illegal (Ross, 1999), and encounters with mixed-race couples were rare. Post-apartheid encounters with mixed-race couples in servicescape contexts can elicit consumer attention if the observed characteristic of these third parties is unexpected and unfamiliar to the consumer:

> My younger sister, a few years ago, she [a Coloured woman] got married
> to a White Afrikaner. . . . But, at first, the people couldn't understand. I
> mean, me myself . . . I said [to my sister] . . . "Are you sure?" . . . *[Nowadays]*
> *you see it [mixed-race couples] in the Waterfront [shopping area], even in*
> *here [Canal Walk, a very large, up-market shopping venue in Cape Town],*
> *how many mixed couples. There was a stage [when] me too [I said], "Wow!*
> *Look at this [White] man and this Black lady [when I would see them here]."*
> (C, M, 40s)

The servicescape provides an opportunity for individuals to observe the social world around them in what Sandikci and Holt (1998, p. 323) describe as "the discreet dance of sociality and accepted voyeurism." Through this voyeurism, the thoughts of the consumer are influenced (see Huston, 1983) by the presence of third parties in the social environment of the servicescape. Still, because the third party is relatively distant from the consumer and there is no direct interaction, the consumer's servicescape experience in a narrow sense is largely unaffected. In a larger sense, repeated observation of changes in the social world would be expected to affect overall attitudes toward what Latané (1997) refers to as salient characteristics, such as observing that couples are mixed race.

"Rubbing shoulders" with third parties in close but superficial contact in the servicescape. In comparison to gazing upon third parties from afar, sometimes third parties come in closer contact with the consumer because they are "sharing the same physical space and time with a group of strangers" (Sandikci & Holt, 1998, p. 323). Similar to Grove and Fisk (1997), who studied tourists visiting U.S. theme parks, these third parties are unknown strangers with whom consumers come in close but limited and superficial physical contact.

Consumers in this study were highly attuned to the race of third-party shoppers in close proximity. In the apartheid era, relating to dissimilar others was highly prescribed and not common in servicescape contexts. With the transition to democracy, coming in close physical contact with dissimilar

Table 10.1 Characteristics of Third-Party Influence on Servicescape Consumers

Process by which Third Party Becomes Salient	Third Party Physically Present in Servicescape?	Third-Party Relationship to Consumer	Level of Contact with Consumer in the Servicescape	Example from Urban Consumers in Apartheid and Post-Apartheid South Africa	Influence Effect
Gazing: Consumer gazes upon third parties from afar, and attends to visible characteristics associated with them	Yes	Stranger	Consumer observes third parties from afar	Observing mixed-race couples at shopping mall	Changes the thoughts of the consumer; provides information to consumer about society but does not necessarily affect consumer's servicescape experience *per se*
"Rubbing Shoulders:" Consumer comes in contact with third party who is nearby in the servicescape and attends to visible characteristics associated with them	Yes	Stranger	Physical proximity may elicit brief and superficial interaction; consumer is close enough to observe third party's servicescape experience	Standing in service line with other shoppers; pushing one's "trolley" past others while shopping; observing how other consumers are treated in servicescape	Affects valence of consumer's experience; may affect consumer's self-esteem (e.g., pride, feeling of being a human being)

Ideating: Consumer activates mental representation of third parties	No	Third parties are represented in consumer's mind by categories and stereotypes	Consumer interacts mentally with the concept of third parties	In the absence of actual observation, consumer considers (mentally) how others were or are treated	Shapes perceptions of encounters in multiple ways, as the activated category is used in information processing (e.g., standard of comparison for evaluating service quality)
Anticipating and Acting: Consumer anticipates and acts on likely actions of categorized third parties	No	Third parties, and their likely behavior, are represented in consumer's mind by categories and stereotypes; possibility of direct interaction is considered	Consumer mentally considers third parties' likely actions, and then acts on them	Beliefs about where and when crimes are likely to be committed, and by whom, affects shopping behavior	Affects consumers' thoughts, feelings, and actions including likelihood of engaging in the servicescape
Interacting: Consumer and third party interact directly while in the servicescape; consumer attends to visible characteristics associated with them	Yes	Known and familiar, or strangers	Consumer interacts directly with person accompanying them, or third-party stranger in the servicescape	Third-party pressure to participate in boycotts of "town" shops	Interpersonal influence on consumer attitudes and behaviors including store, product, and brand choice

others can be a novel situation. Consistent with theories of social cognition, consumers attend to those with unexpected or unfamiliar characteristics (Fiske, 1993; Latané, 1981), such as being of a different race.

> There are a lot of changes [from apartheid to contemporary times]! Lots!
> . . . . We've got all these things now. . . . *I can sit with a White next to me, I don't worry. I don't think that . . . "I'm sitting next with a White lady." I'm talking, I'm sharing, we share [with] each other something. But before [during apartheid], you'd never done that.* (B, F, 40s)

A number of shoppers of color describe positive affect associated with being in close proximity to dissimilar shoppers, such as Nolu [B, F, 30s]: "Another thing [during apartheid], when we were in the banks, we had our own queues. White people had their queue. Now that has improved because I am no longer discriminated against. . . . *It makes me feel good* because now I know that I am a human being." Indeed, in contrast to the view of "the psychological costs that consumers expend while waiting for service" (Zhou & Soman, 2003, p. 517), South African consumers of color perceive some positive benefit—and experience positive affect—arising from being in a queue in the presence of dissimilar third parties who had previously been off limits. This is in line with two components of "normalcy" sought by consumers with visual impairments: participating in and being perceived as an equal in the marketplace (Baker, 2006; Baker, Holland, & Kaufman-Scarborough, 2006).

Other consumers perceive changes in the social milieu and proximal behavior to be a negative-affect experience:

> [In the post-apartheid era] we've got a lot of Indians in the area that we never had before. . . . [The grocery store] Pick N Pay is a nightmare. . . . I hate it. I've become—I sound like a racist but *there are so many Indians in Pick N Pay. . . . I hate myself for saying that. I really, really hate myself for saying that, but it's a nightmare and they don't just go [shopping] like I go [shopping], on my own shopping. The whole bloody family goes and the kids are all pushing the little trolleys, and then dad's there because he's the one who's got the wallet.* I don't know if the Indian women are allowed money. The man has the wallet and he pays for everything but the whole bloody family goes. (F, W, 50s)

Consistent with Grove and Fisk (1997), when a consumer shares time and space with third parties in the servicescape, the experience is affected by adherence to, or violation of, their perception of behavioral norms. Consumers

experience negative affect when third parties violate what Grove and Fisk (1997) refer to as "protocol," or categorical scripts for appropriate behavior in the context.

Negative affect also stems from consumers being close enough to hear and observe the service treatment of other customers, including the "subtle degradation" that can be experienced by third parties (see Chapter 9, this volume). As part of a study of U.S. federal district court decisions regarding consumer discrimination complaints, Harris et al. (2005) state that subtle degradation occurs when people of color are allowed to participate in the servicescape but are provided with, in an indirect or somewhat ambiguous way, something less than what other (White) customers receive. Toppie [B, M, 40s] recalls the subtle degradation of third parties near to him in retail service settings.

> There is this sad thing which makes one bitter. You know, sometimes to be educated can be very [pause] can be [pause] cannot be pleasing in a normal way. . . . *You see these subtle innuendoes, these small racisms. Like maybe you go to town, maybe you go to a bank, expecting a service and then there you just pick up the atmosphere, and then you see the next person who is not educated, he doesn't [pause]. He is not aware of what they've done to him. . . . That change in attitude, that atmosphere, you just feel it in the air, you know? . . . That's what eats me up, man, inside. I wish I . . . didn't have that thing to [be able to] pick these things up.*

Toppie's experience points toward an extension of consumer discrimination identified by Harris et al. (2005), by highlighting that discriminatory service also affects others in the servicescape. This phenomenon is further distinguished from the third-party Complainer role identified by McGrath and Otnes (1995) because no complaint about service is directed from the third party to the informant-consumer. Rather, the informant is merely a witness to ill treatment that may not have registered with the third party. Consistent with the definition of influence (Huston, 1983), Toppie's emotions are changed by the presence of third parties in the servicescape; he is saddened and distressed by observing what he perceives to be discriminatory service delivery to others. Toppie further distinguishes between the encounters he witnesses, and the way such an encounter would unfold if he himself were the target of ill treatment: "But now the good part—I tell them where to get off. But before [during apartheid] I was voiceless. Now I tell them where and when to get off. I can tell them that." Consistent with Hirschman's (1970) exit/loyalty/voice framework, Toppie now feels he would be free to give voice to his dissatisfaction, if he were the target rather than witness of ill treatment.

Ideating, or invoking category knowledge or stereotypes about third parties. Whereas the processes described thus far arise from third parties' physical presence in the servicescape, sometimes consumers activate mental representations of third parties even when the third parties are not present. These mental representations are associated with category labels (e.g., "Whites," "Blacks", "Darkies") and knowledge of such groups that may or may not be biased and stereotyped (Fiske, 1993; Hilton & von Hippel, 1996). Similar to other consumption situations where category-based knowledge is activated, when the consumer invokes these mental representations, servicescape experiences can be shaped in multiple ways.

Donovan [B, M, 40s] activates categorical knowledge about the shopping experiences of Whites and uses it as a standard of comparison:

> It was so difficult. It was so difficult. . . . *It was just painful because we knew that some other [White] people were not going through that [discrimination and denial of opportunities during apartheid].* And we had a hope that that would stop. . . . [During apartheid] there were places whereby you [as a Black person] cannot go in. . . . It used to say "Whites only," "Non-Whites" and that. The buses [etc.]. All those things. It was torture.

That this informant invokes a standard of comparison—beliefs about treatment received by Whites—is consistent with the findings of Grier and Brumbaugh (2005), who found that higher-status third parties serve as a norm against which people gauge their own and others' responses to advertising. In their study in a South African context, Whites were judged by all race groups as the highest-status race group, and Whites were used as the normative standard of comparison. A similar process is observed here in the servicescape context.

Anticipating and acting on (perception of) likely action of others. Unlike the previous third-party influence, where consumers activate category knowledge of a third party to make a social comparison judgment and evaluate service experience, sometimes consumers anticipate in advance what they believe third parties will actually *do* and how they will *behave* in the future. Consumers' beliefs are, again, based on a mental, categorical representation of such third parties, and may or may not be biased and stereotyped. Based on category knowledge of the third party's likely actions, consumers adjust their own behavior. Thus, this third-party influence is behavior-based, even if the anticipated third-party behavior never comes to pass.

This influence process is exemplified by a common perception today among South Africans of all walks of life that crime, and the individuals

who engage in crime, are a serious threat to quality of life (Boshoff & van Eeden, 2001). Jeff [W, M, 50s] bemoaned his loss of "window shopping" since the end of apartheid, largely due to his perceptions of the threat of crime per-petrated by third-party criminals in the central business district of his city. Similarly, Butana [B, M, 40s] stated that "township life is hard even for your kids, for everybody, because you send your son to buy you bread, and then you find out he's shot there by the shops [by criminals]." Others expressed a similar sentiment about the threat of criminals' actions and its dampening of marketplace behavior.

> You're not safe anywhere. *We can't take the car and go out. We can't go to the shopping center. You can't do anything. So the best thing is to pick up a phone. You're safer with a phone. You're in your house. Nothing is going to happen. . . . .* At a shopping center, at a robot [traffic light], *you can never get anywhere without looking behind your shoulder that someone is going to come for you.* (I, F, 30s)

Categorical representations of crime and criminals, along with category knowledge of where and when crime is likely to happen, exert strong influ-ences on shopping behavior in the country. Donald [W, M, 30s] owns a secu-rity firm and travels to townships to install mesh roof security systems in retail shops, where thieves break in through the roof to steal "easily sellable items, like cigarettes, food stuffs. . . . There's a lot of small shops . . . very popular stealing out of them. . . . Ja, *shabeens* [and] *spaza* shops." When traveling to and from work sites, Donald no longer carries his cell phone and says, "*I don't carry cash money with me. I keep it bare minimum, so if I've got 50 Rand [about $10 U.S.] with me at any given point in time, it's a lot.* They rob you very often and very quick in some locations." Self limiting of financial resources obviously deters retail purchase and consumption.

Interacting directly with third parties.   Consistent with findings in the United States, South African consumers are affected by direct interaction with unfamiliar strangers in the servicescape (Grove & Fisk, 1997; McGrath & Otnes, 1995) as well as family and friends (Childers & Rao, 1992; Lowrey, Otnes, & Ruth 2004; Mangleburg, Doney, & Bristol, 2004). Direct interaction with third parties can influence consumers' thoughts, feelings, and actions including store, product, and brand attitudes and behaviors.

Annie's [B, F, 50s] story reflects the direct intrusion of a third party into her consumer/service provider interaction:

> [During apartheid] we as Africans couldn't come into a place. It always non-Whites and Whites. There are places where we didn't go. In shops you

couldn't do that. [Even now] if a White person sees you buying something expensive, they have that thing in their mind that you can't afford it. It is only them who can buy something of that sort. *If you quarrel with the teller by the till, they [the third-party White observers] always have the remark, "You go to [tell your problems to Nelson] Mandela." They always have that remark.*

Moreover, consistent with *Ideating*, Annie invokes a stereotype centered on her beliefs about Whites' biased perceptions of Blacks' shopping behavior. This is consistent with Chin (1998) who observes that some Black shoppers in the United States believe that shop owners in non-Black areas sometimes believe that Black shoppers are unable to afford purchases, and receive ill treatment because of these stereotyped beliefs. Not surprisingly, knowledge of how one is viewed by others affects emotions and behavior; not being accepted elicits negative emotions and self beliefs (Leary, 2005).

A potent example of directly interacting with third parties comes in the form of consumer boycotts Blacks organized during the apartheid era to pressure the government through disruption of economic activity. Mandisi [B, M, 50s] describes boycotts that were organized in the 1980s:

We [Blacks] had a buying power. [During apartheid] we had to go . . . to town and buy. [But] we said that people must keep their money and not go to buy in town. They must buy here in the [township] location. They must support the [Black-owned] shops in the location. . . . *Those [township] boys were monitoring the whole thing. If they find [a person had] come to town, buying groceries, soap, washing powder, fish oil [they'd say], "Old man, don't you know that it was said that nobody must go to town to buy? You decided to go to town and buy some fish oil?" [The old man responds] "Yeah. Fish oil, yeah." [The third-party influencers would then] open it [the fish oil] up and say, "Drink it."* . . . *It was bad, the old man must drink the fish oil.* . . . Now in this new . . . democracy, they are building the [large, formal-sector chain grocery store called] Shoprite. They are bringing the shops to the people. Now there's no way that people must travel to town. They can buy here [in the township].

This reflects consumer behavior fashioned by normative political ideology, or a worldview of values, ideas, and political stances that shape and are shaped by society (Crockett & Wallendorf, 2004). Here, normative political ideology is expressed by third-party township youngsters who enforced—through direct interaction with the consumer—the apartheid-era ideology of buying in the township and from Black-owned businesses.

In post-apartheid times, Kristin [C, F, 20s] observed a third party who unwittingly denied another consumer an opportunity to make a servicescape statement [from field notes]:

> It had been her sister's birthday. They'd gone out to dinner and there were maybe ten of them all seated around. And the service was really bad . . . other tables that had come after them where White people were eating, those people received much better service than they did, and in fact, her sister, the birthday girl, never did receive her meal. . . . Kristin was saying to her sister, "No, no! You should tell them off, or I'll tell them off!" And the sister said, "No, no. I'll just ask for my food in a doggie bag." And then the sister proceeded to leave the doggie bag at the table as a statement about what the service was like and what the feeling was like. It turns out that the postscript to the story is that *Kristin's sister's mother-in-law . . . couldn't bear to see food wasted, and so her mother-in-law took the doggie bag and the statement was not made.*

In *Rubbing Shoulders* with others, Kristin's sister experienced the subtle degradation of obtaining service that was not up to the service delivery standard obtained by another group (Harris et al., 2005) that was visually identified and labeled by race (Fiske, 1993; Hilton & von Hippel, 1996). Kristin's sister opted to voice her resulting dissatisfaction (Hirschman, 1970) vis-à-vis her doggie bag behavior, but a third party with whom she is well acquainted silenced her voice.

Discussion

Noziga [B, F, 40s] points out, "It's only now that we see what that [apartheid] time was like" and how it affected all facets of life, including shopping and retail service consumption. The third-party influence processes and effects explicated here are derived from consumers' recollections about their lived experience in a country that experienced decades, if not centuries, of minority White domination over people of color, who were and still are in the majority. Although legacies of apartheid are certainly still felt today, the South African marketplace has been both a window for shoppers to observe change, as reflected in the third-party influence process arising from consumer gazing, as well as a mechanism that enacts change, as in the new-found servicescape access (rather than denial) experienced by South Africans of color. Nokwazi [B, F, 40s] recalls:

Things are very much different [today]. . . . We grew up in a society where you [would] stay at home. . . . We were made to have only social life [at home]. Things were not open for us to go anywhere. The only place that we could [go], it's going to town, it's going shopping and you buy maybe fish or Kentucky [Fried Chicken] and you bring it home for your kids to eat. . . . For us, restaurants were not [for us] . . . we were not exposed to that kind of life. . . . We only met at restaurants where your mother is working there, and you would have to go and see your mother in the restaurant. We never thought that it's a place where also you go and eat. But now it's different. People are free to go anywhere. . . . Even the malls are open, some for about 24 hours, some up to 9 o'clock, and everybody is welcome.

The changes in South Africa have provided a window for examining effects of the social milieu of the servicescape. Further insights are offered on third-party influence processes, race and other visible consumer characteristics, and issues in retailing.

Insights on Third-Party Influence Processes

This study has shown five different types of third-party servicescape influences, stemming from observation of race, that vary by prior relationship between consumer and third party, whether the third party is physically present, and if so, in what capacity. Not surprisingly, this analysis suggests that when consumers gaze upon third parties, thought patterns are affected because of attention to salient, visually-accessible characteristics. However, emotions and shopping behavior remain relatively unchanged. As the level of direct contact increases, a broader range of consumer experience is shaped by third parties, both those who are physically present as well as those who are reflected in activated mental representations.

Consistent with past research, strangers as well as friends and family can influence shoppers' store, product, and brand choices, as well as other components of consumer experience such as feelings (see Dahl et al., 2005; Lowrey et al., 2004). Still, merely activating a categorical representation of a particular type of third party (e.g., race groups)—or the actions the third party is likely to take (e.g., beliefs about crime and people who are likely to commit crime)—can influence consumer behavior to the point of curtailing shopping because of fear.

This study also provides a counterpoint to some extant literature on third-party influence in consumer behavior and on shopping behavior in particular. Past research has tended to emphasize direct interpersonal influence on consumer decision making, information processing, and persuasion (see Childers & Rao, 1992; Mangleburg et al., 2004). The results of this study underscore the importance of strangers in the servicescape, and consumers' attention to strangers from afar or those whose presence allows closer observation or superficial interaction. Moreover, the direct interaction roles observed by McGrath and Otnes (1995)—such as seeking or receiving advice—were not prominent in this study. Perhaps because "shoppers tend to observe the actions and interact with others whom they visually judge to be like themselves" (McGrath & Otnes, 1995, p. 269), South African consumers may have limited direct interaction with strangers who are perceived to be dissimilar. Alternatively, direct interaction with strangers may occur among South African shoppers who are similar (e.g., by race) and may not have been memorable or remarkable in the context of this study. However, a new direct interaction role of Degrader emerged for the consumer who received unsolicited, derisive commentary from a third-party shopper.

This research also adds to our understanding of the imagined presence of others in the servicescape in two ways. First, based on the notion that embarrassment is a socially-based emotion, Dahl et al. (2005) found that shoppers experience greater embarrassment in certain situations (e.g., buying condoms) if they believe that third parties are physically nearby. South African consumers evidenced the generation of a different emotion—fear—when *Anticipating and Acting* on the notion that criminals might be present in a servicescape. This result extends the effects of imagined social presence beyond so-called social emotions, such as embarrassment, to one that does not necessarily have a social basis to it such as fear (see Leary, 2000). Although emotions have been the subject of much research in advertising and other consumer settings (e.g., Edell & Burke, 1987), there is an opportunity to learn more about the drivers and effects of consumers' emotions elicited by third parties in servicescape settings. It might be fruitful to expand beyond a single emotion—such as embarrassment—to capture a broad range of emotions that are elicited by interactions with others in the servicescape, much like the work done on emotions in interpersonal relationship contexts such as gift giving (Ruth, Otnes, & Brunel, 1999; Ruth, Brunel, & Otnes, 2002).

Second, the influence process arising from *Ideating* a third party differs from the mere presence effect observed by Dahl et al. (2005). In *Ideating*, circumstances of the sociocultural environment and servicescape combine to prompt the consumer to self-activate the imagined third party (rather than researcher-manipulated imagined presence). In addition, rather than the generalized other in Dahl et al. (2005), where the study participant believed that "someone" could possibly observe the consumer's purchase, the imagined third party in *Ideating* is a specific sort of imagined third party (e.g., Whites), and one that elicits certain types of beliefs as a result of categorization and stereotyping. Moreover, it is not necessary for consumers to believe that the third party (e.g., Whites) might be physically present in the servicescape. *Ideating* also did not involve the threat of the third-party other observing and possibly evaluating the consumer's behavior. Instead, consumers merely activate beliefs about a social category's likely treatment in an equivalent servicescape and use it as a standard of comparison.

Insights on Race and Other Visible Consumer Characteristics

Although the laws creating and sustaining apartheid may have been uniquely extensive and pervasive, many markets share a background of discrimination that may be associated with stereotypes and ill treatment today (see Harris et al., 2005; Henderson et al., 2005). Not only should consumer researchers and marketers attend to the processes whereby discrimination occurs within the consumer/service provider dyad, but also the effects *of* third parties and effects *on* third parties who witness such interactions. Indeed, race-related stress occurs within the consumer/service provider interaction (Crockett, Grier, and Williams, 2003) but also in others who witness these incidents, as shown by this study.

The characteristic through which these third-party processes were revealed in South Africa may also exist in other countries and cultures. It would be useful to examine these findings in other shopping contexts where race may be salient (e.g., Hispanic and Native American shopping experiences in the United States: Shim & Gehrt, 1996; servicescapes in Singapore: Henderson et al., 1999). In addition, these third-party influence processes arise in the context of sensitivity to race but they are likely to generalize to other visible characteristics that are categorized and attention-getting by cultural norm. For example, research indicates that third parties in United States servicescapes gaze upon consumers with visible disabilities (Baker, Holland, & Kaufman-Scarborough, 2006). Fiske (1993) notes that age is also a highly visible characteristic, and so perhaps processes associated with gazing might apply to "old" people in servicescapes associated with young people such as Hollister, or men in gendered servicescapes such as bridal salons, or women in barbershops (Fischer, Gainer, & Bristor, 1998).

Insights on Retail Servicescape Experiences

Haytko and Baker (2004, p. 73) observed that safety was a factor in young girls' mall patronage decisions, but also noted that "safety is a construct that has been ignored in previous retail patronage models." Very few of the informants in this study had been the victims of crime, but perception of crime was a salient issue in servicescape patronage across all groups. This study has uncovered one possible framework and theoretical foundation for the study of this phenomenon, namely categorical representations and processes associated with consumer safety, crime, and criminals. Future research may be able to apply theories about categorization and stereotyping to explicate the construct of consumer safety and to develop frameworks for understanding how consumer knowledge of safety and crime develop, and how theory can be applied to change categorical knowledge and stereotypes associated with these concepts.

Conclusion

This research demonstrates that the servicescape provides a public landscape where people have an opportunity to come in contact with dissimilar others, and to learn about one another in new ways. The comments of Josephine [I, F, 30s] reflect this notion, when she describes that during apartheid, she and her family were denied access to non-Indian servicescapes, stating "We could only go where there was an Indian restaurant and things like that. [Now] everybody is allowed anywhere and I think that's good. Everybody needs to associate and learn each other's culture and be unity in life. I think that's very good."

The results of this study suggest that marketers should not underestimate the importance of the servicescape as a public arena for social activity among a society and her peoples. Indeed, the marketplace may provide social opportunities not afforded in other settings such as residential areas, religious communities, and other communities and organizations that are based on voluntary participation and self-selection. By focusing on consumer attention to a visible characteristic of others in the servicescape—namely, race—this study has not only identified five processes of third-party influence but has also provided insight into cognitive and emotional processes that are likely shared by consumers in other countries and contexts characterized by sensitivity to salient visible characteristics such as race and ethnicity, age, gender and the like.

References

Argo, J. J., Dahl, D. W., & Manchanca, R. V. (2005). The influence of a mere social presence in a retail context. *Journal of Consumer Research, 32*, 207–212.

Arnold, M. J., & Reynolds, K. E. (2003). Hedonic shopping motivations. *Journal of Retailing, 79*, 77–95.

Babin, B. J., Darden, W. R., & Griffin, M. (1994). Work and/or fun: Measuring hedonic and utilitarian shopping value. *Journal of Consumer Research, 20*, 644–656.

Baker, S. M. (2006). Consumer normalcy: Understanding the value of shopping through the narratives of consumers with visual impairments. *Journal of Retailing, 82*, 37–50.

Baker, S. M., Holland, J., & Kaufman-Scarborough, C. (2006). How consumers with disabilities perceive "welcome" in retail servicescapes: A critical incident study. *Journal of Services Marketing*, forthcoming.

Bitner, M. J. (1992). Servicescapes: The impact of physical surroundings on customers and employees. *Journal of Marketing, 56*, 57–71.

Bloch, P. H., Ridgway, N. M., & Dawson, S. A. (1994). The shopping mall as consumer habitat. *Journal of Retailing, 70*, 23–42.

Boshoff, C., & van Eeden, S. M. (2001). South African consumer sentiment towards marketing: A longitudinal analysis. *South African Journal of Business Management, 32*, 23–33.

Burgess, S. M., & Harris, M. (1999). Social identity in an emerging consumer market: How you do the wash may say a lot about who you think you are. In E. J. Arnould & L. M. Scott (Eds.), *Advances in consumer research* (pp. 170–175), Provo, UT: Association for Consumer Research.

Childers, T. L., & Rao, A. R. (1992). The influence of familial and peer-based reference groups on consumer decisions. *Journal of Consumer Research, 19*, 198–211.

Chin, E. (1998). Social inequality and the context of consumption: Local groceries and downtown stores. In J. F. Sherry (Ed.), *Servicescapes: The concept of place in contemporary markets* (pp. 591–617). Chicago: NTC Business Books.

Crockett, D., Grier, S. A., & Williams, J. A. (2003). Coping with marketplace discrimination: An exploration of the experiences of black men. *Academy of Marketing Science Review, 4*, 1–18.

Crockett, D., & Wallendorf, M. (2004). The role of normative political ideology in consumer behavior. *Journal of Consumer Research, 31*, 511–528.

Dahl, D. W., Manchanda, R. V., & Argo, J. J. (2001). Embarrassment in consumer purchase: The roles of social presence and purchase familiarity. *Journal of Consumer Research, 28*, 473–481.

Edell, J. A., & Burke, M. C. (1987). The power of feelings in understanding advertising effects. *Journal of Consumer Research, 14*, 421–433.

Fischer, E., Gainer, B., & Bristor, J. (1998). Beauty salon and barbershop: Gendered servicescapes. In J. F. Sherry (Ed.), *Servicescapes: The concept of place in contemporary markets* (pp. 565–590). Chicago: NTC Business Books.

Fiske, S. T. (1993). Social cognition and social perception. *Annual Review of Psychology, 44*, 155–194.

Grier, S., & Brumbaugh, A. M. (2006). Compared to whom? The impact of norms on predictions of persuasion. *Journal of Consumer Behavior,* forthcoming.

Grier, S., & Deshpandé, R. (2001). Social dimensions of consumer distinctiveness: The influence of social status on group identity and advertising persuasion. *Journal of Marketing Research, 38,* 216–224.

Grove, S. J., & Fisk, R. P. (1997). The impact of other customers on service experiences: A critical incident examination of "getting along." *Journal of Retailing, 73,* 63–85.

Harris, A-M. G., Henderson, G. R., & Williams, J. D. (2005). Courting customers: Assessing consumer racial profiling and other marketplace discrimination. *Journal of Public Policy & Marketing, 24,* 163–171.

Haytko, D. L., & Baker, J. (2004). It's all at the mall: Exploring adolescent girls' experiences. *Journal of Retailing, 80,* 67–83.

Henderson, G. R., Williams, J. D., Grantham, K. D., & Lwin, M. (1999). The commodification of race in Singapore: The customer service implications of the other-race effect on tourism and retailing. *Asia Pacific Journal of Management, 16,* 213–228.

Hilton, J. L., & von Hippel, W. (1996). Stereotypes. *Annual Review of Psychology, 47,* 237–271.

Hirschman, A. O. (1970). *Exit, voice, and loyalty.* Cambridge, MA: Harvard University Press.

Huston, T. L. (1983). Power. In H. H. Kelley et al. (Eds.), *Close relationships* (pp. 169–219). New York: W. H. Freeman.

Latané, B. (1981). The psychology of social impact. *American Psychologist, 36,* 343–356.

Latané, B. (1997). Dynamic social impact: The societal consequences of human interaction. In G. McGarty, & S. A. Haslam (Eds.), *The message of social psychology* (pp. 200–221). London: Blackwell.

Leary, M. R. (2000). Affect, cognition, and the social emotions. In J. P. Forgas (Ed.), *Feeling and thinking: The role of affect in social cognition* (pp. 331–356). New York: Cambridge University Press.

Leary, M. R. (2005). Interpersonal cognition and the quest for social acceptance. In M. W. Baldwin (Ed.), *Interpersonal cognition* (pp. 85–103). New York: Guilford Press.

Lowrey, T. M., Otnes, C. C., & Ruth, J. A. (2004). Social influences on dyadic giving over time: A taxonomy from the giver's perspective. *Journal of Consumer Research, 30,* 547–558.

Mangleburg, T. F., Doney, P. M., & Bristol, T. (2004). Shopping with friends and teens' susceptibility to peer influence. *Journal of Retailing, 80,* 101–116.

McCracken, G. (1988). *The long interview.* Newbury Park, CA: Sage.

McGrath, M. A., & Otnes, C. (1995). Unacquainted influencers: When strangers interact in the retail setting. *Journal of Business Research, 32,* 261–272.

Ruth, J. A. (2006). *The "changeover" and the changed: The meaning of product consumption in post-apartheid South Africa,* working paper.

Ruth, J. A., Otnes, C. C., & Brunel, F. F. (1999). Gift receipt and the reformulation of relationships. *Journal of Consumer Research, 25,* 385–402.

Ruth, J. A., Brunel, F. F., & Otnes, C. C. (2002). Linking thoughts to feelings: Investigating cognitive appraisals and consumption emotions in a mixed-emotions context. *Journal of the Academy of Marketing Science, 30,* 44–58.

Ross, R. (1999). *A concise history of South Africa.* New York: Cambridge University Press.

Sandikci, O., & Holt, D. (1998). Malling society: Mall consumption practices and the future of public space. In J. F. Sherry (Ed.), *Servicescapes: The concept of place in contemporary markets* (pp. 305–336). Chicago: NTC Business Books.

Sherry, J. F. (1998). Understanding markets as places. In J. F. Sherry (Ed.), *Servicescapes: The concept of place in contemporary markets* (pp. 1–24). Chicago: NTC Business Books.

Shim, S., & Gehrt, K. C. (1996). Hispanic and Native American adolescents: An exploratory study of their approach to shopping. *Journal of Retailing, 72,* 307–324.

Smith, T. B., Stones, C. R., & Naidoo, A. (2003). Racial attitudes among South African young adults: A four-year follow-up study. *South African Journal of Psychology, 33,* 39–43

Sparks, A. (1995). *Tomorrow is another country: The inside story of South Africa's road to change.* Chicago, IL: The University of Chicago Press.

Statistics South Africa. (2005). *Mid-year population estimates, South Africa.* Pretoria, South Africa: Statistics South Africa. Retrieved from http://www.statssa.gov.za/publications/P0302/P03022005.pdf

Wakefield, K. L., & Baker, J. (1998). Excitement at the mall: Determinants and effects on shopping response. *Journal of Retailing, 74,* 515–540.

Webster's New World Dictionary. (1988). New York: Simon & Schuster.

Wiese, C. (1997). An overview of retailing in South Africa. In J. Reuvid & I. Priestner (Eds.), *Doing business in South Africa.* London: Kogan Page Ltd.

Zhou, R., & Soman, D. (2003). Looking back: Exploring the psychology of queuing and the effects of the number of people behind. *Journal of Consumer Research, 29,* 517–529.

IV

METHODOLOGICAL INNOVATIONS FOR STUDYING SHOPPING BEHAVIOR

11

VIDEO-CUED THOUGHT PROTOCOLS— A METHOD FOR TRACING COGNITIVE PROCESSES AT THE POINT OF PURCHASE

Oliver B. Büttner
Günter Silberer

Georg-August-Universität Göttingen, Germany

*T*HE STORE PLAYS A crucial role in consumer decision making. Many purchases are decided directly on the spot, that is, at the point of purchase (Cobb & Hoyer, 1986; Rook, 1987). Hence, management in retailing as well as in marketing needs to know how customers really interact with the store environment and what guides their behavior in the store (Bitner, 1992; Silberer, 1989; see also the keynote address in this volume). One key to success is the atmosphere of a store (Donovan, Rossiter, Marcoolyn, & Nesdale, 1994; see also Crader & Zaichkowsky in this volume). Consequently, various studies have examined the influence of store characteristics such as scent or music on shopping behavior (e.g., Chebat & Michon, 2003; Mattila & Wirtz, 2001; see also Allan in this volume).

Despite the common assumption that the processes underlying consumer behavior are dynamic in nature (Bettman, Luce, & Payne, 1998; Jacoby et al., 1994), most research is still conducted using static methodological approaches (Jacoby, Johar, & Morrin, 1998). While certain techniques for tracing process have been established for the laboratory (Simonson, Carmon, Dhar, Drolet, & Nowlis, 2001), studies incorporating such methods at the point of sale are scarce. This situation is unsatisfactory because the point of sale offers a variety of possible stimuli that might exert an influence during the whole shopping episode. Influences and mechanisms that can be established in the lab have to be examined as to whether they are also crucial inside the store or are just part of the "noise" (Simonson, 2005). Hence, if consumer research claims to explain and predict actual shopping behavior, consumer research also has to apply process tracing techniques *in situ*, that is, inside the store.

In this chapter, we will address how process tracing methods can contribute to enhanced knowledge about consumers' cognitive processes while shopping in a store. First, we will discuss process tracing techniques that have hitherto been applied to research on cognitive processes at the point of sale. Then we will present video-cued thought protocols as an alternative technique for tracing consumer cognition in the store. This technique is illustrated by three studies that used video-cued thought protocols. Finally, we will discuss implications for further research and for management in retailing and marketing.

Two other chapters in this volume address related issues. Paulson (Chapter 12) presents an interview method that deals with re-creating shopping scenarios. Silberer (Chapter 13) provides a review of methods for recording consumers' behavior in the store.

Traditional Techniques for Tracing Cognitive Processes

Eye-fixation Analysis and Cognitive Processes

Eye-fixation analysis is a process tracing technique that is commonly used in the laboratory. Visual acuity is best in a small region of the visual field, that is, the *foveal* region; this means that eye movements and attention are closely linked (Rayner, 1998). Consequently, eye movements that occur during the visual processing of stimuli can be used as indicators of cognitive processes (Guan, Lee, Cuddihy, & Ramey, 2006). Some studies in consumer research applied eye tracking for analyzing consumer cognition (for a more general discussion of eye tracking in retailing research, see Chapter 13 in this volume). For instance, Russo and Leclerc (1994) identified stages in product choice at shelves by analyzing patterns of eye fixations. Pieters and Warlop (1999) examined the influence of time pressure and task motivation on strategies that consumers use when choosing between brands. Chandon (2002) addressed the relationship between visual attention and memory for brands. Schröder, Berghaus, and Zimmermann (2005) focused on consumers' search processes and identified shelf regions that catch consumers' attention.

Among the tracking devices available for measuring eye movement (Rayner, 1998), those that use infrared corneal reflection are most commonly used in consumer research (e.g., Chandon, 2002; Pieters & Warlop, 1999). Due to the restrictions imposed by the technical equipment, eye tracking is hardly feasible in the field. For instance, reflections from lights in the store can impair the measurement of the infrared corneal reflection. Moreover, walking through the store with an eye-tracking device will influence participants' behavior and will draw the attention of other customers as well. Consequently, consumer research has used eye-fixation analysis almost exclusively in the laboratory. Russo and Leclerc (1994) set up a supermarket simulation in the laboratory, and recorded consumers' eye fixations on certain products on shelves by a video camera through a one-sided mirror. The authors report that none of the participants were aware that their behavior was being filmed, but concede that the procedure is not feasible in a real supermarket. Pieters and Warlop (1999), as well as Chandon (2002), used slides as a surrogate for actual shelves. Schröder et al. (2005) used eye-tracking at shelves in actual supermarkets. Nevertheless, they concede limitations regarding the reliability of their data because of problems, amongst others, with calibration and data transmission.

In-Store Behavior and Cognitive Processes

Eye-fixation analysis permits the examination of which pieces of information consumers have focused their attention on, but is problematic when trying to infer whether the information really was sought after or processed. Other observation procedures have been developed to capture consumers' information processing in a more straightforward manner. In behavioral process analysis (Jacoby et al., 1994), researchers observe which of the available pieces of information is sought after by a participant from an information display matrix and analyze this behavior using such parameters as breadth or sequences of the information acquisition. As this kind of technique usually requires a structured decision-making task, its value for "real-world" research at the point of sale is limited (Payne & Ragsdale, 1978).

Using less formalized observations of consumers' interaction with the store environment, however, might also prove insightful. The approaches and the methods that can be used for observing customers' in-store behavior are abundant (for an overview, see Chapter 13 in this volume). Consumers' interactions with products (e.g., touching them, taking them out of shelves) can be used to analyze consumers' choice processes. For instance, Hoyer (1984) presents results from an observation at a shelf that provide insights into consumers' deliberations during brand choice.

The observation of navigation behavior can also give clues to cognitive processes. For instance, approach or avoidance behavior can be used as an indicator of positive or negative evaluations of areas in the store, respectively (Bitner, 1992; Donovan et al., 1994). Indirect evidence of a relationship between the way consumers move through the store and attractiveness is presented by Milliman (1982): The results suggest that customers who move more slowly tend to buy more. Certain navigational patterns can also provide clues as to the cognitive processes that underlie orientation in the store: Iyer (1989) found that backtracking, "measured as the motion, in a direction opposite to the forward movement, required to purchase/inspect an item" (p. 47), was more pronounced when consumers visited an unknown store.

In general, however, data assessed by the observation of in-store behavior suffers from ambiguity. For instance, when customers spend a long time contemplating a shelf, this might be an indicator of their involvement with the product class or simply show that they cannot find what they are looking for. More unequivocal insights into the relationship between in-store behavior and the underlying reasons can be provided by techniques that combine in-store observation and post interviews (Lowrey, Otnes, & McGrath, 2005; Otnes, McGrath, & Lowrey, 1995). Another possibility is to collect thought protocols, that is, customers' verbal reports on their cognitive processes (e.g., Titus & Everett, 1996).

Verbal Reports and Cognitive Processes

When digging deeper into information processing, verbal reports are the "classic" method in research on cognitive processes (for a review see Ericsson & Simon, 1993; Silberer, 2005). Concurrent verbal reports—known as "thinking aloud"—have been frequently used by consumer research in the laboratory (e.g., Bettman & Park, 1980; Kivetz & Simonson, 2000). This kind of reporting requires participants to verbalize their thoughts while performing a task (e.g., choosing between competing brands) and has already been applied in research at the point of purchase. In these studies, data was collected on cognitive processes by asking participants to think aloud while walking through a store; it was typically supplemented by data from observation. Both King (1969) and Bettman (1970) used thought protocols collected from a small number of participants to model consumers' in-store information processing. Payne and Ragsdale (1978) present descriptive analyses of consumers' use of strategies and product attributes during grocery shopping derived from in-store thought protocols. Another study that combined thinking aloud and observation was conducted by Titus and Everett (1996) to examine the cognitive processes that underlie navigational search behavior at the point of purchase. Reicks et al. (2003) used thinking aloud to examine factors influencing in-store grocery purchase decisions.

The advantage of these verbal reports is that they provide rich, sequential information about cognitive processes (Payne, 1994). However, a crucial argument against them is the reactivity of the method, that is, the underlying cognitive processes might be altered by the procedure of assessing the data (Russo, Johnson, & Stephens, 1989). Although advocates of the thinking aloud method report results indicating that thinking aloud slows down the process but does not alter it (Ericsson & Simon, 1993; Payne & Ragsdale, 1978), there is also evidence that reactivity reaches beyond task speed and that the effects are contingent upon the task to be solved (Dickson, McLennan, & Omodei, 2000; Russo et al., 1989; Schooler, Ohlsson, & Brooks, 1993; van den Haak, de Jong, & Schellens, 2003). Research on attention and performance shows that performing two tasks simultaneously results in interferences between the tasks (Pashler, Johnston, & Ruthruff, 2001). The complex tasks involved in shopping (e.g., wayfinding, thinking about needs and budget) in such a rich environment as a store can be assumed to require more resources than solving puzzles or making decisions in the laboratory. Consequently, we expect that reactivity due to the interference between the shopping task and the verbalization task are even more pronounced when applying thinking aloud at the point of sale. Indeed, Reicks et al. (2003) mention anecdotal evidence for reactivity on shopping behavior when customers were asked to think aloud.

In addition, there are also problems with thinking aloud at the point of purchase that are more mundane. For instance, people may not be used to verbalizing their thoughts and feelings while shopping. Talking about such issues in public might create an awkward situation for them and hinder verbalization. Moreover, practical reasons such as interfering music or loud voices in the store complicate the application of thinking aloud in the store. Finally, thinking aloud is not applicable for studying customers' social interactions—it would interfere with the normal communication.

Verbal reports can be collected retrospectively to counter these problems (Ericsson & Simon, 1993; Shiv & Fedorikhin, 1999; Wright & Rip, 1980). This eliminates the danger of reactivity, but it fosters the problem of nonveridicality, that is, no or loose correspondence between verbal reports and original processes (Gibbons, 1983; Russo et al., 1989). The first reason is that the thoughts have to be retrieved from long-term memory and hence are prone to forgetting. The results of Fidler (1983) show that retrospective reports are indeed of lower quality compared to concurrent reports. Second, interpretation on the part of the subjects is more likely (Harte & Koele, 1997) and can lead to the fabrication of mental events (Russo et al., 1989). Finally, the sequential order of the verbalized thoughts is less strict and cannot be accurately assigned to the participant's behavior. All these problems become graver with increasing time between the shopping episode and the retrospective verbalization.

Supporting the verbalization with an aid that contains cues to facilitate recall can be a solution (Omodei, McLennan, & Wearing, 2005; Silberer, 2005; see also Paulson in this volume). For this purpose, cueing retrospective reports with video observations of the informants' shopping behavior presents an alternative. We refer to this technique as "video-cued thought protocols" and will discuss it in detail in the remaining sections of this chapter.

Video-Cued Thought Protocols

The Technique

The core idea of video-cued thought protocols is to use a video of the shopping episode as a recall aid when assessing verbal reports on cognitions retrospectively. The technique originates from laboratory research on consumer behavior towards online shops (Silberer, 2000; Silberer, Engelhardt, & Wilhelm, 2003). Here, the consumer's interaction with an online shop is recorded in a video, either by using a head-mounted camera (Silberer et al., 2003) or software to record the screen content (Büttner, Schulz, & Silberer, 2006). The video is presented to the participants afterwards and paused each time they click on a link to another web page. Participants are then asked to report what they had in mind while surfing the page.[1]

For the use in brick and mortar shops, the technique had to be elaborated because of peculiarities of the shopping environment (Silberer, 2005). The procedure is as follows: An observer follows a customer with a video camera (at a discreet distance) and films the customer's behavior in the store. The participants are informed about the observation for ethical and practical reasons. Directly after the shopping episode, the video is presented to the customer using a laptop as output device. Participants are asked to comment on the video with the thoughts and feelings they can remember from the former shopping episode. In order not to provoke justifications or "false memories" (Russo et al., 1989), the interviewer adopts a nondirective manner and only intervenes by repeating the instructions when the participant stops verbalizing. Both interviewer and interviewee have the possibility to

---

[1] The focus of this chapter is on applying the technique in brick and mortar retailing. For more detailed discussions and illustrations of using the technique in online environments, see Silberer (2000), Silberer et al. (2003), or Büttner et al. (2006).

pause the tape if necessary. Video and audio tracks are combined after the interview, resulting in a video tape with the pictures from the original shopping episode and the audio track from the interview. Participants' thought protocols are then coded and analyzed in the laboratory. Moreover, the video can be used to analyze behavioral data. The coding schemes for participants' thoughts and behavior are based on the scope of the research. If the existing coding schemes do not fit the research question, one might either adapt one of them or develop a new one.

Similar techniques have evolved in other domains than consumer research. Kalbermatten (1984) reports on a method called "self-confrontation" (*Selbstkonfrontation*). Video recordings of behavior are used to elicit verbal comments from the actors in contexts such as teaching, counseling, or sports. Wagner, Uttendorfer-Marek, and Weidle (1977) term their approach "retrospective thinking aloud" (*nachträgliches lautes Denken*). They use video recordings from school lessons that are commented on by teachers or pupils. While these approaches have in common that they record the behavior from the view of an external observer, there are also approaches that use a head-mounted camera to collect videos in naturalistic situations: Odomei and colleagues apply "own-point-of-view recordings" to recall the decision-making of professionals such as firemen (Omodei et al., 2005). In usability research, recordings of the screen content have been used to elicit participants' thoughts on their interaction with software (e.g., Bowers & Snyder, 1990).

In the following, we will address the feasibility and the validity of using video-cued thought protocols for research at the point of sale. Moreover, as the effort for applying video-cued thought protocols is rather high, we will examine whether the technique can yield useful insights for consumer research. We will discuss these issues using results from a study that was conducted in a store for electrical and electronic goods (for details see Büttner, Rauch, & Silberer, 2005). In this study, we focused on differences between browsing visitors and visitors with a particular intent to purchase, and explicitly addressed questions of validity (study 1, $N = 128$). We will support the discussion with an analysis of two other studies, thereby illustrating the variety of research questions that can be addressed using video-cued thought protocols. Study 2 ($N = 48$) examined consumers' in-store purchase decisions in a supermarket (Marienhagen, 2005), whereas study 3 ($N = 66$) focused on couples' shopping behavior in a toy store (Weitemeyer, 2006).

Feasibility

Whether video-cued thought protocols can be used reasonably depends on both the acceptance by the store's management and customers (i.e., the potential participants; Silberer, 2005). In all three studies, the management readily agreed to support the studies. The customers' willingness to participate was also good, although we did not pay any money for participation but handed out small incentives such as candy bars. In all studies, the interviewers approached customers at the entrance to the store. Given the invasiveness of the technique, the participation rates are surprisingly high: 22 percent of the customers approached by our interviewer in study 1 agreed to participate. The participation rate was even higher in studies 2 and 3: 38 percent and 29 percent of those asked, respectively, agreed to participate. Nevertheless, we expect participation rates to be significantly lower for shopping situations that involve time pressure (e.g. gift shopping before Christmas) or that emphasize the customers' need for privacy (e.g., buying condoms; see Dahl, Manchanda, & Argo, 2001).

The technical equipment—laptop computer, digital video camera, microphone, and software—can be handled easily in the field situation. In study 1, five of the data sets had to be discarded because of corrupt audio tracks. Overall, however, technical problems rarely occurred. We had good experiences with the in-store recording of participants' behavior, although it was not always possible to keep track of all movements exactly. Furthermore, the video compressions (MPEG) that were necessary for archiving after recording the videos did not cause significant delays in the course of the studies. They were started while participants filled out a final questionnaire and the compression algorithms used to produce both an acceptable image quality as well as file size do not consume too much time when using up-to-date computers. Certainly, archiving the videos on DVD is an additional yet important aspect, and thoroughly cleaning the laptop from temporary video files at regular intervals is indispensable because of the large file sizes.

When combining the audio track with the video, the video has to be in the same format as presented to the participant. We achieved this by recording the video presentation itself (i.e., including all pause, rewind, and forward operations) in another video. In the first two studies, we used the video-editing software Pinnacle Studio™ for this purpose. In study 3, we switched to Camtasia Studio™, a software solution for screen recording; the procedure turned out to be even easier to handle. Both procedures resulted in a video that includes the original video in the way it was presented to the participant (video from a video) and a synchronized audio track.

Validity

Threats to validity. The validity of verbal reports can be jeopardized in two ways—by reactivity and nonveridicality (Russo et al., 1989). *Reactivity* means that the underlying process (i.e., cognitive processes) is altered by assessing it (i.e., by eliciting verbal protocols). Although it is a common finding that reactivity is a minor issue in thinking aloud when carried out properly (Ericsson & Simon, 1993; Payne, 1994), certain results suggest that the effects might be underestimated (Dickson et al., 2000; Russo et al., 1989; Schooler et al., 1993). This should be especially crucial in a field situation where the self-awareness of the informant is higher due to other visitors observing him or her verbalizing. Moreover, having to perform two tasks simultaneously (i.e., shopping and verbalizing) can result in interference between the tasks (Pashler et al., 2001). In a usability study, van den Haak et al. (2003) compared thinking aloud and retrospective video-cued thought protocols. They found participants who were thinking aloud to be less successful in solving tasks. Moreover, verbalizations from the thinking aloud participants proved less helpful than verbalizations from the video-cued thought protocols in identifying usability problems. The findings suggest that both the primary and the verbalization task suffer from the interference between them when participants think aloud. The advantage of video-cued thought protocols is that verbalization itself cannot affect the original process because it is done afterwards (Ericsson & Simon, 1980, p. 234). Nevertheless, the problem shifts to the question as to whether filming the subject while shopping alters the external and inner behavior.

Nonveridicality arises when the verbalized process does not correspond to the underlying processes. This might be produced by forgetting or the fabrication of mental events (Russo et al., 1989). Compared to uncued retrospective reports, video-cued thought protocols are less prone to nonveridicality because the video facilitates recall. This assumption is supported by the crucial role that contextual factors play in recalling information from episodic memory (Raaijmakers & Shiffrin, 1992). Moreover, anchoring the verbalization with the video both preserves the sequential order of the thoughts and leaves less room for interpretation, thereby reducing the fabrication of mental events. Guan et al. (2006) provide evidence that fabrication is not very prevalent in cued retrospective reports. They also report results indicating a high level of omissions in cued retrospective reports, but concede that the amount might be greatly overestimated because of differences in the level of abstraction between thought protocols and data on eye fixation.

However, the biggest nonveridicality challenge for all techniques using verbal reports is whether people are really able to report on their mental processes. This has been subject to debate since the early days of psychology (Massen & Bredenkamp, 2005). In German *Denkpsychologie* of the early 20th century, Bühler (1907) favored introspection as a method for the study of thought processes. This view was attacked by Wundt (1907) with the argument that monitoring one's inner processes is not possible because these processes themselves bind those cognitive resources (i.e., attention) that are necessary for the monitoring.

In the 1970s, Nisbett and Wilson (1977) contended after reviewing various studies that people cannot adequately report on mental processes but, when asked to do so, "construct" these processes by relying on naïve theories. This conclusion has been criticized for several reasons. Ericsson and Simon (1980, 1993), for instance, argue that the studies reviewed by Nisbett and Wilson (1977) cannot provide insight into people's ability to report on their mental processes because they neglect the characteristics of the cognitive system. Ericsson and Simon (1980, 1993) developed a theory for predicting the validity of verbal reports based on characteristics of the cognitive system and argue that verbal reports can produce valid insights when applied properly. One central premise is that people can only report on mental processes that have been conscious, that is, have passed short-term memory. The assumption that people have a privileged access to their conscious inner states is now also acknowledged by former critics (e.g., Wilson, 2002, p. 106).

If consciousness is a prerequisite for valid verbal reports, then the role of nonconscious processes might limit their applicability. Research on unconscious processes is currently experiencing a renaissance: people in general and in their role as consumers have been found to be far more subject to unconscious processes than previously assumed (Bargh, 2002; Dijksterhuis, Smith, van Baaren, & Wigboldus, 2005). There are, however, good arguments to assume that the influence of unconscious processes might be overestimated by current research (Chartrand, 2005; Simonson, 2005). According to Simonson (2005, p. 214), this view is supported by the wide range of phenomena that can be explained by conscious processes (e.g., Payne, Bettman, & Johnson, 1993).

All in all, one has to accept that video-cued thought protocols cannot provide insights into all cognitive processes and thus might be incomplete. However, as Ericsson and Simon (1980) point out, it "does not invalidate the information that is present" (p. 243). Moreover, it is not a sole characteristic of this technique but applies to all other methods as well (e.g., thinking aloud, eye-fixation analysis). Overall, the risk of forgetting and fabrication is less crucial for video-cued thought protocols than for uncued retrospective reports, yet higher than in concurrent thinking aloud. In return, the technique is less invasive than thinking aloud and therefore less prone to reactivity. In uncued retrospective reports, reactivity is even less prominent. These limitations have to be kept in mind when using video-cued thought protocols to examine cognitive processes. As with all research methods, the adequateness of video-cued thought protocols has to be judged with regard to the scope and purpose of the research endeavor.

Testing reliability and validity. For verbal reports in general, whether they are collected retrospectively or concurrently, the concept of reliability as founded in the Classical Test Theory is not applicable, because "it is not possible to separate measurement error from the 'true decision' process" (Harte & Koele, 1997, p. 25). Retests with the same subjects are not adequate as this implies that the ongoing process and the corresponding thoughts would be the same. It is evident that such a retest would alter the shopping process as well. As dynamic processes are necessarily inconsistent over time, consistency measures like split-half reliability are not applicable either. Consequently, the concept of reliability is rarely addressed in process tracing research (Harte & Koele, 1997), except for the coding scheme as inter-rater reliability. As this is not an issue concerning the method *per se*, we will drop this issue here and refer to the literature on content analysis (e.g., Krippendorff, 2004; Neuendorf, 2002).

As a first step in assessing validity, we focused on the reactivity resulting from the video observation. In all three studies, most participants indicated that they had been not at all or only slightly disturbed (seven-point rating scale, 1 = not disturbed, 7 = very much disturbed; $M_1 = 2.7$, $M_2 = 2.1$, $M_3 = 2.3$). Younger people felt less disturbed in study 1 and study 2 ($r_1 = -.18$, $r_2 = -.24$, all $ps < .05$); this relationship is of comparable size in study 3 ($r_3 = -.18$, $p = .16$), but is not significant. No differences between men and women regarding reactivity were found in any of the studies.

In study 2, we directly probed for perceived changes in participants' shopping experiences. About one third of the participants indicated that they had spent less time in the store because of the video observation. Changes in feelings were reported by 31 percent of the participants (they experienced some kind of negative feelings or "felt observed"). The perceived changes in other dimensions are less pronounced: 20 percent examined fewer products, 14 percent thought less intensively about their purchases, and 11 percent indicated that they had purchased fewer products because of the observation. Overall, this suggests that reactivity exists to some degree, but is not a major threat to the validity of video-cued thought protocols.

Testing the validity of verbal reports directly is no trivial task, as it is nearly impossible to find a perfect criterion for validation which is not based on some other form of verbal reports (Russo et al., 1989; for an example see Biehal & Chakravarti, 1989). Many studies use differences in task completion and solution time between different verbalization conditions as indicators (e.g., Dickson et al., 2000; Russo et al., 1989; Schooler et al., 1993). In our study 1, we observed behavior that is supposed to be an indicator for certain cognitive processes as criteria for the verbalized thoughts referring to the same cognitive processes (i.e., product evaluation, decision-making).

The correlation pattern between behavior and cognition allowed us to check for convergent and discriminant relationships (Campbell & Fiske, 1959): The correlations should be high between thoughts and behavior that reflect the same processes and low between thoughts and behavior that pertain to different cognitive processes. For instance, behavior that is an indicator of the product evaluation, such as thoroughly looking at or touching products, was assumed to correlate with verbalized thoughts referring to product evaluation, but not (or at least lower) with thoughts referring to orientation in the store. The correlation pattern in our study turned out to be in accordance with our expectations: 17 out of 21 correlations support the respective convergent and discriminant relationships (Büttner et al., 2005).

A similar approach has been used by Jacoby, Chestnut, Hoyer, Sheluga, and Donahue (1978), but the other way around: They examined the validity of behavioral process data by using verbal protocols. Furthermore, Guan et al. (2006) compared retrospective verbalizations on information processing sequences with observed data on eye fixations. Both studies reflect the results from our study: Verbal reports and behavioral process data correspond, but the relationship is not perfect.

A further procedure in proving the validity of verbal reports is to derive a network of relationships between constructs from theory that includes constructs measured by verbal reports (nomological validity). In our study 1, we applied a design which would allow a theory-driven postulation of differences in cognitions between two groups: those who come to the store with a purchase intent and those that come to browse in the store without a particular purchase in mind (Bloch, Ridgway, & Sherrell, 1989). According to the theory of action phases and mind-sets (Gollwitzer, 1990, 1996), we predicted that browsing customers would be more open-minded regarding new information and would process information regarding the desirability of certain goals, whereas customers with a purchase intent try to ensure the realization of their chosen goal (i.e., the purchase). These differences are supposed to resurface in differences in the cognitive activities reported in the video-cued thought protocols of the two groups. Five of the seven hypotheses tested are in accordance with these predictions: Browsing customers report more thoughts on perceiving alternatives and on evaluating alternatives; customers with a purchase intent report more thoughts on orientation, the selection of alternatives, and problems with achieving their goal (Büttner et al., 2005).

To sum up, the results on convergent and discriminant as well as on nomological validation evidence that video-cued thought protocols can be valid measures of consumers' cognitive processes while shopping in a store. This also implies that nonveridicality and reactivity are not serious threats when applying video-cued thought protocols. Participants' self-reports on reactivity support this conclusion.

Utility

So far, we have reported evidence on the feasibility and validity of the method. But is using the technique also worthwhile? Typically, the effort required for video-cued thought protocols, as with other process tracing techniques, is high. Consequently, we shall discuss further whether video-cued thought protocols can provide insights into consumers' in-store behavior that compensate for the amount of effort required.

In study 1, we addressed the utility of the method by examining whether data provided by video-cued thought protocols can predict one of the pivotal outcomes of the visit to a store: whether a customer buys something or not. Twenty-five percent of the customers with purchase intent did not buy anything. By using logistic regression, we found that data on cognitive processes derived from the video-cued thought protocols can distinguish between those who did act upon their original intention and those who did not (Büttner et al., 2005).[2] The more thoughts the participants verbalized on the selection of alternatives and on the evaluation of goal achievement, the more likely they were to purchase. While these two predictors are quite obvious, the third predictor reveals more interesting insights: The more thoughts participants reported on searching/perceiving alternatives, the less likely they were to buy. This is consistent with other findings on an inverse relationship between number of options and likelihood to purchase (Iyengar & Lepper, 2000).

In study 2, video-cued thought protocols were collected from shoppers in a grocery store. The protocols were used to analyze shoppers' cognitive processes at the level of individual purchase decisions (Marienhagen, 2005). These purchase decisions were analyzed with regard to reasons for the purchase. Among other results, in-store stimuli were more frequently mentioned as reasons for individual purchases in the thought protocols when customers had less clear ideas about what to buy before entering the store. Moreover, individual purchase decisions were rated with regard to the decision involvement. Most purchase decisions were classified as low involvement decisions based on criteria such as the amount of information processing, interest in the product, or reported social influence. High involvement decisions were found to be most prevalent when customers decided not to buy a product that they had originally planned to purchase. In contrast, nearly all unplanned

---

[2] The analysis is restricted to the purchase intent group because the number of browsing customers who purchased a product was too small to conduct reasonable analyses.

purchases were classified as low involvement purchases. The variability of involvement during a shopping trip can easily be dismissed when relying only on overall measures: The actual ratio of high involvement compared to low involvement decisions was not reflected in an overall rating of purchase decision involvement.

Study 3 focused on the shopping behavior of couples (Weitemeyer, 2006). Video-cued thought protocols were assessed for the person identified as the "main shopper." While they commented on the video, their shopping partners were asked to listen to a CD using headphones. After the initial interviewee had finished, the waiting shopping partner watched the video and took the perspective of the initial interviewee: They were asked to comment on the video with the thoughts they believed the initial interviewee had during the shopping episode. We conducted further analyses of the data provided by Weitemeyer (2006) and found that participants can guess their partner's thoughts at least to some degree: Concordance ranges from 5 percent to 45 percent ($M = 18$ percent). The partner also plays an important role during the shopping trip: About 9 percent of all verbalized thoughts refer to the shopping partner. The results from this exploratory study highlight that video-cued thought protocols have the potential to give interesting insights into the interpersonal processes that underlie shopping behavior.

Conclusions and Outlook

The range of phenomena that can be examined using video-cued thought protocols is wide. Some of those, such as in-store decision-making (King, 1969; Payne & Ragsdale, 1978) or search and navigation behavior (Titus & Everett, 1996), have already been studied using thinking aloud. Here, video-cued thought protocols present an alternative to the problematic thinking aloud method. A further research area for which video-cued thought protocols might be particularly valuable is the study of social interaction at the point of purchase. Thinking aloud is by no means reasonable for this purpose, because it would interfere with the normal communication. Moreover, the video has an important benefit: It can be analyzed for nonverbal behavior.

Nevertheless, methodological aspects remain on the research agenda; scrutinizing the influence of the video observation on customers' behaviors and identifying corresponding moderators, such as type of product or shopping orientation, appear at the top of the list. Testing other ways of generating videos for recall, such as a head-mounted camera that records from the participant's point of view (Belk & Kozinets, 2005; Omodei et al., 2005), offers further interesting perspectives—both at the methodological and theoretical level.

The use of video-cued thought protocols, however, is not restricted to academic research; management in marketing and retailing can benefit from data generated by video-cued thought protocols as well. Data on cognitive processes that are supplemented with data derived from the video recordings on consumers' paths and interaction behavior (see Chapter 13 in this volume) can draw a more complete picture of the interplay between shoppers and store environment than data provided by static methodologies. Retailers can use it for diagnostic purposes, for instance, when testing store designs or promotions.

Video-cued thought protocols can be combined with other techniques for studying shopping behavior. For instance, Otnes et al. (1995; see also Lowrey et al., 2005) have developed a procedure for shopping with consumers that integrates steps such as multiple shopping trips and interviews. The rapport that can be established when applying such a multi-step framework facilitates the use of a video camera. Within this approach, video-cued thought protocols could replace the manual notes of observations and verbalizations during the shopping episode. Moreover, the video could be used by the researcher to generate questions for later in-depth interviewing.

The latter example also highlights another issue: Although developed within the information processing paradigm, video-cued thought protocols can be used within interpretive paradigms—the main difference is the way in which the material is analyzed. Especially in ethnographic research, video records of consumer behavior are highly valued both as data (Belk, Wallendorf, & Sherry, 1989) and as a way of communicating results (Belk & Kozinets, 2005). Using the same material (i.e., the video from the shopping episode) by researchers from different paradigms may help bridge the often lamented gap between positivist and interpretive approaches in consumer research (Otnes et al., 1995; Simonson et al., 2001) and provide a richer understanding of shopping behavior in brick and mortar stores.

Overall, the preceding analysis leads to an optimistic conclusion: Video-cued thought protocols are a promising technique for research at the point of purchase. The technique is feasible in the field situation in the store, and, more importantly, it provides insights into consumers' cognitive processes that are both valid and useful.

Notes

Acknowledgments: The authors appreciate the comments and suggestions from Tina Lowrey, the anonymous reviewer, and the participants of the 25th Advertising and Consumer Psychology Conference.

References

Bargh, J. A. (2002). Losing consciousness: Automatic influences on consumer judgment, behavior, and motivation. *Journal of Consumer Research, 29,* 280–285.

Belk, R. W., & Kozinets, R. V. (2005). Videography in marketing and consumer research. *Qualitative Market Research, 8,* 128–141.

Belk, R. W., Wallendorf, M., & Sherry, J. F. (1989). The sacred and the profane in consumer behavior: Theodicy on the odyssey. *Journal of Consumer Research, 16,* 1–38.

Bettman, J. R. (1970). Information processing models of consumer behavior. *Journal of Marketing Research, 7,* 370–376.

Bettman, J. R., Luce, M. F., & Payne, J. W. (1998). Constructive consumer choice processes. *Journal of Consumer Research, 25,* 187–217.

Bettman, J. R., & Park, C. W. (1980). Effects of prior knowledge and experience and phase of the choice process on consumer decision processes: A protocol analysis. *Journal of Consumer Research, 7,* 234–248.

Biehal, G., & Chakravarti, D. (1989). The effects of concurrent verbalization on choice processing. *Journal of Marketing Research, 26,* 84–96.

Bitner, M. J. (1992). Servicescapes: The impact of physical surroundings on customers and employees. *Journal of Marketing, 56,* 57–71.

Bloch, P. H., Ridgway, N. M., & Sherrell, D. L. (1989). Extending the concept of shopping: An investigation of browsing activity. *Journal of the Academy of Marketing Science, 17,* 13–21.

Bowers, V., & Snyder, H. L. (1990). Concurrent versus retrospective verbal protocol for comparing windows usability. *Proceedings of the Humans Factors Society 34th Annual Meeting,* 1270–1274.

Bühler, K. (1907). Tatsachen und Probleme zu einer Psychologie der Denkvorgänge. I. Über Gedanken [Facts and problems regarding a psychology of thought processes. I. On thoughts]. *Archiv für die gesamte Psychologie, 9,* 297–365.

Büttner, O. B., Rauch, M., & Silberer, G. (2005). *Consumer cognition at the point of sale: Results from a process tracing study* (Contributions to Tracking Research No. 11). Göttingen: Institute of Marketing and Retailing, Georg-August-Universität Göttingen.

Büttner, O. B., Schulz, S., & Silberer, G. (2006). Perceived risk and deliberation in retailer choice: Consumer behavior towards online pharmacies. In C. Pechmann & L. L. Price (Eds.), *Advances in consumer research* (Vol. 33, pp. 197–202). Duluth, MN: Association for Consumer Research.

Campbell, D. T., & Fiske, D. W. (1959). Convergent and discriminant validation by the multitrait-multimethod matrix. *Psychological Bulletin, 56,* 81–105.

Chandon, P. (2002). *Do we know what we look at? An eye-tracking study of visual attention and memory for brands at the point of purchase* (Working paper No. 2002/60/MKT). Fontainebleau, France: INSEAD.

Chartrand, T. L. (2005). The role of conscious awareness in consumer behavior. *Journal of Consumer Psychology, 15,* 203–210.

Chebat, J.-C., & Michon, R. (2003). Impact of ambient odors on mall shoppers' emotions, cognition, and spending: A test of competitive causal theories. *Journal of Business Research, 56,* 529–539.

Cobb, C. J., & Hoyer, W. D. (1986). Planned versus impulse purchase behavior. *Journal of Retailing, 62,* 384–409.

Dahl, D. W., Manchanda, R. V., & Argo, J. J. (2001). Embarrassment in consumer purchase: The roles of social presence and purchase familiarity. *Journal of Consumer Research, 28,* 473–481.

Dickson, J., McLennan, J., & Omodei, M. M. (2000). Effects of concurrent verbalization on a time-critical, dynamic decision-making task. *Journal of General Psychology, 127,* 217–228.

Dijksterhuis, A., Smith, P. K., van Baaren, R. B., & Wigboldus, D. H. J. (2005). The unconscious consumer: Effects of environment on consumer behavior. *Journal of Consumer Psychology, 15,* 193–202.

Donovan, R. J., Rossiter, J. R., Marcoolyn, G., & Nesdale, A. (1994). Store atmosphere and purchasing behavior. *Journal of Retailing, 70,* 283–294.

Ericsson, K. A., & Simon, H. A. (1980). Verbal reports as data. *Psychological Review, 87,* 215–251.

Ericsson, K. A., & Simon, H. A. (1993). *Protocol analysis: Verbal reports as data* (rev. ed.). Cambridge, MA: MIT Press.

Fidler, E. J. (1983). The reliability and validity of concurrent, retrospective, and interpretive verbal reports: An experimental study. In P. Humphreys, O. Svenson & A. Vári (Eds.), *Analyzing and aiding decision processes* (pp. 429–440). Amsterdam: North-Holland.

Gibbons, F. X. (1983). Self-attention and self-report: The "veridicality" hypothesis. *Journal of Personality, 51,* 517–554.

Gollwitzer, P. M. (1990). Action phases and mind-sets. In E. T. Higgins & R. M. Sorrentino (Eds.), *Handbook of motivation and cognition: Foundations of social behavior* (Vol. 2, pp. 53–92). New York: Guilford Press.

Gollwitzer, P. M. (1996). The volitional benefits of planning. In P. M. Gollwitzer & J. A. Bargh (Eds.), *The psychology of action: Linking cognition to motivation and behavior* (pp. 287–312). New York: Guilford Press.

Guan, Z., Lee, S., Cuddihy, E., & Ramey, J. (2006). The validity of the stimulated retrospective think-aloud method as measured by eye tracking. *Proceedings of the SIGCHI conference on Human Factors in computing systems,* 1253–1262.

Harte, J. M., & Koele, P. (1997). Psychometric and methodological aspects of process tracing research. In R. Ranyard, R. Crozier & O. Svenson (Eds.), *Decision making: Cognitive models and explanations* (pp. 21–34). London: Routledge.

Hoyer, W. D. (1984). An examination of consumer decision-making for a common repeat purchase product. *Journal of Consumer Research, 11*, 822–829.

Iyengar, S. S., & Lepper, M. R. (2000). When choice is demotivating: Can one desire too much of a good thing? *Journal of Personality and Social Psychology, 79*, 995–1006.

Iyer, E. S. (1989). Unplanned purchasing: Knowledge of shopping environment and time pressure. *Journal of Retailing, 65*, 40–57.

Jacoby, J., Chestnut, R. W., Hoyer, W. D., Sheluga, D. A., & Donahue, M. J. (1978). Psychometric characteristics of behavioral process data: Preliminary findings on validity and reliability. In H. K. Hunt (Ed.), *Advances in consumer research* (Vol. 5, pp. 546–554), Chicago: Association for Consumer Research.

Jacoby, J., Jacard, J. J., Currim, I., Kuss, A., Ansari, A., & Troutman, T. (1994). Tracing the impact of item-by-item-information accessing on uncertainty reduction. *Journal of Consumer Research, 21*, 291–303.

Jacoby, J., Johar, G. V., & Morrin, M. (1998). Consumer behavior: A quadrennium. *Annual Review of Psychology, 49*, 319–344.

Kalbermatten, U. (1984). Selbstkonfrontation. Eine Methode zur Erhebung kognitiver Repräsentationen [Self-confrontation. A method for examining cognitive represantations]. In H. Lenk (Ed.), *Handlungstheorien interdisziplinär* (Bd. 3: Verhaltenswissenschaftliche und psychologische Handlungstheorien, Halbbd. 2, pp. 659–679). München: Fink.

King, R. H. (1969). A study of the problem of building a model to simulate the cognitive processes of a shopper in a supermarket. In G. H. Haines (Ed.), *Consumer behavior. Learning models of purchasing* (pp. 22–67). New York.

Kivetz, R., & Simonson, I. (2000). The effects of incomplete information on consumer choice. *Journal of Marketing Research, 37*, 427–448.

Krippendorff, K. (2004). *Content analysis: An introduction to its methodology* (2nd ed.). Thousand Oaks, CA: Sage.

Lowrey, T. M., Otnes, C. C., & McGrath, M. A. (2005). Shopping with consumers: Reflections and innovations. *Qualitative Market Research, 8*, 176–188.

Marienhagen, A. (2005). *Videogestützte Untersuchung des Kundenerlebens am Point of Sale* [Using video to study customers' experiences at the point of sale]. Unpublished diploma thesis, Institute of Marketing and Retailing, Georg-August Universität Göttingen.

Massen, C., & Bredenkamp, J. (2005). Die Wundt-Bühler-Kontroverse aus der Sicht der heutigen kognitiven Psychologie [The Wundt-Bühler-controversy from the perspective of contemporary cognitive psychology]. *Zeitschrift für Psychologie, 213*, 109–114.

Mattila, A. S., & Wirtz, J. (2001). Congruency of scent and music as a driver of in-store evaluations and behavior. *Journal of Retailing, 77,* 273–289.

Milliman, R. E. (1982). Using background music to affect the behavior of super-market shoppers. *Journal of Marketing, 46,* 86–91.

Neuendorf, K. A. (2002). *The content analysis guidebook.* Thousand Oaks, CA: Sage.

Nisbett, R. E., & Wilson, T. D. (1977). Telling more than we can know: Verbal reports on mental processes. *Psychological Review, 84,* 231–259.

Omodei, M. M., McLennan, J., & Wearing, A. J. (2005). How expertise is applied in real-world dynamic environments: Head-mounted video and cued-recall as a methodology for studying routines of decision making. In T. Betsch & S. Haberstroh (Eds.), *The routines of decision making* (pp. 271–288). Mahwah, NJ: Lawrence Erlbaum Associates.

Otnes, C. C., McGrath, M. A., & Lowrey, T. M. (1995). Shopping with consumers: Usage as past, present and future research technique. *Journal of Retailing and Consumer Services, 2,* 97–110.

Pashler, H., Johnston, J. C., & Ruthruff, E. (2001). Attention and performance. *Annual Review of Psychology, 52,* 629–651.

Payne, J. W. (1994). Thinking aloud: Insights into information processing. *Psychological Science, 5,* 241–248.

Payne, J. W., Bettman, J. R., & Johnson, E. S. (1993). *The adaptive decision maker.* Cambridge: Cambridge University Press.

Payne, J. W., & Ragsdale, E. K. E. (1978). Verbal protocols and direct observation of supermarket shopping behavior: Some findings and a discussion of methods. In H. K. Hunt (Ed.), *Advances in consumer research* (Vol. 5, pp. 571–577). Chicago: Association for Consumer Research.

Pieters, R., & Warlop, L. (1999). Visual attention during brand choice: The impact of time pressure and task motivation. *International Journal of Research in Marketing, 16,* 1–16.

Raaijmakers, J. G. W., & Shiffrin, R. M. (1992). Models for recall and recognition. *Annual Review of Psychology, 43,* 205–234.

Rayner, K. (1998). Eye movements in reading and information processing: 20 years of research. *Psychological Bulletin, 124,* 372–422.

Reicks, M., Smith, C., Henry, H., Reimer, K., Atwell, J., & Thomas, R. (2003). Use of the think aloud method to examine fruit and vegetable purchasing behaviors among low-income African American women. *Journal of Nutrition Education & Behavior, 35,* 154–160.

Rook, D. W. (1987). The buying impulse. *Journal of Consumer Research, 14,* 189–199.

Russo, J. E., Johnson, E. J., & Stephens, D. (1989). The validity of verbal protocols. *Memory & Cognition, 17,* 759–769.

Russo, J. E., & Leclerc, F. (1994). An eye-fixation analysis of choice processes for consumer nondurables. *Journal of Consumer Research, 21,* 274–290.

Schooler, W. J., Ohlsson, S., & Brooks, K. (1993). Thoughts beyond words: When language overshadows insight. *Journal of Experimental Psychology: General, 122,* 166–183.

Schröder, H., Berghaus, N., & Zimmermann, G. (2005). Das Blickverhalten der Kunden als Grundlage für die Warenplatzierung im Lebensmitteleinzelhandel [Customers' eye movements as basis for the placement of products in food retail]. *der Markt, 44,* 31–43.

Shiv, B., & Fedorikhin, A. (1999). Heart and mind in conflict: The interplay of affect and cognition in consumer decision making. *Journal of Consumer Research, 26,* 278–292.

Silberer, G. (1989). Die Bedeutung und Messung von Kauferlebnissen im Handel [Importance and measurement of shopping experiences in retailing]. In V. Trommsdorf (Ed.), *Handelsforschung 1989: Grundsatzfragen* (pp. 59–76). Wiesbaden: Gabler.

Silberer, G. (2000). Marketingforschung und Electronic Commerce: Die Interaktionsanalyse als innovativer Ansatz der Nutzungsforschung [Marketing research and electronic commerce: Interaction analysis as an innovative approach in usage research]. In C. Wamser (Ed.), *Electronic Commerce. Grundlagen und Perspektiven* (pp. 169–184). München: Vahlen.

Silberer, G. (2005). Die videogestützte Rekonstruktion kognitiver Prozesse beim Ladenbesuch [Video-cued reconstruction of cognitive processes during the visit to a store]. *Marketing ZFP, 27,* 263–271.

Silberer, G., Engelhardt, J.-F., & Wilhelm, T. (2003). *Der Kundenlauf im Web-shop bei unterschiedlicher Besuchermotivation* [Customers' routes through a web shop and their dependance on the motivation for the visit] (Contributions to Tracking Research No. 7). Göttingen: Institute of Marketing and Retailing, Georg-August Universität.

Simonson, I. (2005). In defense of consciousness: The role of conscious and unconscious inputs in consumer choice. *Journal of Consumer Psychology, 15,* 211–217.

Simonson, I., Carmon, Z., Dhar, R., Drolet, A., & Nowlis, S. M. (2001). Consumer research: In search of identity. *Annual Review of Psychology, 52,* 249–275.

Titus, P. A., & Everett, P. B. (1996). Consumer wayfinding tasks, strategies and errors: An exploratory field study. *Psychology & Marketing, 13,* 265–290.

van den Haak, M. J., de Jong, M. D. T., & Schellens, J. P. (2003). Retrospective vs. concurrent think-aloud protocols: Testing the usability of an online library catalogue. *Behavior & Information Technology, 22*, 339–351.

Wagner, A. C., Uttendorfer-Marek, I., & Weidle, R. (1977). Die Analyse von Unterrichtsstrategien mit der Methode des "Nachträglichen lauten Denkens" von Lehrern und Schülern zu ihrem unterrichtlichen Handeln [Analyzing teaching strategies by using the "retrospective thinking aloud" method with teachers and pupils on their classroom behavior]. *Unterrichtswissenschaft, 3,* 244–253.

Weitemeyer, A. (2006). *POS Pärchentracking: Möglichkeiten und Probleme im Lichte einer Pilotstudie* [Tracking couples at the POS: A pilot study on chances and problems]. Unpublished diploma thesis, Institute of Marketing and Retailing, Georg-August-Universität Göttingen.

Wilson, T. D. (2002). *Strangers to ourselves: Discovering the adaptive unconsciousness.* Cambridge, MA: Belknap.

Wright, P., & Rip, P. (1980). Retrospective reports on consumer decision processes: "I can remember if I want to, but why should I bother trying?" In J. C. Olson (Ed.), *Advances in consumer research* (Vol. 7, pp. 146–147). Ann Arbor, MI: Association for Consumer Research.

Wundt, W. (1907). Über Ausfrageexperimente und über die Methoden zur Psychologie des Denkens [On interview experiments and the methods of the psychology of thinking]. *Psychologische Studien, 3,* 301–360.

CARTOON SEQUENCE RESEARCH: ADDRESSING THE MYSTERY OF CONSUMER DECISION-MAKING AND RATIONALE

Dale G. Paulson

Allegiance Research Group

*C*ARTOON SEQUENCE RESEARCH (CSR) was developed to answer the question, "How can we get into the minds of consumers without asking leading questions?" CSR uses non-verbal stimuli in the form of cartoon pictographs to re-create the shopping scenario allowing respondents to explain their thinking and emotions at each step of the process. Usually 15 to 20 pictographs are given to respondents. This methodology can be useful for understanding a variety of purchase and usage scenarios such as the decisional calculus related to comparing e-shopping to brick-and-mortar shopping. Development of pictographs is based on identifying decision points in these scenarios.

CSR cartoon pictographs are like storyboards. But unlike storyboards, used so often to explain a movie or an ad to prospective consumers before being released, these are used so the consumer can explain a story *totally* from their point of view. The key here is that the researcher asks *no leading questions*.

The Challenges

When designing consumer research there are many challenges. These include the polluting effects of leading questions and the ambiguity of language, as well as the need to account for demographics including age, gender, and ethnicity. The cartoons address demographic differences by depicting different types of people. Then the cartoons replace leading questions and ambiguous language, and to see why this is important the limitations of language need to be briefly addressed.

The Limitations of Language

Words are imprecise tools. For example, they have three levels: a *denotative* element-what we think they mean; a *connotative* element-what is implied; and an *emotive* element-what is felt when words are used.

I am reminded of Mae West's line in the movie "My Little Chickadee" when the presiding judge asked, "Are you showing contempt for this court?" She replied, "No your honor, I'm doing my best to hide it." (Weintraub, 1967) Undoubtedly, Ms. West's *connotation* was meant to elicit an *emotional* response from the judge. Such is the problem with words when conducting research. I suggest that CSR may be a good alternative.

Theory and Background

CSR is an extension of Thematic Apperception Testing (TAT) and the central question for this chapter is: can TAT methodology be modified to be useful for understanding the decision-making process related to consumer behavior (purchasing)? TAT is a projective methodology in the psychoanalytic tradition (Aronow, Altman, & Reznikoff, 2001). Like the Rorschach inkblot test, TAT does personality assessment by using visual stimuli (Janda, 1998). CSR uses visual stimuli but its purpose is to understand consumer behavior, not to assess personality. Another important difference in these methodologies is the amount of context in the images. The Rorschach provides little or no context, TAT provides some context usually with one image that is subject to a variety of interpretations, and CSR provides more context with a series of images and the continued emphasis on interpretation.

Donoghue (2000) describes the benefits and limitation of projective research. Projective techniques were originally developed by clinical psychologists. It was assumed that projective techniques, which use vague, ambiguous, and unstructured stimuli, allow the subject to "project" his or her personality and self-concept to give the situation some structure. In this context, they were used to understand the unconscious desires and feelings of the subject. As a diagnostic technique, its usefulness depended on acceptance of a particular school of thought and on the skill of the interviewer.

From the almost totally vague technique of the Rorschach (inkblots), projective techniques evolved as follows:

> to the more contextual, including TAT with a single somewhat vague picture;
> to word association;
> to pictographic story-telling;
> to bubble drawings (that show what the person in the cartoon is saying);
> to sentence completion; and
> to role-playing which can include play-acting, drawing, or painting.

Projective techniques can also include asking why a subject answered in the way that they did. For example, can you rank these items in terms of "most important" to "least important" and why.

The primary disadvantage of projective techniques is the complexity of the data and the corresponding skill of the researcher in interpreting them (Burns & Lennon, 1993). There is no tabulation or scoring, yet the technique does provide a wealth of information. On the plus side, this information is garnered without asking leading questions because the respondent must interpret the stimuli prior to responding. With this approach, "there's gold in them thar hills," but the researcher still must recognize the nuggets.

CSR seeks to understand consumer behavior by providing visual stimuli that is sufficiently contextual, yet still open to subjective interpretation. Figure 12.1 describes the role that context plays in the process.

The y-axis on the graph goes from Rorschach to TAT to CSR, and the x-axis goes from the Psychoanalytic to Marketing and Consumer Research. The ascending line indicates that as context increases, we move away from Rorschach and Psychoanalytic to CSR and Marketing and Consumer Research. Therefore context is critical to understanding the value of cartoon sequencing as a tool for exploring consumer behavior.

Specifying Context

The cartoons need to provide detail and yet be vague enough to allow for a variety of interpretations. The respondent needs to identify with the cartoons and the cartoons must reflect a usage or buying scenario. The process starts by specifying shopping or usage scenarios. Examples include understanding the car purchasing scenario at a specific car dealership, purchasing

Projective Methodology Using Images

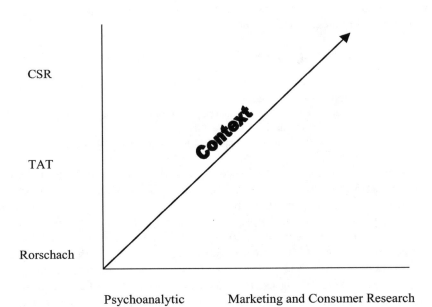
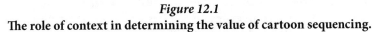

Figure 12.1
The role of context in determining the value of cartoon sequencing.

a new home from a home builder, using an ATM machine, retail shopping in different environments, and so forth.

Next, the decision-points in the purchase or usage scenario are specified. A decision point can be defined as the opportunity for the consumer or respondent to say "no". For the car-purchasing scenario, decision-points may include "looking at a dealership ad in the newspaper" or "when the sales person first greets the customer" or "when the customer first looks at the price sticker on the new automobile." There can be many decision-points and the researcher needs to be overt in identifying "probable" decision-points. As the research develops, respondents will usually describe additional decision-points. *This research methodology is evolutionary and dynamic and should reflect the respondent's orientation and suggestions.*

Once the decision points are specified, an initial set of cartoons are developed and tested with "typical" consumers. With the car-purchasing scenario, a middle-aged couple was depicted in the initial set. Experience suggests that

15 to 20 cartoons work well and that different sets need to be made to try and match the prospective respondents in terms of demographics such as age, gender, ethnicity, and shopping style.

The respondent should feel that the individual(s) depicted in the cartoon-pictographs represent themselves. Typically, the following cartoon sets would be utilized: (1) male and female of various ages including young, middle age, older; and (2) various group settings such as single or married with children of various ages. The research question and the audience to be investigated determine the cartoon sets. In most instances eight to ten different demographic sets of cartoon-pictographs are utilized. From a technical standpoint, this is fairly easy because we simply insert different people into the backgrounds.

Overall, the respondent needs to: (1) understand the situation; (2) interact in some way to other people or situations; and (3) have an opportunity to reflect on their experience—hopefully without prompting by the researcher. Therefore, three types of cartoons are utilized: *situational; interactive; and reflective.* Tom Gorski, Executive Director of a national association and an accomplished artist, designed the cartoons in this chapter. He has an excellent understanding of marketing and CSR and contributed many insightful ideas to its development.

Situational Cartoons

This situational cartoon shows a wide shot of a shopping mall. An escalator, foliage, stores, and shoppers are depicted. This Cartoon is designed to encourage respondents to talk about the general environment of a shopping mall. For example, this shows openness and the opportunity to experience the outdoors in a warm controlled environment. This is one of the appeals of the Mall of America in Minnesota—that is, the opportunity to experience an outdoor-like summer experience in the winter. This cartoon addresses what may be termed the broader environmental aspects of the mall experience.

This situational cartoon shows a young woman perusing a mall directory. It provides a little more context than the cartoon described above, but still provides the opportunity for broad interpretation. For example, we could learn about signage, decisions related to which stores interest her, or her overall impression of how easy it is to find things in this particular mall. Again, there remains considerable opportunity for interpretation.

This situational cartoon shows several people at the entrance of a store, presumably a restaurant. Notice that two people are looking at a directory or menu and one person is waiting. Thus we have a little more context, and there are three people with which the respondent can identify. Opinions can be offered on a variety of things such as the outside décor of the store or restaurant, the contents of the directory or menu, and the actions of the people. The respondent tends to zero in on that which they believe is the most significant.

Overall, situational cartoons tend to depict an environment that is germane to the research question that generally has to do with purchasing or usage, and are contextually understood and sufficiently generalized so as to allow for a variety of interpretations. Other examples could include cartoons of the outside of the mall or a road sign announcing the mall entrance. The purpose of this type of cartoon is to "set the scene" or to establish context. Oftentimes these types of cartoons will go from the general to the more specific. For example, they may start by showing an advertisement for a store or product. This may be the first impression that the respondent has concerning the store or product.

Interactive Cartoons

Interactive cartoons depict face-to-face experiences. This interactive cartoon shows a car shopper looking at the sticker on a new car. The goal of this type of cartoon is to encourage the respondent to "react" to the interaction or relationship in the cartoon. The interaction can be to an object or an individual. Cashiers or salespersons are often depicted. Interactive cartoons can also show a customer using or examining a product. This cartoon is a close-up of the sticker, and the entire car or type of car is not shown. The emphasis is on the sticker.

This interactive cartoon simply shows a man looking at a computer screen. The placement of this cartoon oftentimes provides additional context. This carton was used to gauge attitudes toward on-line shopping because the preceding cartoons in this set addressed on-line shopping. This type of cartoon can also elicit attitudes toward computers in general.

This interactive cartoon was used to determine attitudes related to the need to wait for delivery of a product when shopping on-line. This is a major difference between brick-and-mortar and on-line shopping. On-line shopping may provide for greater "written" detail about a product than in-person shopping, but it does not provide "touch and feel" plus the consumer must wait for the merchandise. This cartoon addressed the "wait" issue.

Reflective Cartoons

This cartoon shows a group discussion and since it is placed after situational or interactive cartoons, the events depicted in previous or set-up cartoons will likely be discussed by the respondents.

This cartoon shows a woman seated at a bench and it again is subject to the type of interpretation that is common in the TAT. She could be talking on a cell phone or she could be holding her head, possibly suggesting a headache or exhaustion. Again the respondent will supply the details and these details usually will reflect back on the previous cartoons.

This could be a situational cartoon depending on its placement. When this was last used this individual was shown waiting in line to make a purchase. This individual is shown leaving without the merchandise. The respondent will interpret "what he is thinking." In a sense this is a cartoon that taps into what an individual is saying to himself.

Overall, reflective cartoons can be a group discussion, one end of a phone conversation or speculation on what a person is thinking. The usefulness of this type of cartoon depends on the cartoons that precede them. Reflective cartoons depict discussion with a spouse, friend, or colleague in person or on the phone. This type of cartoon will provide the respondent the opportunity to discuss situational or interactive cartoons.

Some Unanticipated Findings

With the permission of the respondent, CSR interviews are recorded (using audio not video) and later a transcript is typed. This methodology works well for individuals or in focus groups. As noted, CSR provides information from the respondent's perspective and it provides this information in the respondent's own words. There are often "unanticipated findings" and it will be useful here to describe some of these findings.

For an Upscale Homebuilder (The Writer Corporation, Denver CO)

This homebuilder acquired land on a lake peninsula overlooking the mountains near Denver, Colorado. The land was so valuable that multi-family housing was the best option. Potential clients would be upper-middle class couples in their fifties and older. The project architect designed upscale duplexes and needed to determine if the prospective buyers would be interested. Cartoons went from the general to the specific. An aerial cartoon was shown to establish location, then some cartoons showing outside designs of the prospective homes, and finally there were various interior cartoons. The scenario was like a home tour. Several changes were needed to satisfy the respondents, but the most serious problem was with the exterior. A recurring theme was captured by this quote when respondents saw the secluded entry ways, "A great place to get mugged!" Initially the architect and builder thought that secluded entrances were a major amenity and in this case CSR provided an answer to a question that might never have been asked.

For a Bank (A Contract with Sam Lusky and Associates, Advertising and PR Firm, working with a Denver Bank)

The executives of a Midwestern bank wanted to know the best strategy to successfully appeal to grandparents to buy certificates of deposits for their young grandchildren. The executives of the bank and the grandparents thought that this was a wonderful investment for the children but to the kids it was just a piece of paper. Can you imagine the reaction of a child receiving a piece of paper with a large number? You might as well say, "This disappointment is brought to you by your local bank." Cartoon pictographs were developed and shown to grandparents and children and the findings suggested that the bank sell certificates of deposit to grandparents by including teddy bears for their grandkids. Even the tagline came from the research, "A future you can hug," and the program was a hit.

For An Auto Dealer (A Denver, Colorado Chrysler Dealership)

A set of cartoons were developed that showed the new-car purchasing scenario starting with the respondent first becoming aware of a particular dealer to driving off the lot with a new car. Recommendations from the research included: establish strategies for developing rapport before discussing a new car purchase; advertise in venues with less direct competition; and determine the subjective purchase strategy of the potential buyer. For example, to establish rapport, it was recommended that the dealership install pictures showing various interests and activities. These could include college and professional sports and leisure activities such as tennis or golf. When prospective buyers showed interest in one of the pictures, the sales people were encouraged to discuss this activity prior to discussing the purchase of a car. This required some reorientation and training of the sales staff and then it helped increase sales.

For a Non-Traditional School (Denver Free University)

This situation presented a unique challenge. This school was somewhat counter-culture because it taught arts and crafts to a group formerly referred to as "hippies." These well-meaning individuals embraced positive values but were not business oriented. The school faced a crisis when it ran out of hippies. CSR was used to reposition the school. When the appropriate cartoons were developed and when the appropriate audiences were identified the school was able to fill a needed niche. The school went from teaching arts and crafts to teaching computer skills. However, the training was not directed to business executives. Traditional schools already filled this need. Rather the training was designed for executive assistants and secretaries. This group was put off by traditional education with its emphasis on competition and grades. CSR research with executive assistants and secretaries found that the phrase, "We teach but we don't grade," resonates with this group. The residual image of the "hippy" school became an advantage.

For a New Home Sales Office (A Contract with Sam Lusky and Associates for a Denver Home Builder)

This research project was more focused because it sought to answer the question, "Why don't prospects buy a home that is 'perfect' for them when they first see it?" CSR explored the decision calculus of the new homebuyer by ensuring that the cartoons in the process met all or most of their needs. Special emphasis was placed on reflective cartoons. Early on it became apparent that potential buyers set for themselves the number of homes to look at before they will buy. A new sales strategy, which included competitive home information, was used to close more deals. Sometimes the sales personnel from our client would accompany the potential buyer to other competitors' projects.

For National and State Associations (Allegiance Research Group)

The association business is a multi-billion dollar industry (according to the trade newspaper, *Association Trends*) but it was not well understood why people join and stay with associations; i.e. why they purchase a membership. Cartoon research was used to let members and potential members explain their motivations and the key cartoon that unlocked these secrets showed a person writing a check. The research uncovered nine basic reasons and they became the basis for segmenting members into nine types. A few examples include: *Shapers*™ who want to participate in policy making; *Altruistics*™ who share the values and mission of the association; *Cognoscenti*™ who want specialized information they can't get elsewhere; *Relevant Participants*™ who want to attend meetings; and *Status Conscious*™ who want the association to enhance the prestige of their profession (Paulson, 1998). Every association has a unique mix of these segments and can develop specific marketing strategies for its dominant segments.

This research also goes one step further. Each of the consumers fills out a short one-page form asking about this purchase, and the results are summarized into a three-digit code that goes into the association's database. Now the organization knows what each member wants, no more guesswork. These segments enable an organization to do target marketing, operate more efficiently, and find new opportunities. For example, when looking for members to serve on a committee look up the *Shapers*™, or when looking for members to volunteer for a fundraiser look up *Altruistics™*. Write different renewal letters for each segment rather than the same letter to everyone. More personalized service leads to more loyalty which in turn leads to increased revenue.

Reliability and Validity

CSR is a projective methodology, and reliability (i.e., can we do it again?) and validity (i.e., are we measuring what we think we are measuring?) remain a challenge. The standard answer is that projective research is good for hypothesis testing and requires validation through triangulation. But it shortchanges CSR somewhat. CSR takes the interrogative researcher out of the process, it matches the cartoons to the respondent's demographics or shopping style, it considers emotional response to be important, it allows the respondents to comment on the "appropriateness" of the cartoons, and it reveals information that is relevant but unanticipated. When respondents respond to similar cartoons in similar ways this suggests that we are getting reliable results and that we are indeed measuring what we think we are measuring. Further testing, such as content analysis and triangulation, are still merited.

Conclusions

This chapter began by suggesting that CSR may be useful in investigating the motivations related to e-shopping versus brick-and-mortar. It is certainly possible to design cartoons depicting the two scenarios. In fact, cartoon research may be one of the best alternatives. Previous research shows that even if the cartoon or purchase scenario is approximate, respondents provide valuable information. Korzybski (1931), when describing how people interpret the world, said "the map is not the territory." Still, a map is very useful for understanding the territory and it is my contention that cartoon pictographs are better than words for understanding usage or buying scenarios.

This methodology provides unintentional and valuable information that is still contextually relevant. Visual provocation results in subjective vocabulary. That is, the respondents explain "their reality" in their own words. Emotional responses, which are common, appear to validate respondents' identification with the purchase or usage scenario. Recurring themes by different respondents appear to be valuable. For example, the cartoon showing the secluded entrance of a home elicited concern for security over and over again. The cartoon showing a price sticker on a new car elicited several similar strong comments. Sense-based vocabulary such as I see, I feel, I hear can be analyzed separately and, finally, content analysis can be utilized to further understand comments. If we assume that the respondent is able to explain their decisional calculus, then a projective methodology in the form of cartoon sequencing offers a good chance to understand the motivations related to e-shopping versus brick-and-mortar shopping.

References

Aronow, E., Weiss, K. A., & Reznikoff, M. (2001). *A practical guide to the thematic apperception test: the TAT in clinical practice*. Philadelphia: Taylor & Francis.

Burns, L. D., & Lennon, S. J. (1993). Social perception: Methods for measuring our perception of others. *International Textile and Apparel Association Special Publication, 5*, 153–159.

Donoghue, S. (2000). Projective techniques in consumer research. *Journal of Family Ecology and Consumer Sciences, 28*, 47–53.

Janda, L. H. (1998). *Psychological testing: Theory and applications*. Boston: Allyn & Bacon.

Korzybski, A. (1931), A non-Aristotelian system and its necessity for rigour in mathematics and physics. Paper presented before the American Mathematics Society at the New Orleans, Louisiana meeting of the American Association for the Advancement of Science, December 28, 1931. Reprinted in *Science and Sanity*, 1933, pp. 747–761.

Paulson, D. G. (1998). *Allegiance®: Fulfilling the promise of one-to-one marketing for associations*. Washington, DC: American Society of Association Executives.

Weintraub, J. (1967). *The wit and wisdom of Mae West*. New York: Avon Books.

13

BEHAVIOR AT THE POS—CLASSICAL AND NEWER METHODS OF RECORDING IT

Günter Silberer

Georg-August-Universität Göttingen, Germany

*M*ANY PRODUCTS ARE STILL bought and sold via stationary retailing, even in the age of the Internet. What underlines the central significance of buyer research in retailing is the fact that countless purchase decisions are only made at the Point of Sale (POS). In any case, it is of interest to all parties involved regarding in which areas of a store customer contacts are made and what these contacts look like. Just as advertising does not reach everyone or realize the desired contact qualities, in-store offers suffer the same fate.

Shopper wayfinding essentially determines the *number of contacts* with the offer, and the shopper's "approach behavior" the *contact quality*. We therefore take a closer look here at these two behavior categories—wayfinding and approach behavior. As a result, we are primarily interested in the possibilities of recording the behavior at the POS. In addition to the classical and newer methods, we also report current trends and, finally, discuss the challenges which POS research faces tomorrow. Closer consideration of the causes and effects of the behavior at the POS is reserved for another article.

General Remarks on Behavior at the POS

The possible methods and difficulties of recording visitor or customer behavior at the POS depend on which behavior is to be recorded. It therefore makes a difference:

1. Whether the intention is to map wayfinding and shopper paths only or also to record approach behavior such as looking (i.e. what is

looked at how often and for how long), touching (i.e. what is picked up and inspected), or replacing and taking away (i.e. what is ultimately purchased);

2. Whether the intention is to examine search behavior only, i.e. the behavior of shoppers intending to purchase specific products, or also browsing, i.e. the behavior of people who enter the store with no intention to buy but simply to look around (see Babin & Darden, 1995; Bloch & Richins, 1983; Iyer, 1989; Kahn & Schmittlein, 1992; Zielke, 2002);

3. Whether behavior throughout the entire store visit is of interest or only parts of this activity (e.g. behavior in a certain department or at a selected shelf);

4. Whether purchase-related behavior only is of interest or also returning empties, changing goods, or redeeming bonus points; and

5. Whether the intention is to record the behavior of individual consumers only or possibly also to note differing wayfinding and approach behavior by groups (e.g. the behavior of couples, parents with children, or same-age groups).

Consequently, important dimensions of shopper behavior are addressed. However, we should also distinguish areas of behavior. In this way, a study can examine visits to shopping centers or other agglomerations, e.g., downtown areas. Furthermore, behavior distributed over several shop visits can be of interest to analyze temporal patterns of behavior.

Within the scope of this chapter, we will concentrate upon behavior during a shop-visit, knowing full well that certain statements on the recording of POS behavior can also be applied to other behavioral areas and longer periods of time.

The Classification and Assessment of the Recording Instruments

A glance at the methodological arsenal of behavioral research, as well as at studies of behavior at the POS to date, soon makes clear that there are several possible research tools (see Granbois, 1968). We can distinguish between the following groups: *observation methods* (i.e. methods using observers), *video recordings* (understood as camera-supported observations), *registration techniques* in which people are not needed for the data collection, and *interview methods* in which test participants are asked for information.

If the instruments which are possible for the recording of POS behavior are considered, not only is their description of interest to us, but also their suitability. As regards *feasibility, social acceptance* on the part of all those involved and affected is to be observed in addition to what is financially, administratively, and technically viable—in the case of the experimentees themselves, other shoppers, employees, and the management. The shopper should agree to the recording in advance or retrospectively. Besides, it has to be considered that potential observees can be perturbed by the measurement of other shoppers' behavior. Furthermore, reservations on the part of the sales and service staff can arise through their being observed or recorded intentionally or by coincidence. If the managers anticipate such reservations in their customers and staff and maybe fear further restrictions, they may refuse to grant permission for the appropriate measuring experiments from the outset.

A further assessment criterion is *internal validity*. This means the suitability in a narrower sense, namely whether an instrument records exactly what it is supposed to record. As evident as this may be, it is difficult to ascertain and verify internal validity. In the formulation of demands on internal validity, it should be considered that methods cannot be criticized with the argument that they cannot describe all aspects of the POS behavior when not all aspects of the behavior at the POS are of interest (cf. Ericsson & Simon, 1980, p. 243).

Finally, the *external or ecological validity* should also be taken into account, as a measurement of shopper behavior as a rule should allow certain conclusions regarding the behavior of comparable shoppers in similar shops and comparable situations. This also applies to the conclusion regarding any situations in which no recording is carried out. Against this background, Wells and LoSciuto's (1966, p. 228) claim that the samples should be representative, cover all aspects of a shop and, furthermore, record different times, is evident. Whether such a high demand should always be imposed upon ecological validity, let alone if it can be realized, remains doubtful. Findings whose reference is restricted according to person, space, and time, can also be extremely helpful.

The Individual Recording Instruments

Observation Methods

In-store shopper movement and approach behavior is open-field behavior. It is consequently obvious that observation should first come to mind as a research method. That no psychological processes such as purchase plans and their revision can be recorded (as discussed, for example by Granbois,

1968), in no way alters the fact that observation is an appropriate method of registering behavior at the POS. The key requirement is the use of suitable, trained observers. They can act passively (passive or non-participating observation) or take part actively in what is happening (participating observation). Moreover, the circumstance of being observed can either be withheld from the shoppers under observation (concealed observation), or they can be made aware of the observation or have it disclosed to them in advance (open observation).

(1) Concealed, Passive Observation. Studies carried out so far have focused mainly on concealed, passive observation. Classic examples are the US studies by Wells and Lo Sciuto (1966) and Granbois (1968), in which customer movement was observed in-store (see Groeppel-Klein, Bartmann & Germelmann, 2006, for a recent European study). Wells and Lo Sciuto (1966) concentrated on episodic behavior in individual stages and only on categories of goods that the relevant shopper showed an interest in purchasing. The observers were tasked with recording which products the test persons looked at, put back or placed in their shopping cart, and also with registering what they paid attention to (e.g., weight and price) and who influenced whom. We are not told whether valid recording of specific interactions with objects was successful (p. 232). Granbois (1968) used observers wearing typical staff or sales assistant outfits, who had to enter the customer's path on maps of the store's layout, and also points at which products were looked at and/or placed in the cart. Of 388 shoppers observed, only one person noticed they were being watched. Similar success is reported, for example, by Botelho (2002) and Baldauf, Srnka, and Wagner (1997) in their studies of customer paths in German and Austrian stores respectively. In the broad-based ISB study (ISB-Studie, 1986, p. 13) there are reports of break-offs because the subjects had realized they were under observation, but these are not quantified. The authors report 819 successful observations from approximately 1,000 observation attempts, indicating a substantial number of failures.

In addition to shoppers' paths, certain forms of interaction can be observed. However, only a very few experiments are available on this topic. For the observation of interaction behavior at a shelf, Hoyer (1984) used an observer dressed as an employee, who had to observe the shopper discreetly and establish which brands were looked at, taken off the shelf and purchased, and how much time this took. Also of interest in this study were across-brand comparisons and within-brand comparisons. Mindful of the fact that, in the case of small-sized products, such processes do not induce visible movements and are consequently difficult to record through observation, Hoyer therefore opted to conduct his research at a detergent shelf.

Given that visual attention cannot as a rule be observed well when the observer is standing behind the test person, the obvious solution is to use a method by which people standing behind the shelf can be observed. For this purpose one-way mirrors have occasionally been used as shelf units (Russo & Leclerc, 1994). But this method works only if the products on the shelves do not interfere with the view of the shopper visiting the shelf.

(2) Open, Passive Observation. Observation is carried out openly if, for example, permission has been requested in advance and granted by the people who are to be observed. If the person known to be the observer tends to behave passively, their influence on what is happening may be negligible; it may, however, also be considerable, because the person being observed might react simply to the fact of being observed (reactance or demand effects; Rosenthal & Rosnow, 1969; Spano, 2006). Consent to being observed by no means rules out reactivity of behavior. To my knowledge, studies in which shoppers were observed openly but passively have not been carried out as yet.

(3) Participating Observation. An observer taking an active part in what is happening may be known as such to the person observed, but not necessarily so. If, for instance, a sales assistant at a service counter is briefed to observe the people served, this does not have to be made public. In cases like this it must be borne in mind that the staff involved, as concealed participating observers, are not always able or willing to make objective judgments. A more sensible approach would therefore be to have the interaction between the sales and service staff on the one hand and shoppers on the other observed by a third party (see Bitner, 1992, on social interaction at the POS).

If observers are to accompany the selected test persons in-store, this can by all means take place openly and also with instructions to influence the shopper's behavior. In the study by Payne and Ragsdale (1978) 19 housewives were accompanied on several weekly shopping trips. The attendants had to observe and record the following in the "candy department:" the customers' paths, the products taken, the use of a shopping list, the use of coupons, and the behavior in the candy department. At the same time, arrangements had to be made for the shoppers to express their thoughts out loud and clearly. The attendants thus had to ensure, constantly and wherever necessary, that thought expression did not cease. The trained observers in the study by Titus and Everett (1996) also had this dual role. They were likewise instructed to accompany shoppers through the store, to observe their search behavior, and to encourage them to express their thoughts out loud. Under observation were test persons with a shopping list containing 21 products that had to be found, not bought, in the store. It is to be hoped that the shoppers and attendants in this study coped well with their by no means easy tasks.

"Shopping with Consumers" is a special variant of participating observation developed and recommended by Otnes, McGrath, and Lowrey (1995; see also Lowrey, Otnes, & McGrath, 2005). Here, the buyer is accompanied on at least two shopping trips following prior arrangement and interview. He/she should be used to the presence of the accompaniment by the second shop-visit and behave as naturally as possible (Lowrey et al., 2005). The information of the test person also serves this purpose—"so participants would not be alarmed during the actual trip" (p. 177).

Evaluation of the Observation Methods. The technical feasibility does not constitute a noteworthy problem in the observation. However, observations are always fairly costly. The observers have to be instructed carefully and trained sufficiently (Lowrey et al., 2005). If necessary, joint shop-visits need to be planned and arranged sufficiently in advance. The social acceptance is more likely to pose problems. Not every buyer wants to be observed, let alone accompanied. Opposition does not only depend upon the age and gender of the accompanying person but also upon which purposes the study serves (whether they are scientific or commercial). Consequently, at least in the case of open and participating observations, it is difficult to avoid the selectivity of the sample and, thus, a reduction of the external validity. The latter also suffers from the influence which the observation can, and indeed does, exert upon the purchase situation and, therefore, the behavior at the POS. Judging from our results, there are indeed customization effects which do not only appear in the second observed purchase but also during the first or only shop-visit. The deciding internal validity of an observation of shop visitors depends primarily upon the suitability of the observer, on their existing capabilities on the one hand (above all, their social intelligence), and on their instruction and training on the other. Observation has to be trained itself but the retention of the observation results should also be practiced.

Film Footage (Videography)

Film footage is equally suitable for the recording of behavior at the POS. This can be described as camera-supported observation, and also as a kind of registration if no camera man is used. At any rate, there are different ways of using film cameras at the POS.

(1) CCTV Cameras. For security reasons closed circuit television (CCTV) cameras are fixtures in many stores. However, they may not be used at will

and everywhere for the purposes of market research. Newman and Foxall (2003) argue in favor of using the CCTV systems already available in many stores to record customer movement in such a way that it does not overstep any legal and ethical barriers. This could be achieved by: first, having a central computer system store the videos recorded by digital cameras; second, evaluating them by means of pattern recognition to record shoppers' pathfinding and attention behavior; and third, making employees' (and customers'?) faces unrecognizable. However, the authors do not say whether their system succeeds in recording individual shopper movement throughout the store and how expensive a system that can track shoppers across more than one room would be. At any rate, initial applications by Newman and Foxall (2003) show that paths in a specific room can be recorded just as successfully as the staff involved can be made anonymous. However, even when tracking is confined to one single room, it is doubtful whether one or more cameras in that room can always be in a position to cover all goods presentation areas and hence to record all conceivable approach behavior by shoppers.

(2) Recordings Made by a Camera Operator.   Pathfinding and attention activities can be recorded successfully if the shopper is "pursued" by a camera operator who attempts to record all important aspects of wayfinding and approach behavior (see Silberer, 2005, and Chapter 11 in this volume). Nowadays, modern, handy digital film cameras enable filming to take place with minimal obtrusiveness. However, with this method not only must the shoppers selected and approached be asked for their approval, but staff who may appear on the footage produced must also give their consent. What is more, shoppers not involved in the procedure must not be placed in a position where they fear appearing in the footage or otherwise develop a sense of being disturbed. That, too, would arguably deter management from allowing studies of this kind. But initial experience with this method shows that careful, unobtrusive use of small digital film cameras is by all means possible, meeting with acceptance mainly among younger generations and open-minded managers.

When the film is shown immediately afterwards on a PC to the people involved, their wayfinding and approach activities can be discussed, e.g. the type and focus of an interaction with a product on the shelf for which the film alone does not provide sufficient information. It must be said, though, that the diagnostic gain with the method using a camera operator in tow and video-supported interviewing on approach activities comes at the cost of certain restrictions in terms of the representativeness of the random sample and the disadvantage of a certain element of reactivity in the case of some test persons.

(3) *Location-Bound Film Footage.* We can distinguish between two types of location-bound, in this case shelf-bound, types of filming: shots towards the front of the shelf and shots from out of the shelf unit. Very early on, Norman Albers (quoted by Hicks & Kohl, 1955) worked with a memomotion or quick motion camera to record customer behavior at the dairy shelf over a period of three weeks. The camera was positioned nearby, attached to another shelf, from where it could film the entire dairy shelf. This delivered evidence on the buyers (sex, age group), their behavior when purchasing products, and evident brand preferences, in each case accompanied by the most precise time data. Hicks and Kohl (1955) stress as the advantages of this method not only the possibility of permanent operation (providing a kind of full census) and low costs, but also the ability to record shoppers' behavior without disturbance and in detail (although the latter may arguably not always hold true).

Occasionally one-way mirrors are installed behind a shelf in order to observe or film customer behavior unnoticed. Russo and Leclerc (1994) worked in the laboratory with a video camera behind the shelf, behind just such a one-way mirror. Their aim was to record as precisely as possible shoppers' perception behavior as visual attention. They needed customers to stand in a particular spot to obtain the necessary, evaluable recordings. Evaluation of the video recordings enabled them to determine eye fixations; although they could not pinpoint the duration of individual fixations, they certainly could determine the duration of certain fixation sequences. Of 47 test persons only one noticed the one-way mirror, but "did not suspect that it concealed a video camera" (p. 276).

(4) *Recordings With the Aid of an "Eye Camera."* A classical technique for recording visual attention or interaction—De Heer, Groenland, and Bloem (2000) speak of "exploratory visual search behavior"—is the "eye camera." It consists of two component systems: one films the field of vision using an extremely small video camera (production of the field of vision video), the other records eye movement, i.e., fixations and saccades (the short and quick movements between the longer fixations). Both systems have to be calibrated for the respective application concerned. However, the demands made of the production of videos that correctly reproduce the field of vision are not as stringent as those made of recording eye flow. That is why, in the case of people with full freedom of movement such as is customary in everyday scenarios, it is easier to capture the field of vision and changes in it successfully than to measure eye movement.

At any rate, most of the eye movement studies conducted so far in the context of POS have taken place in the laboratory. Chandon, Hutchinson, and Young (2001, 2002) and Young (2002), who report on procedures at the U.S. company

Perception Research Services, do go into stores, but they work in laboratory-like on-site facilities there, and not at the shelves. In these facilities they show interviewees photos of products or brands in slide shows to capture visual attention reactions and assess consumer acceptance by interviews. The time until the first eye fixation, the number of fixations, the length of gazes, and the total viewing duration, among other things, are measured for each product or brand.

Leven (1992) also investigated visual shelf attention using shelf slides shown in a laboratory. Pieters and Warlop (1999) likewise worked with shelf slides. Schröder and Berghaus (2005), on the other hand, used a reproduction of a real cake and pastry shelf. Leven (1992) was interested in the hit rate with the search for certain magazine titles and the "structure" of the search. Pieters and Warlop (1999) even determined intra-brand saccades and inter-brand saccades but had to eliminate 10 test persons because of calibration problems, and Schröder and Berghaus (2005) had the test persons search for three products they were potentially prepared to buy so as to capture their eye movement in the process. The video recording was successful, but not the projected, computer-aided recording of eye movement, which had to be reconstructed by manual transcriptions. Even so, this approach did reveal the number of gazes: first, on the shelf space; second, on the products taken from the shelf; and third, on other objects.

One of the rare eye movement studies at the shelf conducted in the field is the research by Schröder, Berghaus, and Zimmermann (2005). In three department stores this dealt with eye movement in the cream cheese category of goods, and here in particular with the frequency and duration of perception of certain shelf spaces and with eye movement and eye movement patterns. Shoppers who intended to buy cream cheese were included in the study. In this research, too, the computer-aided recording of eye movement was unsuccessful, and once again the eye movements had to be reconstructed "manually."

(5) Recordings Made by a "Field of Vision Camera." If the recording of visual fixation and eye-tracking always reaches the limit but the direction of the field of vision should be lifted, the sole use of a "field of vision camera" is obvious. Here, today's miniaturized technology offers an interesting possibility, namely the assembly of a small, inconspicuous lens on, for example, the badge of a baseball cap (Belk & Kozinets 2005, p. 131) which is connected to an equally small recorder on the belt or in the coat pocket. In this, it is important that a calibration of the field-of-vision recording is carried out and examined during the shop-visit.

Evaluation of the Video Recording Methods. The great potential of video recordings arises from the fact that they reproduce sequences of events extremely realistically, record sound and noises in addition to pictures, provide indications of behavioral situations, and can be evaluated afterwards as often as required and thus with better insights, be it by the researcher alone or enlistment of the experimentees and their commentation. Belk and Kozinets (2005, p. 137) describe the "story telling potential" of the videography.

The videography's individual options are assessed very differently. The demands on technology already vary considerably. Digital surveillance cameras may be purchased and assembled easily, but bringing the recordings together within the scope of customer tracking is just as difficult as the automatic anonymization of the people recorded—the customers and employees. In the case of a cameraman in tow, there is the enormous challenge of playing back the digital video immediately on a big enough screen and managing the possibility of parallel recording of the commentation in such a way that the customer video and the points of reference can be related to each other for later evaluation. Shelf-bound cameras should be installed inconspicuously and in such a way as to permit a view over all attention reactions. The use of a camera behind a shelf becomes especially costly if it is to be both inconspicuous and effective. The greatest difficulties are linked to attempts to record the eye movements in the shop with eye-camera recordings. Several attempts at this have failed. In comparison, the chances of a technical realization of the registration of the field of vision without recording eye movements are considerably better.

The social acceptance of the videography is bound to reach its limits. Security cameras are not installed for the purposes of market research and are not allowed to be converted everywhere. Even if lawyers do not have misgivings, the fear is that the customers do not like it. Negative private communication could play into the hands of competitors. Maybe the informed and decided consent from customers and employees feasible in special shops designated for experiments can be achieved. Such consent has to be requested if shelf-bound cameras allow the identification of people, even if this is not the purpose. Informed consent is a matter of course for recordings with eye and field of vision cameras.

The internal validity of video recordings depends considerably upon the classification of recordings and people, and the calibration. The higher the demands on the completeness and accuracy turn out to be, the easier it will be to query the validity of the videography. Optimism is then particularly appropriate if only wayfinding patterns and the attention to relatively large areas are to be surveyed. Furthermore, it will also be easier to secure the validity of attention analyses in the laboratory and in laboratory-like settings than in every-day shopping environments (Belk & Kozinets, 2005, mention "naturalistic observations" here). The assessments regarding the external validity of video recordings have to turn out appropriately differentiated. A low willingness to allow oneself to be accompanied by a cameraman (approximately 20 percent in our study), or wear an eye camera or an "equipped baseball cap" is not surprising. The reactions of the experimentees towards such measurements also contribute to the limitation of the external validity. The following consolation applies in this case: By doing without possibilities of generalization (restriction of the external validity), a veritable increase in the explanatory power (increase in the internal validity) is achieved.

Registration Techniques

For the purposes of this chapter, registration is taken to mean the recording of facts without the use of personnel. On closer consideration this also applies to certain video techniques (e.g. for the recordings made by a surveillance or CCTV system or a fixed shelf camera), so that the classification into videography and registration selected here cannot be entirely free from overlapping.

Registration techniques can also be introduced at the POS. In doing so, contact counters at particular points should be considered (e.g. in recording the visitor's arrival using light barriers and in recording visitor flows by way of footprints on the floor, should it be raining, or signs of wear and tear on the flooring).

To record shopper wayfinding and shoppers' examination of products on shelves or in displays, registration techniques capable of capturing behavioral sequences at the individual level are more of a possibility. We have already mentioned the computer-aided use of CCTV. Also conceivable and feasible are position-finding systems. Using communication networks such as cell phones as a kind of long-range radio, and radio frequency identification (RFID) as a kind of short-range radio, appropriately equipped shopping carts, shopping baskets, and possibly also people can be located and their movements followed. This also applies to the tracking of products, the more so as RFID was developed and constructed for this purpose. RFID technology is very promising. The RFID tags, which respond to radio signals and keep ID data at the ready, can be installed in shopping baskets or carts but also in fidelity cards or bonus vouchers. The corresponding sender and registration apparatus can be stored in the floor and/or in shelves (information-processing shelves and floors). The position of the RFID tag and thus the shopping cart can be determined via the retrace time of the signal. Authors like Sorensen (2003) and Larson, Bradlow and Faden (2005) are primarily concerned with tracking shopping carts. Larson et al. (2005) see a good approximation to the wayfinding behavior of the visitors in the movement of the shopping cart because they are located in close proximity to the cart in the movement phase and in its vicinity in the stationary phase (p. 396).

And if the RFID tags are built into store cards, behavioral patterns can be identified for repeat visitors to the shop. If the RFID tag can be transferred to voluntary shop visitors as part of a voucher, which can be cashed in, for example, at the cash-desk following the visit, the identification of the person would not be required. The risk of customers being a fully "transparent customer," (i.e., loosing privacy due to customer data bases, which also contain tracking data), would be far lower in this case than with RFID chips in the store cards.

In principle, the following applies: The closer the registration points are distributed in the shop, the easier it is to follow the path of a customer, shopping basket, or cart, and to estimate the duration of stops or breaks. Registration points at the entrance, the cash-desks, and exits are of primary importance in order to determine the exact duration of the visit.

Evaluation of the Registration Techniques.   Although location systems for tracking purposes are regarded as technically feasible nowadays, they nevertheless require a lot of initial investment and also certain maintenance costs. The enormous rise in the amount of data can be reduced via sample programs, and information overload avoided by using suitable data-processing programs. The social acceptance could be compromised by cautioning against the "transparent customer" and the discussion on this topic is in full swing. Consequently, it will make a large difference as to whether personal, accountable data or personal but unaccountable data is extracted and saved. At any rate, the danger that shopping basket data in the scanner system and tracking data can be amalgamated via the procedure so that the anonymization can suffer from data fusion should be taken into account.

A great advantage of recording is evident in the internal and external validity. The measurements are reliable and not reactive, excepting the open person tracking and the reaction of particular customers to the criticism of tracking in the media. A restriction can also be made where the wayfinding is concluded from the cart path. As yet, there is no clear evidence to justify such a conclusion. We can assume that the cart path and the wayfinding by no means always coincide. And, as far as the external validity is concerned, it can be said that the registration through anonymous location systems permits full recordings of behavior in realistic situations.

Interviewing Methods

Behavior is open to self-observation and hence also to interviewing. Basically, however, this calls for a certain degree of self-attentiveness and the willingness to communicate one's behavior to others. However, if the behavior took place some time before, a certain degree of memory skill is required. The same applies where longer shop-visits and various attention reactions should be recalled. Let us consider some interviewing variants and classify them according to their temporal detachment into later reports, immediate reports, and parallel reports.

(1) Later Reports. Interviews on behavior at the POS, which take place retrospectively and presumably at another location, quickly reach their limits. Nevertheless, they can still be suitable for the provision of rough clues: approximate information on the path behavior and reports on important attention reactions, such as the location of a long-sought-after product, the impulsive purchase of a special offer, consultation with a member of the sales or service staff, and the exchange of a defective product. If several people have made purchases, data regarding various actors can be compared.

(2) Immediate Reports. In the case of short shopping trips or during a visit to a particular department, an immediate interview is more likely to be successful than a later interview as the powers of recollection are not exercised to the same extent. This is different in the case of longer visits and numerous behavioral actions. Suitable memory jogs can be implemented here, suitable meaning those which evoke the behavioral process and the individual environment, such as the videography outlined above, e.g., footage shot by a cameraman (Silberer, 2005). Initial experiences, which we were able to gather with this approach, have been most successful (see Chapter 11 in this volume).

(3) Parallel Reports. Whenever low involvement and/or low powers of recall are to be expected, a just-in-time report can also be implemented besides the immediate report. Here, the customer is asked to impart his/her behavior during its execution. For this purpose, a Dictaphone, which immediately records such information, or an attendant, who makes a note of the statements, can be used. At face value, the use of a Dictaphone has the advantage that the presence of an attendant is unnecessary. However, there is the danger that the experimentee may find the just-in-time information to be a burden and therefore neglect or forget it completely.

POS research is familiar with attempts to record behavior using the "acting aloud method" (e.g., Thelen & Hermetsberger, 2006). With Payne and Ragsdale (1978) mothers had to talk to a young companion on several weekly shopping trips. The test persons had to say where they were going, what they were doing, what they were looking for, and what products or brands they had just noticed or were looking at. This was complicated by the fact that the women also had to report what thoughts came to mind in each case. This meant that two things not only had to be recorded, but also put into words.

At any rate, the companion was tasked with repeatedly encouraging the test person—where necessary—to say what they were thinking and doing.

Titus and Everett (1996) confronted their test persons with a task of similar magnitude. The test persons were supposed to search the store for the products contained in a shopping list, saying in the process where they were searching, why they were specifically looking there, what pointers they use to find their way around the store and whatever else occurred to them. In this case, too, the interviewees were accompanied by an attendant to keep the articulation of their thoughts and behavior going, whenever necessary.

Evaluation of the Interviewing Methods.   General possibilities and limitations of the interviewing methods are widely known and will not be described here (e.g., see Cannel & Kahn, 1968, or Fontana & Frey, 1994). The indication of the limitations of self-perception, memory, formulation of statements, and the willingness to communicate will have to suffice. However, we maintain that the feasibility of interviews and the use of technical equipment do not cause many problems, and that by no means all of the possibilities of a cued interview are used today. Besides, it is apparent that the social acceptance suffers if there is not any time available, a companion interferes with the shop-visit and/or an insight into personal things is not wanted. Therefore, the internal validity is also constantly at risk. This also applies to the external validity as not everyone participates gladly in an interview (selectivity) and not every behavioral situation remains unaffected by the behavior assessment, especially in the parallel interview by a companion or in the recording of "loud reports" about one's own behavior.

Selected Method Combination Options

The combination of different measuring methods can serve different purposes: on the one hand, the verification of methods if they appear to measure the same thing (validation aim), on the other hand, the enhancement of the recognition potential if the methods measure different things and thus compliment each other (synergy aim). This combination for the purpose of work division or cooperation will be the focus of attention here. Let us begin with the method combinations within a method group before turning to group-spanning combinations.

On Method Combinations Within a Method Group

(1) Observation Mix.   An example of a useful observation combination is provided by any case where the researcher observes selected shoppers in their

wayfinding behavior passively and, if necessary, undercover whilst employees at the self-service and service counters observe the same customers, also undercover but actively (doing their usual job).

(2) Video Mix. While a CCTV system records the wayfinding and identifies wayfinding patterns, the concrete approach behavior at particular shelves can be recorded via fixed shelf cameras. It is also conceivable that the behavior at the shelf be recorded with two cameras, where one camera records the customer from the back and the other is placed behind the shelf and placed behind a one-way mirror in order to record visual attention.

(3) Registration Mix. A coarse-meshed location system (analog for the GPS) could record shopper wayfinding and wayfinding patterns (e.g. in a shopping center), and be complemented or supported by a close-meshed RFID system in the precise recording of wayfinding paths at especially interesting points (e.g., in a particular retail store). A combination of the location of people and the determination of the location would also be conceivable regarding the shopping cart: By this means, we could analyze when and where the cart and customer separate, when they are reunited, how long the separation lasts, and where the person has been during this period.

(4) Interview Mix. Should the retailer be interested in the path taken by the customer until he/she reaches a particular shelf and the behavior at this shelf, he/she could consider the following method combination: Parallel interviewing and acting aloud methods at the shelf and open or supported interviewing regarding the previous wayfinding path.

Method Combinations Across Method Groups

(1) Observation and Other Methods. As regards the use of observation techniques in combination with other methods, there are many conceivable possibilities. Let us single out two: The observation of the behavior in the shop can be linked to the interview regarding the path which was taken to get to the shop in question. A combination of observation and interview is also to be found in "shopping with consumers" (Lowrey et al., 2005; Otnes et al., 1995), repeated shopping accompaniment (observation) with parallel in-depth interviews and a subsequent interview on the shopping behavior. A second example would be to combine the use of observation and videography, for example, recording visual attention at the shelf.

(2) Videography, Recording, and Interview. Videography and recording could be combined in such a way that light barriers in front of a shelf assume the

selection of customers and their behavior is then recorded by a shelf-camera. There is combination of videography and interview where a cameraman records the wayfinding and these recordings subsequently serve the closer determination of the attention behavior via video-enhanced memory. The situation where a location system records the wayfinding and the attention behavior at particular shelves is subsequently inquired is similar. This would be a combination of recording and interview.

The Realization of the Method Combinations. The combination of diverse methods can be the responsibility of different people but can also be affected by a single person. For example, in a study on customer behavior in the Christmas department of a store, two persons were involved: One of them assumed the undercover observation, the other the subsequent interview (Silberer, 2006). Equally, several tasks were assumed by one and the same person in Iyer's analysis (1989): They drove the customer to the shop of his/her choice and took them back home. Moreover, they had to interview the passenger as to his/her purchase plans at the beginning and record the products purchased at the end. And during the shopping trip, this person also had to follow the shopper inconspicuously and observe them equally as inconspicuously whilst shopping so that he/she was extremely busy.

Sequence Analysis as a New Method for Data Processing

When describing the behavior at the POS adequately, it is not simply a question of the validity of the data recording but also the usefulness of the data processing. Not only do the wayfinding and attention behavior have to be recorded but also appraised as such. Therefore, the obvious question is whether groups exist which are similar in their wayfinding and approach behavior. However, such analyses have been a scarce commodity as yet. Nevertheless, recently there have been initial attempts to analyze the wayfinding behavior at the POS through the analysis of contact sequences by way of sequence clustering (Ruiz, Chebat, and Hansen [2004, p. 335]; Larson et al. [2005, pp. 397–412]).

In the case of sequence clustering, which also represents a relatively new data analysis method in other fields of consumer and marketing research, specific questions arise which have to be answered. These questions above all include the following: how can sequences which differ in length be compared? How can similarities and distances be operationalized and which measures of distance or similarity come into question? And how can a sequence cluster or search for behavioral patterns account for the circumstance that wayfinding and attention sequences relate to different levels of behavior but are nevertheless to be considered together?

In the analysis of a wayfinding study in a supermarket, we attempted to determine sequence clusters. The sequence of area contacts served as an illustration of the behavior sequences (approach activities recorded were not taken into account). We calculated the distance between wayfinding and area contact sequences by way of the Levenshtein Algorithm (Levenshtein, 1965), which means that a distance is all the greater the higher the number of operations required in the transformation of one sequence into another.

The search for homogenous sequence clusters and distinguishable patterns of behavior (using the Ward Method; Hair, Anderson, Tatham, & Black, 1998) produced three distinguishable groups. These three wayfinding clusters can be described briefly by way of the following *centroids*:

> *Cluster 1* (*n* = 44): fresh fruit & vegetables >>> bakery products >>> frozen products >>> food dry & packaged >>> frozen products >>> cash desk area,
> *Cluster 2* (*n* = 14): fresh fruit & vegetables >>> bakery products >>> frozen products >>> food dry & packaged >>> beverages >>>> frozen products >>> cosmetics and hygiene articles >>> cash desk area,
> *Cluster 3* (*n* = 22): food dry & packaged >>> frozen products >>> bakery products >>> fresh fruit & vegetables >>> cash desk area

In order to illustrate the more or less homogenous wayfinding behavior of these three clusters as a behavior pattern, we selected five wayfinding sequences which, compared to the usual wayfinding sequences, exhibited the lowest distances to the centroid. These "centroid proxies" can be represented graphically and are reproduced in Figures 13.1–13.3. As regards this representation of the results, it should be noted that it is a question of a simplified, schematic representation of the wayfinding paths.

Current and Future Trends in POS Research

Having revealed important possibilities of behavior research at the POS, recognizable and expected trends are being addressed in POS research. The current trends above all include the following:

1. The interest in behavior at the POS is increasing. This is not only true in practice but also for science, as increasing calls for articles in publications and contributions at conferences demonstrate.

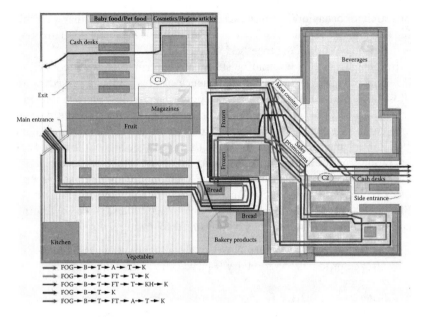

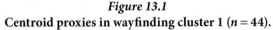

Figure 13.1
Centroid proxies in wayfinding cluster 1 ($n = 44$).

2. The analysis of customer behavior at the POS is being intensified. Having always carried out the analysis of customer reactions by way of in-store marketing, the number of studies which are concerned directly with wayfinding and the approach behavior of the shopper, more or less independent of POS measures, is increasing. The analysis of the click and view behavior on the Internet acted as a model at least in some studies.

3. Newer attempts of POS research increasingly recognize the new opportunities which arise from the use of digital location, recording, and presentation technology. Above all, mobile radio, RFID technology, video technology, and software on fixed and mobile appliances are worth mentioning.

And further developments can be expected in the future, namely:

1. The testing of previously unused methods and method combinations;
2. The use and development of appropriate data analysis processes, in particular sequence analysis and sequence clustering;

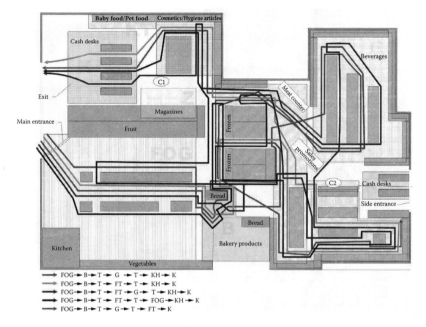

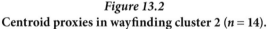

Figure 13.2
Centroid proxies in wayfinding cluster 2 (*n* = 14).

3. The fusion of records from the scanner, customer data bases, and direct inquiries regarding POS behavior; (and closely linked to this);
4. An intensified discussion of the legal and ethical issues which are linked to the accumulation and use of personal data regarding POS behavior; and finally
5. It is to be expected that, alongside the detection of the behavior at the POS, intensified attempts to explain new findings regarding this behavior will also be undertaken, namely to investigate their causes. This means two things: the attention to corresponding investigation designs, such as conducting experiments and quasi-experiments (e.g. the direct change of shelf arrangements and the implementation of in-store promotions); and the recourse to newer theories on situative thinking, feeling, and acting (see e.g. Smith & Semin, 2004).

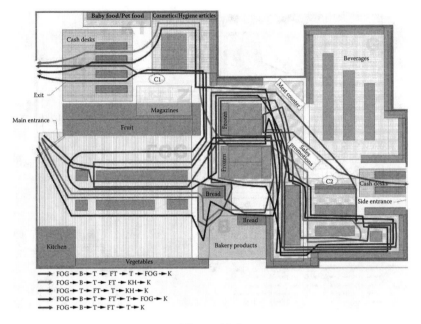

Figure 13.3
Centroid proxies in wayfinding cluster 3 (*n* = 22).

Challenges for Scientific POS Research

Whereas individual company and commercial research will be interested in such analyses in the future and translate their results directly into goal-orientated marketing measures, academic or scientific research can and must consider fundamental issues. For example, in the development and assessment of a method arsenal, these basic issues include on the one hand, the assessment of individual recording instruments and, on the other hand, the assessment of goal-oriented method combinations. In more detail, this means: (1) examining the technical feasibility and the cost of time, money, and staff more closely (but also the know-how); (2) determining the social acceptance of particular measurement processes by customers, employees, and managers (but also in society, including legislation and judicature); (3) testing the validity of the methods under consideration of the respective use modalities; and (4) permitting statements on the ecological validity in which the selectivity effects in the samples and the reactivity in the behavior of the test persons is examined. Striving for the internal validity of measurements of the POS behavior, even if it is accompanied by the greatest challenges, has to be of great importance in this. However, we can edge closer to this goal by beginning with face validity or the consultation of measurement experts whilst intensifying the search for measurable external criteria, thus preparing tests for criterion validity and finally turning to nomological validity. The latter means that we are striving after a theory which provides information as to which measurement instruments and method combinations provide correct information concerning the virtual POS behavior for specific applications.

Notes

Acknowledgments: The author would like to thank Alexander Gorbach, Institute for Marketing and Retailing, Georg-August-Universität Göttingen, for his collaboration in the calculation and description of wayfinding clusters. Special thanks to Tina Lowrey and the anonymous reviewer for helpful comments.

References

Babin, B. J., & Darden, W. R. (1995). Consumer self-regulation in a retail environment. *Journal of Retailing, 71,* 47–70.

Baldauf, A., Srnka, K. J., & Wagner, U. (1997). Untersuchung eines neuartigen Shop-Konzeptes mittels Kundenlaufstudie [Examination of a new store concept by analyzing customers' paths]. *der markt, 36,* 142–143; 103–111.

Belk, R. W., & Kozinets, R. V. (2005). Videography in marketing and consumer research. *Qualitative Market Research: An International Journal, 8,* 128–141.

Bitner, M. J. (1992). Servicescapes—The impact of physical surroundings on customers and employees. *Journal of Marketing, 56,* 57–71.

Bloch, P. H., & Richins, M. L. (1983). Shopping without purchase: An investigation of consumer browsing behavior. In R. P. Bagozzi & A. M. Tybout (Eds.), *Advances in consumer research* (Vol. 10, pp. 389–393). Ann Arbor, MI: Association for Consumer Research.

Botelho, V. M. (2002). *Analyseverfahren zum Kundenlauf* [Methods for analyzing customers' paths]. Unpublished diploma thesis, Institut für Marketing und Handel, Abteilung Marketing, Georg-August-Universität, Göttingen, Germany.

Cannel, C. F., & Kahn, R. L. (1968). Interviewing. In G. Lindzey & E. Aronson (Eds.), *The handbook of social psychology* (pp. 526–595). Reading, MA: Addison-Wesley.

Chandon, P., Hutchinson, W. J., & Young, S. H. (2001). *Measuring the value of point-of-purchase marketing with commercial eye-tracking data* (Working Paper No. 2001/19/MKT). Fontainebleau: INSEAD.

Chandon, P., Hutchinson, W. J., & Young, S. H. (2002). *Unseen is unsold: Assessing visual equity with commercial eye-tracking data* (Working Paper No. 2002/85/MKT). Fontainebleu: INSEAD.

De Heer, J., Groenland, E., & Bloem, S. (2000). To be or not to be included in the consideration set? The effects of brand conspicuity on exploratory visual search behavior and memory. In J. Inman, K. Tepper, & T. Whittler (Eds.), *Proceedings of the society for consumer psychology winter conference*. San Antonio, TX: Society for Consumer Psychology.

Ericsson, K. A., & Simon, H. A. (1980). Verbal reports as data. *Psychological Review, 87*, 215–251.

Fontana, A., & Frey, J. H. (1994). Interviewing: The art of science. In N. K. Denzin & Y. S. Lincoln (Eds.), *Handbook of qualitative research* (pp. 361–376). Thousand Oaks, CA: Sage.

Granbois, D. H. (1968). Improving study of customer in-store behavior. *Journal of Marketing, 32*, 28–33.

Groeppel-Klein, A., Bartmann, B., & Germelmann, C. C. (2006). Mental maps of retail spaces and their relevance for consumers' well-being while shopping. In H. Timmermans (Ed.), *Book of abstracts: 13th recent advances in retailing & services science conference, July 2002, Budapest* (p. 76). Eindhoven, The Netherlands: Technische Universiteit.

Hair, Jr., J. F., Anderson, R. E., Tatham, R. L., & Black, W. C. (1998). *Multivariate data analysis* (5th ed.). Upper Saddle River, NJ: Prentice-Hall.

Hicks, J. W., & Kohl, R. L. (1955). Memomotion study as a method of measuring consumer behaviour. *Journal of Marketing, 20*, 168–170.

Hoyer, W. D. (1984). An examination of consumer decision-making for a common repeat purchase product. *Journal of Consumer Research, 11*, 822–829.

Iyer, E. S. (1989). Unplanned purchasing—knowledge of shopping environment and time pressure. *Journal of Retailing, 65*, 40–57.

ISB-Studie (1986). Kundenlauf-Studie in einem SB-Warenhaus [Studying customers' paths in a self-service department store]. In BdSW—Bundesverband der Selbstbedienungs-Warenhäuser (Ed.). Köln: Institut für Selbstbedienung und Warenwirtschaft.

Kahn, B. E., & Schmittlein, D. C. (1992). The relationship between purchases made on promotion and shopping trip behavior. *Journal of Retailing, 68*, 294–315.

Larson, J. S., Bradlow, E. T., & Fader, P. S. (2005). An exploratory look at supermarkt shopping paths. *International Journal of Research in Marketing, 22*, 395–414.

Leven, W. (1992). Warenpräsentationen im Einzelhandel, dargestellt am Beispiel der Zeitungs- und Zeitschriftenpräsentation [Presentation of products in retail considering as example newspapers and journals]. *Marketing ZFP, 14,* 13–22.

Levenshtein, V. I. (1965). Binary codes capable of correcting deletions, insertions and reversals. *Doklady Akademi Nauk SSSR, 163,* 845–848.

Lowrey, T. M., Otnes, C. C., & McGrath, M. A. (2005). Shopping with consumers: Reflections and innovations. *Qualitative Market Research, 8,* 176–188.

Newman, A. J., & Foxall, G. R. (2003). In-store customer behaviour in the fashion sector: Some emerging methodological and theoretical directions. *International Journal of Retail & Distribution Management, 31,* 591–600.

Otnes, C. C., McGrath, M. A., & Lowrey, T. M. (1995). Shopping with consumers: Usage as past, present and future research technique. *Journal of Retailing and Consumer Services, 2,* 97–110.

Payne, J. W., & Ragsdale, E. K. E. (1978). Verbal protocols and direct oberservation of supermarket shopping behavior: Some findings and a discussion of methods. In H. K. Hunt (Ed.), *Advances in consumer research* (Vol. 5, pp. 571–577). Chicago, IL: Association for Consumer Research.

Pieters, R., & Warlop, L. (1999). Visual attention during brand choice: The impact of time pressure and task motivation. *International Journal of Research in Marketing, 16,* 1–16.

Rosenthal, R., & Rosnow, R. L. (Eds.) (1969). *Artifact in behavioral research.* New York: Academic Press.

Ruiz, J.-P., Chebat, J.-C., & Hansen, P. (2004). Another trip to the mall: A segmentation study of customers based on their activities. *Journal of Retailing and Consumer Services, 11,* 333–350.

Russo, J. E., & Leclerc, F. (1994). An eye-fixation analysis of choice processes for consumer nondurables. *Journal of Consumer Research, 21,* 274–290.

Schröder, H., & Berghaus, N. (2005). Blickaufzeichnung der Wahrnehmung am Regal—Methodendemonstration am Beispiel Süßgebäck [Recording of eye-fixation at shelves—Demontration of the method considering as example cookies]. In V. Trommsdorff (Ed.), *Handelsforschung 2005. Neue Erkenntnisse für Praxis und Wissenschaft des Handels* (pp. 315–335). Stuttgart: Kohlhammer.

Schröder, H., Berghaus, N., & Zimmermann, G. (2005). Das Blickverhalten der Kunden als Grundlage für die Warenplatzierung im Lebensmitteleinzelhandel [Customers' eye movements as basis for the placement of products in food retail]. *der Markt, 44,* 31–43.

Silberer, G. (2006). *Selectivity and reactivity of customer observation and interviews at the point of sale.* Göttingen, Germany: Institute of Marketing and Retailing. Georg-August-Universität Göttingen.

Silberer, G. (2005). Die videogestützte Rekonstruktion kognitiver Prozesse beim Ladenbesuch [Video-cued reconstruction of cognitive processes during the visit to a store]. *Marketing ZFP, 27,* 263–271.

Smith, E. R., & Semin, G. R. (2004). Socially situated cognition: Cognition in its social context. *Advances in Experimental Social Psychology, 36,* 53–117.

Sorensen, H. (2003). The science of shopping. *Marketing Research, 15,* 30–35.

Spano, R. (2006). Observer behavior as a potential source of reactivity: Describing and quantifying observer effects in a large-scale observational study of police. *Sociological Methods & Research, 34,* 521–553.

Thelen, E. M., & Hemetsberger, A. (2006). Losing direction—consumers' wayfinding and instore search behavior. In H. Timmermans (Ed.), *Book of abstracts: 13th recent advances in retailing & services science conference, July 2002, Budapest* (p. 77). Eindhoven, The Netherlands: Technische Universiteit.

Titus, P. A., & Everett, P. B. (1996). Consumer wayfinding tasks, strategies and errors: An exploratory field study. *Psychology & Marketing, 13,* 265–290.

Wells, W. D., & Lo Sciuto, L. A. (1966). Direct observation of purchasing behavior. *Journal of Marketing Research, 3,* 227–233.

Young, S. (2002). Winning at retail. *Global Cosmetic Industry (GCI), 10,* 61–64.

Zielke, S. (2002). *Kundenorientierte Warenplatzierung* [Customer-oriented placement of products]. Stuttgart, Berlin, Köln: Kohlhammer.

AUTHOR INDEX

Page references followed by *f* indicate figures.
Page references followed by *t* indicate tables.
Page references followed by *n* indicate footnotes.
Page references in *italics* indicate reference section.

A

Aaker, D. A., 112, 113, *122*, 136, 137, 140, *147*
Adaval, R., 112, *122*
Aiken, K. D., 110, 111*t*, *122*
Ajzen, I., 136, *147*
Akerlof, G. A., 131, *147*
Allen, J., 79, *82*
Alpert, F., 141, *147*
Alpert, J. I., 33, *49*
Alpert, M. I., 33, *49*
Altman, K., 244, *255*
Altsech, M. B., 45, *50*
Ambady, N., 17, 18, 19, 20, 21, 22, 23, 25, 26, 28, *29*, *30*
Ambler, T., 112, *122*
Anderson, N. H., 132, 133, *147*
Anderson R. D., 88, 100, *104*
Anderson, R. E., 273, *278*
Andrews, M. L., 115, *122*
Ansari, A., 221, *238*
Areni, C. S., 35, 37*t*, 42, 45, 46, 47, *49*
Argo, J. J., 199, *215*, *216*, 228, *237*
Arnold, C., 99, *104*
Arnold, M. J., 197, *215*
Arnold, S. J., 5, 9, *13*, 65, *80*, 161, *166*
Arnold, T. J., 91, *104*
Aronow, E., 244, *255*
Aronson, J. E., 57, *81*
Atwell, J., 224, 225, *239*

B

Ba, S., 115, *122*
Babin, B. J., 35, 41*t*, 42, 44, 45, 47, *49*, 72, *79*, 197, *215*, 258, *277*
Babin, L. A., 72, *79*
Baker, J., 35, 37t, 40*t*, 42, 44, 46, *49*, 56, 57, 75, *79*, 197, 214, *217*, *218*

Baker, S. M., 206, 214, *216*
Baldauf, A., 260, *277*
Banister, E. N., 79, *79*, *80*
Bargh, J. A., 20, *29*, 230, *236*
Barker, S., 27, *29*
Bart, Y., 108, 109, 110, 111*t*, 112, *122*
Bartmann, B., 260, *278*
Barwise, P., 137, *148*
Bean, L., 174, *192*
Belanger, F., 110, 112, *122*
Belk, R. W., 4, *13*, 154, *165*, 234, 235, *236*, 265, 266, *277*
Bell, G. D., 72, 76, *79*
Bellizzi, J., 92, *104*, 160, *165*
Bem, S. L., 65, *79*
Benedicktus, R. L., 110, 111*t*, 115, 117, 119, 120, *122*
Benet-Martínez, V., 25, *30*
Bergeron, J., 117, *124*
Berghaus, N., 222, *240*, 265, *279*
Berlyne, D. E., 35, *49*
Bernieri, F. J., 18, *28*
Bettman, J. R., 28, *29*, 221, 224, 230, *236*, *239*
Beynon, J., 155, 157, 158, 160, *165*
Biddle, G. C., 133, *148*
Biehal, G., 231, *236*
Bitner, M. J., 33, *49*, 116, *127*, 197, 202, *216*, 221, 224, *236*, 261, *277*
Black, W. C., 103, *105*, 273, *278*
Bloch, P. H., 78, *80*, 91, 96, 103, *104*, *105*, 197, *216*, 232, *236*, 258, *277*
Bloem, S., 264, *278*
Bohner, G., 114, *123*
Bolton, G. E., 114, *122*
Borghini, S., 5, *15*
Boshoff, C., 198, 209, *216*
Botelho, V. M., 260, *277*
Bottomley, P. A., 136, 137, 138, *147*
Bourke, J., 155, *165*

SUBJECT INDEX

Page references in *italics* indicate figures.
Page references in **boldface** type indicate tables.